The Wisconsin Project on American Writers

Frank Lentricchia, General Editor

HUCKLEBERRY FINN AS IDOL AND TARGET

The Functions of Criticism in Our Time

JONATHAN ARAC

THE UNIVERSITY OF WISCONSIN PRESS

The University of Wisconsin Press
2537 Daniels Street
Madison, Wisconsin 53718

3 Henrietta Street
London WC2E 8LU, England

Library of Congress Cataloging-in-Publication Data

Arac, Jonathan, 1945–
    Huckleberry Finn as idol and target: the functions of criticism in our time /
Jonathan Arac.
        264 pp.   cm.—(The Wisconsin project on American writers)
        Includes bibliographical references (p. 225) and index.
        ISBN 0-299-15530-7 (cloth: alk. paper).   ISBN 0-299-15534-X (pbk.: alk. paper)
        1. Twain, Mark, 1835–1910.   Adventures of Huckleberry Finn.
    2. Junior high school students—United States—Books and reading.
    3. National characteristics, American, in literature.   4. American
    fiction—Study and teaching (Secondary)   5. Literature and society—
    United States—History.   6. Mississippi River—In literature.
    7. Race relations in literature.   8. Afro-Americans in literature.
    9. Racism in literature.   10. Boys in literature.   11. Canon
    (Literature)   I. Title.   II. Series.
    PS1305.A89   1997
    813'.4—dc21   97-15550

Contents

Preface

This book joins my concerns as a citizen and as a scholar. As a scholar, I am concerned by bad arguments about an excellent and important book, *Huckleberry Finn*, and as a citizen I am concerned because these arguments inform discussion in the public press on important matters—how we think about questions of race and how we understand the United States.

As a work of criticism, my book has a strong animus. I am fed up with reading that *Huckleberry Finn* is the "quintessentially American book," and that it is a "devastating attack on racism." These terms are not good descriptions of the book, and they are not the best terms for appreciating the book. I do not argue that *Huckleberry Finn* is racist or un-American. Rather, I explore how Twain's book came to be endowed with the values of Americanness and antiracism, and with what effects.

In the later 1940s there began a process I call "hypercanonization." That is, within the canon of American classics that was defined in the academy at this time, *Huckleberry Finn* was placed at the very top. Academic excess would not itself be important, but in this case the academic judgments fueled newspaper and magazine articles when public controversy arose about the desirability of requiring *Huckleberry Finn* in junior high schools. The excessive media response in defense of *Huckleberry Finn* I call "idolatry."

This book details and analyzes the emergence of hypercanonization in the academy—it occurred in the years from 1948 to 1964—and demonstrates its role in idolatry, largely since 1982. This is a work of academic scholarship and critical argument, but I hope it may be useful for parents who want to fight the idolatry that routinely answers them when they complain that their early-teenage children are being made to study and admire a text in which the title character, hero, and narrator, Huck, uses the term *nigger* hundreds of times. As a member of the ACLU, I hope too that my materials and arguments will persuade local chapters to seek discussion, not just confrontation, with protesting voices. To challenge the required status of *Huckleberry Finn* does not threaten the First Amendment. It does call into question a set of recent educational assumptions that this book tries to explain. I do not want to ban *Huckleberry Finn*. I do want to see fairer, fuller, better-informed debates when the book comes into question.

The construction of this book is somewhat unusual. In order to make critical arguments, I work closely with historical detail from three distinct periods: the pre–Civil War decades of Huck's fictional life; the later nineteenth century when Twain wrote *Huckleberry Finn;* and the middle of the twentieth century when academic hypercanonization occurred. Most chapters draw evidence from all three periods. I use writings by polemicists, novelists, critics, scholars, and journalists, as well as much work by historians, who in the last several decades have greatly deepened our knowledge of nineteenth-century American history, particularly the history of slavery and its aftermath. The first three chapters mainly discuss recent journalism, together with research and judgments drawn from historians, brought to bear on *Huckleberry Finn.*

Among my historical concerns, I care very much about the place of *Huckleberry Finn* in the history of prose fiction, both in the United States and more widely. Within the history of fiction in the United States, I argue that *Huckleberry Finn* participated in a nineteenth-century cultural conflict between two modes of prose fiction, what I call "literary" narrative and what I call "national" narrative. This contrast of narrative modes leads me to considerable discussion of *Uncle Tom's Cabin* (1852), especially in chapter 4. Stowe's "national" narrative gained great acclaim in the nineteenth century, but by the 1930s it was devalued as "protest" fiction, against which the value of Twain's "literary" narrative was asserted. In chapter 6, I discuss how critics "nationalized literary narrative" in order to find in *Huckleberry Finn* lessons for America, and in so doing to demote the explicitly national concerns of James Fenimore Cooper's *The Pioneers* (1823). In chapter 7, I investigate Twain's prose style, including some comparison with French writing of his time, and in chapter 8 I sketch yet broader, global, perspectives.

To understand how academic hypercanonization has fueled journalistic idolatry, I have studied closely the critics whose work proved most important in the hypercanonizing: in chapter 5 Lionel Trilling; in chapter 6, Henry Nash Smith as critic together with the scholarly edition of *Huckleberry Finn,* headed by Walter Blair; in chapter 7 Leo Marx; and in chapter 8 Ralph Ellison (who was not an academic when his first critical writings appeared but who spent many years in university positions). I have serious arguments with all of these critics, but I have also learned a great deal from each of them.

My own critical premises are largely in the line that I am criticizing. Trilling, Smith, Marx, and Ellison all think, as I do, that writing is a highly skilled performance to be judged by asking how well it accomplishes its imaginative goals. They also all believe, as I do, that a writer's chosen goals are not immune to criticism, and that imaginative goals are always linked, in complex and important ways, to the society and history in which the writing occurs. Moreover, all of these critics are open, as I am, to the resources of other disciplines. Enduring literary works, they and I agree, are widely important, and therefore the criticism that treats them must not be restricted to a narrowly defined aesthetic sphere. They all share, as do I, the view of Matthew Arnold that literature is a criticism of life and that criticism has a special responsibility to challenge the complacency of the society in which it arises. One reason I can and must criticize them so strongly is that their views have so greatly prevailed: what might have been a challenge to complacency in the 1950s, in the 1990s has become the voice of authority. This was a process Trilling painfully acknowledged later in his career. And, of course, my work may be analyzed and criticized just the way I have done in criticizing these other critics. Self-criticism has its limits. Finally, you have to write it the way you see it, and leave the critique to your readers.

Unless otherwise noted, all citations from *Huckleberry Finn* are from the University of California Press edition (1988).

HUCKLEBERRY FINN AS IDOL AND TARGET

Introduction

In 1959, to celebrate the seventy-fifth anniversary of the publication of *Huckleberry Finn,* the *New York Times* Sunday book review section published a feature by the brilliant young critic Norman Podhoretz, in which he proclaimed, "Sooner or later, it seems, all discussions of 'Huckleberry Finn' turn into discussions of America—and with good reason. Mark Twain was the quintessential American writer." Decades later, in 1992, in a letter to the *Times,* the correspondent declared, "Huckleberry Finn is not only the most representative American boy in our literature, he is also the character with whom American readers—white American readers—have most deeply identified" (Howe). In a prestigious recent anthology of essays on Twain, the editor authoritatively described *Huckleberry Finn* as "an autobiographical journey into the past" that at the same time "also told the story of the nation" (Sundquist 10). These kinds of claims are commonly made in discussion of *Huckleberry Finn.* I hope to persuade critics to stop doing it and readers to stop liking it.

If Huck is representative, it can't be in the sense of average or typical, or "it was just like that." If most Americans before the Civil War had felt about slavery the way Huck does about Jim, there would have been no war. As Harriet Beecher Stowe had urged in *Uncle Tom's Cabin,* Americans would have brought themselves to "feel right," and those who owned slaves would have freed them. Huck, in the widespread critical commonplace, represents a morally idealized best American self, as is suggested in the memorial judgment with which William Dean Howells concluded *My Mark Twain:* "he was the Lincoln of our literature." Yet Lincoln has a more shaded reputation on race matters than Huck enjoys. The

3

historian David Potter, in a highly admired synthesis of the process that led to the Civil War, finds Lincoln's views "ambiguous." Based on his position in the debates with Stephen Douglas, "Lincoln was a mild opponent of slavery and a moderate defender of racial discrimination." But considering the direction that Lincoln's thought was moving, Potter concludes, "he held a concept of humanity which impelled him inexorably in the direction of freedom and equality" (*Impending* 354).

Why can't we treat our literary heroes with the same critical nuance we use for our political heroes? Harry Truman, himself from Missouri and an admirer of Mark Twain's work, became in 1948 a "Mark Twain character" of "grinning, cocky, vernacular, give 'em hell" (Podhoretz, *Doings* 302). Truman established the governmental momentum that led to the civil rights movement, but he proved no supporter of the movement once it turned to protest. Or take another political hero of civil rights, the Texan Lyndon Johnson. Everyone knows Johnson's faults, and yet his political commitment and skill made possible the laws on which most current bans on discrimination depend.

Why have we for decades recirculated a single idealizing set of claims about Mark Twain and *Huckleberry Finn*? I think of an anecdote from the career of the Southern writer George W. Cable, a friend of Twain. His historical novel *The Grandissimes* (1880), set in Louisiana around 1800, was being serialized in *Scribner's* magazine, and members of the editorial staff queried a certain passage of dialogue that set forth white supremacist beliefs. They doubted that any character would actually have "thought of uttering such a truism"—that is, they held that the prejudicial views went without saying. Cable, who had grown up in Louisiana and fought for the Confederacy, asserted his knowledge of what things had been like: "The old false beliefs . . . were only sustained by incessant reiterations. I heard them myself from my earliest childhood, up" (A. Turner 97). My book is concerned with a set of incessant reiterations, and it tries to suggest the work done by such repetitions.

As a road map, I need to offer a very brief historical sketch of the reception, by literary authorities, of Mark Twain and *Huckleberry Finn*. Twain is widely valued nowadays for his opposition to the established culture of his time; we recall the library committees that refused to carry *Huckleberry Finn* because of its unsavory setting and uneducated language. But there are higher authorities than library committees. Twain was greatly admired by, and his career supported by, the two most important and prestigious editors of the leading high-culture magazines of his time. In the 1870s, William Dean Howells, as editor of the *Atlantic Monthly*, wrote highly favorable reviews of Twain's work and actively recruited Twain for his pages. In the 1880s, Richard Watson Gilder, as editor of *Century* magazine, made recruiting Twain a top priority, and published excerpts from *Huckleberry Finn* for three months.

The two defining books for the twentieth-century discussion of Twain were *The Ordeal of Mark Twain* (1920) by Van Wyck Brooks, and *Mark Twain's America* (1932) by Bernard DeVoto. Brooks treated Twain as a sorry case study in the failure of America to produce great culture. Twain, in Brooks's view, lost the critical edge that his outsider's perspective might have brought, because he too readily yielded to the comforts and limitations of the established genteel culture. DeVoto, in contrast, considered Twain not as someone who had failed to fulfill his genius but as the writer who most fully expressed the American heartland of his time. The two, however, shared something that sets them apart from the criticism of the last fifty years: neither offered much specific or detailed critical argument concerning *Huckleberry Finn*. In 1935, Ernest Hemingway claimed, in a sentence in *The Green Hills of Africa*, that all modern American literature comes from *Huckleberry Finn*. Only in the postwar years did scholars begin unpacking in detail the implications of this claim.

At the moment of Hemingway's sentence, one hundred years after Samuel Clemens had been born, fifty years after *Huckleberry Finn* had been published, twenty-five years after Twain's death, the image of Mark Twain held a privileged place in American cultural memory, but *Huckleberry Finn* had not yet become one of the great books of the world. Twain was part of the atmosphere of American culture, not someone whose standing depended on closely attentive reading of whole works. In the last years before his death in 1910, Twain had already been widely identified in the United States as "our" Mark Twain and represented by cartoonists in imagery that made him equivalent to the national icon of Uncle Sam (Budd, *Our* 12, 171). In the 1920s the leading critic of his generation, Edmund Wilson, observed of Twain that "the man is more impressive than his work" (*Shores* 227), and in a feature piece for the centennial of Twain's birth in 1935, Newton Arvin judged that Twain was immortal "less as a writer" than "as a figure," a "grand, half-legendary personality," loved for his "largeness and sweetness" (126–27). Over sixty years later, Twain remains a massive figure in our culture. As the *San Francisco Examiner* wrote in 1994, concerning an exhibit of Twain memorabilia, "Some writers are respected, some are worshipped, some are even feared. But there is only one American writer who is universally loved, Mark Twain" (Kamiya).

After Twain's death, *Huckleberry Finn* was admired by avant-garde and oppositional writers as various as Gertrude Stein, H. L. Mencken, Sherwood Anderson, and Hemingway, but for the culture at large it was a beloved boy's book. The several decades after the Second World War transformed the cultural standing of *Huckleberry Finn*. In the 1940s *Huckleberry Finn* became a universally assigned college text and the focus of a huge amount of academic scholarship and critical discussion. Scholars and critics established terms for valuing *Huckleberry Finn* as a masterpiece of world literature and as the highest image of America. This is the process I call "hypercanonization."

Hypercanonization involved teaching students to appreciate *Huckleberry Finn* in ways that it had never been appreciated before. One particular skill emphasized in literary study at this time involved the detailed close analysis of specific passages. For *Huckleberry Finn*, two particular passages became the hypercanonized parts within the hypercanonical whole. The opening page of chapter 19 sets forth how Huck and Jim "put in the time" as they made their escape downriver on the raft; this passage has been highlighted in critics' discussions of Huck's American "vernacular" language. In the middle of chapter 31, Huck contemplates writing to Miss Watson about how she could recover her escaped slave, Jim, but he finds that he can't do it and would rather "go to hell"; this passage has been highlighted in critics' discussions of Twain's moral vision. I make each of these passages the centerpiece of a chapter: chapter 31 in my chapter 2; chapter 19 in my chapter 7.

There is no sign that hypercanonization lessens. In 1987 one of the major textbook anthologies of American literature included, along with two massive hardbound volumes, a shrink-wrapped paperback "centennial facsimile" of *Huckleberry Finn*, marked "This edition is packaged with and is a part of *The Harper American Literature*, volume II. Not for sale separately." This collectible neatly resolved the problem of how you include a substantial complete novel within an anthology. In 1990 the *Heath Anthology of American Literature* was published, also in two volumes. This 5,800-page collection avowedly grew from the radical concerns of the 1960s, and it asserted its commitment to feminist and multicultural transformations of the canon. The *Heath* enforced its principles so strongly that out of over fifty contemporary poets and fiction writers it included who were younger than John Updike (b. 1932), only two were white males. Yet in this same volume, which reached from the Civil War to the present, Mark Twain occupied nearly ten percent of the total pages. No other writer of the nineteenth century had eighty pages; no twentieth-century writer had even fifty pages; William Faulkner had twenty-five pages, and *Huckleberry Finn* was printed in its entirety. It's the same in high schools. In the 1990s, only Shakespeare was more assigned than *Huckleberry Finn*. Some three-quarters of high schools required *Huckleberry Finn*, which was taught more than any other novel, more than any other long work (such as a play by Shakespeare), and more than any other work of American literature (Applebee 28).

Hypercanonization started with three professors. The New York-based cultural critic Lionel Trilling (b. 1905), the Chicago scholar Walter Blair (b. 1906), and the Berkeley historical critic Henry Nash Smith (b. 1907) now can be seen to have joined forces, across the continent, at the forefront of a generation—born early in the century, formed between the wars, and coming to their full powers around 1950—who linked a book to a nation at a key moment in history. Through their insight and scholarship a widespread critical and cultural understanding of *Huckleberry Finn* was codified that is still familiar in schools and newspapers: Despite some readers' trouble with the ending, *Huckleberry Finn* is "almost perfect" in "form and style" (Trilling, *Liberal* 110), not only "one of the central documents of American culture," but also "one of the world's great books" (Trilling, *Liberal* 101) for the "vernacular protest" (Smith, *Development* 115) of its prose and plot, which permit an "exploration of Huck's psyche" (Smith, *Development* 120) and convey a morality of the "uncoerced self" against the "social conformity" (Smith, *Development* 122–23) satirized throughout.

That moment of academic hypercanonization ran from 1948 to 1964, from Trilling's introduction to the first college text of *Huckleberry Finn* in 1948, through college texts edited by Smith, Blair, and others, to Blair's massive contextual study *Mark Twain and Huck*

Finn (1960); Smith's *Mark Twain: The Development of a Writer* (1962), which contained what many still consider the best single overall discussion of *Huckleberry Finn;* and *The Machine in the Garden* (1964) by Leo Marx (b. 1919), whose essays of the 1950s had already set an agenda for subsequent Twain studies.

This period from 1948 to 1964, from Truman to Johnson, included the onset of the Cold War and the emergence of the civil rights movement. It ended with the passage of the most important civil rights legislation since Reconstruction, and the erosion of the Cold War liberal coalition. In 1948 Truman so effectively coopted the civil rights concerns of Henry Wallace's third-party candidacy that Strom Thurmond, then the Democratic governor of South Carolina, led Southern "Dixiecrats" in protest out of the party convention. In 1964, things went the other way. Johnson was so worried about Barry Goldwater's potential exploitation of what was already becoming known as "white backlash" that he refused to accept the challenge to the establishment convention delegates by the Mississippi Freedom Democratic Party. In addition, the impact of the war in Vietnam, and the beginning of violent urban agitation by African Americans, further contributed to end this historical phase. Yet the hypercanonization persists, a wishful residue of values that were once connected to concrete attempts to improve the life of the United States.

In the chapters that follow, I study in detail both the academic arguments made on behalf of *Huckleberry Finn* and the circulation of these arguments in the public press. There is a painful paradox at the heart of my undertaking. When Lionel Trilling declared that Huck and Jim formed a "community of saints" (*Liberal* 104, 106), a new moral value was attributed to *Huckleberry Finn* and to America at a time when an increasing number of white people wanted to believe that racial prejudice was a thing of the past. Yet this interpretation of Huck and Jim, by idealizing their relation, powerfully invites complacency. When readers, teachers, and critics follow Trilling in identifying the relation of Huck and Jim as the pinnacle of human community, it is as if "we" uttered in self-congratulation: "Americans have spiritually solved any problems involved in blacks and whites living together as free human beings, and we had done so already by the 1880s; all that remains is to work out the details." But many African Americans have not wanted to join that "we." No sooner had *Huckleberry Finn* begun to achieve hypercanonization, in part because it could so effectively serve as an icon of civil rights consciousness, than it also began to be challenged in the schools by African Americans—the very people on whose behalf, it was imagined, the book was functioning. If civil rights means anything, shouldn't it mean that African Americans ought to have a real voice in public definitions of what counts as a model of enlightened race relations?

What distresses me in these controversies in the media is the structure that I call "idolatry"—the journalistic by-product of hypercanonization. News about African American protests against the required place of honor held by *Huckleberry Finn* in the classroom—especially at the junior high level—began to appear in the press as early as 1957, in the very midst of the first phase of Southern white protests against school integration, but only in 1982 did this topic first become big news, rapidly reaching television. John Wallace, an African American educator based at the Mark Twain Intermediate School in Fairfax, Virginia, denounced *Huckleberry Finn* as "racist trash" (Moore 1)—above all for its several hundred repetitions of the word *nigger*. And the fight was on.

One incident in this controversy focused the connections between academic arguments and arguments in the news. The 1982 *Washington Post* editorial "Selling Huck Down the River" demonstrated the long-enduring power of the hypercanonical moment of *Huckleberry Finn*. After rebutting Wallace, the editorial concluded on a somewhat conciliatory note. The officials of Mark Twain Intermediate School at least "do literature the honor of taking it seriously." Indeed, the *Post* went on, it is true that "'Huckleberry Finn' is dangerous," because Huck, "in helping Jim escape to freedom, discards the conventional 'moral' code he has always taken for granted." The editorial concluded:

> No one who has seriously read or understood his story should be able to accept without irony or question the less reputable, so-called "moral" assumptions of the society in which he lives.

If this editorial formulation had appeared in a freshman essay, it would have brought the student close to plagiarism charges. For in his 1948 introduction, Trilling had claimed that *Huckleberry Finn* was "subversive," and the analysis was the same:

> No one who reads thoughtfully the dialectic of Huck's great moral crisis will ever again be wholly able to accept without some question and

some irony the assumptions of the respectable morality by which he lives. (*Liberal* 108)

It is understandable that Trilling's nuanced qualifications ("wholly," "some") should be lost in an editorial, but I am awed by the success of his essay in defining the terms by which authoritative public debate on *Huckleberry Finn* would be conducted, more than three decades after the essay was published, nearly a decade after Trilling's own death. And it is a perfect irony that, as they repeated Trilling's position thirty-four years later, there was no sign that these public moral authorities had been in any way provoked by Huck's crisis of conscience to consider that a book they hailed as the "quintessentially American masterpiece" could possibly be scarred by, rather than wholly rising above, the history of American racial oppression. Contrary to their assertion of its power, the book had failed to shake the conventional moral code they took for granted.

Idolatry continues in the rhetoric with which newspapers frame stories about challenges to the hypercanonical status of *Huckleberry Finn*. In the summer of 1995, the museum housed in the mansion that Mark Twain built in Hartford, Connecticut, held a workshop for schoolteachers. Look at the headlines: in the *Pittsburgh Post-Gazette*, "Mark Twain Museum Mounts 'Huckleberry Finn' Defense"; and in the *New York Times*, "Huck Finn 101, or How to Teach Twain without Fear." The *Post-Gazette* casts the workshop as "coming to the rescue" of beleaguered teachers (Berland), and the *Times* explains that "for the lovers of Mark Twain, the event is a preemptive effort to bolster the nerve of teachers" (Rabinovitz). In the *Post-Gazette* story, a display quote from a scholar proclaims, "It's a weapon in the battle against racism that we can't afford to take out of our classrooms."

Why must the book be rescued from African American parents and students for their own good? Why must they be the objects of preemptive cultural strikes? Why is it so obvious to so many authorities that their complaints cannot be taken seriously? Why must the parents and students be told repeatedly by authorities that they are bad readers, rather than being acknowledged as voices in a genuine debate over what works against racism in the classroom? Here is what one authority, in the journal *Teaching Tolerance*, thinks it means for *Huckleberry Finn* to operate as a weapon against racism.

He explains that if *Huckleberry Finn* is not required in the classroom, "young readers won't get to see how Huck comes to regard the runaway slave, Jim, as a real person" (Carnes). Is this all that it means to fight racism in the 1990s? And is this all a literary masterpiece is good for? Must students be taught that even white boys at the verge of puberty can treat African Americans as human? If this premise of humanity is not already shared, what can a single book do?

The structure of idolatry—that is, the assault by the establishment when African Americans challenge the prestige of *Huckleberry Finn*—reminds me of a larger pattern that James Baldwin defined in 1964: "The impulse in American society . . . has essentially been to ignore me when it could, and then when it couldn't to intimidate me." Only if intimidation failed might "concessions" follow (Steinberg 111). Albert Murray, a strong critic of Baldwin, made a similar point in 1970, referring more specifically than Baldwin had to the quality of interchange on intellectual matters of shared concern: "On principle, white liberals give or 'grant' sympathetic assistance to the civil rights movement, to be sure, but few Negroes are convinced that this indicates a comprehensive commitment to equality or even represents a truly intimate intellectual involvement with the fundamental issues of citizenship in an open, pluralistic society" (224). As the historian Barbara Jeanne Fields put it in 1990, "ideology" does not consist in "the 'handing down' of the appropriate 'attitudes'" but rather in "the ritual repetition of the appropriate social behavior" (113). To apply her view to the controversies over *Huckleberry Finn*, what counts is not the attitudes that the book supposedly teaches, but rather the opportunity the book provides for the incessant reiteration, the ritual repetition, of practical behavior: whenever blacks complain about *Huckleberry Finn*, the authorities proclaim that they're wrong. My point is not simply that they are right. My point is that the ethics of scholarship and the ethics of citizenship require careful engagement with the intricate issues of history, culture, and politics that the complaints arise from. Idolatry means that cultural authorities rely on poor arguments and pseudo-facts to bury the complaints.

From 1948 to 1964, the years that set hypercanonization in place and that also framed the rise and triumph (but not the complete success) of the civil rights movement, liberal intellectuals seemed to imagine that everything necessary had already happened, and that therefore African Americans didn't need to do any political work for themselves. This message is repeated in the structure of idolatry around *Huckleberry Finn*.

As early as 1948, Elizabeth Hardwick, later a founder of the *New York Review of Books*, writing on William Faulkner, displayed this liberal perspective in the pages of *Partisan Review*. The "final emancipation of the Negro" from decades of subordination was already "real and historical." Only "Stalinists" felt "compelled to underestimate" this triumph. Only "sadistic passion" on the part of Communists and a corresponding masochism on the part of a few African Americans produced the "frenzy of indescribable perversity" in which "lynchings" and "humiliating segregation" were dwelt upon (229). Hardwick praised Faulkner for his criticism of such radicals, but she thought he was wrong to believe that there existed Southern reactionaries who would obstruct the course of the future. She considered it not only "historically ridiculous in terms of America today" but even "inconceivable" that any Southerners "are prepared . . . to risk their lives, their wealth, or even their time in any sustained, hopeless revolt against the will of the country to which they are tied" (230). Less than a decade later, the policy of "massive resistance" to desegregation closed public schools all over the South, led to murders and bombings, and brought federal troops to the South for the first time since Reconstruction.

And in the midst of all this, in 1957, the most authoritative American historian of ethnic groups, Oscar Handlin, in a work intended for a wide, general readership, wrote of the liberal triumph as if it had already occurred. According to Handlin, in the 1930s, "Americans ceased to believe in race" and "hate movements began to disintegrate" (141). Although African Americans in the 1950s "still suffer from injustices and still have legitimate grievances," the "integrity of the patterns of segregation has decisively been broken" (142). In North and South alike, African Americans "no longer labor under the fear of violent reprisal." Even in the absence of antidiscrimination laws, "Negroes have moved steadily and with relatively light friction, into skilled, clerical, and managerial jobs and into the professions." These claims were wholly unwarranted, but they emphatically made the point that things had already been taken care of.

In the next decade, Daniel Patrick Moynihan's report (1965), attributing African American poverty to broken families, provoked much controversy. One critic of the report offered a perspective that casts light on the role that *Huckleberry Finn* was being made to play, and still plays, in the schools. William Ryan, who popularized the phrase "blaming the victim," saw the report as a way of "copping a plea." He explained: "As the murderer pleads guilty to manslaughter . . . liberal America is pleading guilty to the savagery and oppression against the Negro that happened a hundred years ago, in order to escape trial for the crimes of today" (464).

This is what the idolatry adds up to. Liberal white American opinion identifies with the wonderful boy Huck. Even though his society was racist, he was not, and so "we" are not. For African Americans to challenge this view is to challenge "us" just where "we" feel ourselves most intimately virtuous, and it is also to challenge Mark Twain, and thereby the America he "quintessentially" represents. I find this structure pernicious.

In its 1982 editorial on the challenge to *Huckleberry Finn* in Fairfax County, the *New York Times* wrote as if racism were only a matter of specific intention to harm, of attitude rather than habitual practice and social structure: "Carry Mr. Wallace's condemnation to its logical conclusion and Huck Finn's audience is also racist—but we'll bet they don't know it." The *Times* proposed that people read *Huckleberry Finn* not for racist reasons but "because it is exciting and beautiful and funny" ("A Little"). I think the *Times* missed the point. Wallace's campaign trusted that people can be brought to recognize that familiar behavior and practices, including some that have been honored for decades, such as requiring *Huckleberry Finn* in schools, may operate in a racially offensive way, and may, therefore, be rejected as racist. Of course people "don't know it" before being engaged in discussion by someone who may succeed in showing them that they were not aware of all the issues.

Moreover, as I have already indicated, contrary to the *Times*, most school instruction does not treat *Huckleberry Finn* simply as an excellent aesthetic object. Leo Marx spelled out this issue in a thoughtful essay on the controversies of the 1980s:

> To claim that it should be required reading because it is a great American book is unconvincing: we don't require students to read most great books. Objections to the requirement become more understandable if we recognize the unique character of the niche Twain's book tends to occupy in the high-school English course. It often is the only book that is centrally concerned with racial oppression. ("Huck" 152)

If *Huckleberry Finn* were read and taught only for pleasure, there would be much less passion in defending its classroom role. The identification of a book not just with a nation, but with the *goodness* of the nation, makes the controversy so painful. Why can we not allow our *selves* to be better than our masterpieces? Is it impossible to grant that we and our children may try to live by standards that Twain and his society could not yet imagine?

The structure of identification and defense is irrational, and such irrationality is evident in contradictions that even scholars are brought to in writing for larger audiences. On the hundredth anniversary of the American publication of *Huckleberry Finn,* in February 1985, protests arose over the opening of *Big River,* the musical drama based on Twain's novel. A scholar wrote to defend the book in the *Times* Op-Ed page. The defense thoughtfully focused on the problem of Twain's irony. An ironist "faces two problems," namely, that the "reader may miss the point" and that "the reader may get the wrong point." But it then concluded, "the novel continues to force us to confront our own hypocrisy and arrogance" (Fishkin, "Twain"). This conclusion in no way follows from the analysis of irony. The trouble with irony, as the essay pointed out, is that many readers for a century have missed or mistaken "the" point. Then how can it be claimed that the book "forces us" to do anything? This is one of many judgments that praise *Huckleberry Finn* for "irony" or "complexity" (critical terms that need reassessment) but then go on to find a very simple lesson that in fact denies complexity and debate.

More recently, another scholar, in the *TLS* (London), began by referring to the Wallace controversy: "It looked as though the fact that *Huckleberry Finn* is one of the fiercest denunciations of racism in American culture would have to be demonstrated all over again" (Fender). This seems a pretty straightforward claim for an authoritative meaning to the book, but the review ended, "what makes *Huckleberry Finn* a classic is not that it embodies some timeless set of values established by the dominant culture, but continues to invite reinterpretation." That is, it continues to invite reinterpretations— unless someone denies the "fact" that it is "one of the fiercest denunciations," and so forth.

My research demonstrates that the belief that *Huckleberry Finn* is "one of the fiercest denunciations," and so forth, is a belief people began to assert only around 1950, just when racial equality was "established" by the "dominant culture" high on its list of "values." To argue against the belief that *Huckleberry Finn* is such a denunciation is not to oppose struggles against racism, but it is to try to take that struggle beyond the stage of 1950.

1 ————

Huckleberry Finn as Idol and Target

Huckleberry Finn is a wonderful book that has been loaded with so much value in our culture that it has become an idol. It is invoked by the upper-middlebrow establishment in endlessly various circumstances to shed its power and elevate the subject under discussion, as I illustrate with a range of instances from the *New York Times*. This idolatry would be a harmless foible, except that it goes along with the novel's required presence in schools, frequently at junior high level, and when parents and children of color complain about the classroom effects of Huck's constant use of the word *nigger*, they are put down with the passion provoked by the defense of an idol. Even though protests are denigrated by asserting the immense good *Huckleberry Finn* does for race relations, in fact the idolatry of the book has served, and—remarkably—continues to serve, as an excuse for well-meaning white people to use the term *nigger* with the good conscience that comes from believing that their usage is sanctioned by their idol (whether Twain, or his book, or Huck) and is made safe by the technique of irony. In this chapter, after illustrating the modes of sanctifying reference in the *Times*, I begin tracing some of the controversy provoked by opposition to the book, focusing on the problem of "Nigger Jim" and the difficulties of the argument from irony.

The Idol

In the *Times*, the novelist Anne Tyler reviewed E. L. Doctorow's *Billy Bathgate*—a novel that shares with *Huckleberry Finn* an early teenaged narrator-protagonist, living in a violent and

16

morally dubious environment close to the time and place of its author's own youth. All this she did not mention, it was so obvious; all she needed to say was that the plot of *Billy Bathgate* was "almost perfectly constructed," that it was "as tightly constructed as that of *Huckleberry Finn*." Few other readers have ever found the plot of *Huckleberry Finn* almost perfect, at least since Hemingway drew attention to the ending as a problem, but when a work is an idol, its memory can be used to supply any desired perfection. For Tyler, Doctorow's book was "darker than Huck and Jim floating down a river together," because the gangster Dutch Schultz is a "scary man" who figures as a "powerful but capricious parent." She did not mention Huck's pap—a drunkard who locks Huck up, beats him, and even threatens to kill him. Pap's grotesque violence has disappeared for Tyler, and she has forgotten the weakness of the plot: idolatry means selective memory.

In the *Times*, the theater critic Frank Rich reviewed the Steppenwolf Company production of *The Grapes of Wrath*. He observed that in this performance, Tom Joad and Jim Casy, "who leave civilization to battle against injustice," are historically the "forefathers of the rock-and-roll rebels in Steppenwolf Productions by Sam Shepard and Lanford Wilson just as they are the heirs to Huck and Jim." What is the respect in which they are similar? "They get their hands dirty in the fight for right"—a sentence that makes me imagine Rich was actually thinking of Gene Hackman in *Mississippi Burning*, a film that evidently remained a point of reference for Rich, since he brought it up again in the context of recent debates over the "N-Bomb."

Sometimes it is not necessary to make any comparison at all; the mere invocation of *Huckleberry Finn* is enough to position audience and writer happily on the same good side. When Veronica Geng reviewed Garrison Keillor's *Lake Wobegon Days*, she reached out to her readers, allowing each individually to share a credo, to be "someone who believes, as I do, that the greatest moment in American literature is when Huckleberry Finn says to himself [at least she remembers that he didn't say it to a vigilante posse], 'All right, then, I'll *go* to hell.'"

It's not just a *New Yorker* parodist who so admires a funny novel. Arthur Schlesinger Jr., an important historian, an architect of Camelot, the author of the prophetic 1960 polemic, *Nixon or Kennedy: Does it Make Any Difference?* shares this belief. Schlesinger not only is an honored historian but has also been for half a century a powerful participant in national political debate, so his voice reaches far beyond the academy. In a *Times* piece titled "The Opening of the American Mind," originally the inaugural address when Vartan Gregorian became president of Brown University, Schlesinger argued, against Allan Bloom's *Closing of the American Mind*, that absolutism is socially dangerous and relativism does much less damage. In his concluding sequence, Schlesinger devoted a half column to the "greatest . . . American . . . of them all," Abraham Lincoln, and then for his finale a quarter column to the "human struggle against the absolute in the finest scene of the greatest of American novels." Schlesinger zeroed in on chapter 31. He recalled Huck's indecision over whether to write to Miss Watson and tell her where she could catch Jim, and Huck's disobedience to the voice of the absolute, speaking as his conscience, which tells him it is wrong to have helped a slave to escape. After quoting the most memorable line of that sequence, "All right, then, I'll *go* to hell," Schlesinger ended, "That, if I may say so, is what America is all about."

Part of what I mean by idolatry is that Schlesinger here joins a long tradition of using *Huckleberry Finn* as the basis for statements proclaiming what is truly American—I have never seen so much use of the term "quintessentially" as in the claims for the Americanness of *Huckleberry Finn*. So to question *Huckleberry Finn* is to be *un*American. For Van Wyck Brooks in the 1920s, as for Bernard DeVoto in the 1930s, as for Lionel Trilling in the 1940s, so for Schlesinger and many others today—whether like Schlesinger combating the "disuniting of America," or like Shelley Fisher Fishkin glorying in "hybridity"—*Huckleberry Finn* figures at the core of what an authoritative "we" takes to be the meaning of America.

Trilling's essay is especially important. In 1948 the newly published *Literary History of the United States* laid out a triumphant nationalist vindication of American literature, and Rinehart published the first college text version of *Huckleberry Finn*, introduced by Trilling, who was to become the most widely respected and influential American critic of the next two decades. Trilling was already known for his sense of nuance and complexity, tempered in the debates of *Partisan Review* over Marxism and modernism, yet his introduction is hyperbolic praise, commonly reprinted under the title "The Greatness of *Huckleberry Finn*." His essay proved the book's open sesame into college canonicity. Once there was a time, for somewhat more than the first half of the book's century of existence, when many public cultural authorities argued against

Huckleberry Finn for its alleged vulgarity or disrespect for social hierarchy and when an avant-garde defended it, while it was also widely read by many who were in neither of these cultural parties. The Second World War brought the United States to an unparalleled place of world power, and it also marked the point at which many previously oppositional intellectuals found their way to accommodation.

As part of this movement, Trilling redefined the relation of a book to our nation at a key moment in its history. Trilling brought to bear on *Huckleberry Finn* comparisons drawn from his years teaching the Columbia College Humanities ("great books") course, and he thereby authenticated the work as a masterpiece of world literature, elevating the popular art form of prose fiction to the elite level of epic, tragedy, and aristocratic verse drama. For Trilling, *Huckleberry Finn* in American culture was like the *Odyssey* in classical Greek culture, a book read in childhood that grows as its reader does. The recurrent ecstatic passages on the river were, for Trilling, like the choral odes of Greek tragedy, and even the ending had the perfect formal aptness of the Turkish masque that ends Molière's *Bourgeois Gentilhomme*. So Trilling asserted.

Moreover his essay's inclusion in Trilling's collection *The Liberal Imagination* made its extravagant praises all the more striking, since Trilling's volume as a whole favored the complex and the "conditioned." In the volume's keynote essay, "Reality in America," Trilling rescued Henry James from charges of effete snobbery by placing James's work at the "dark and bloody crossroads where literature and politics meet" (8). Likewise, Trilling rescued Twain from Van Wyck Brooks's charges of moral timidity, by asserting that Huck and Jim form a "community of saints." Since Trilling's landmark hymn of praise, *Huckleberry Finn* remains an object for debate and analysis in the academy, but the public authorities have made it an idol. Just as socially marginal and culturally avant-garde ethnics like Trilling (who Columbia planned to dismiss in 1936 because as "a Jew, a Marxist, a Freudian" he couldn't be happy there—see Diana Trilling 274) became authorities, so the book that was an underdog has become an overlord.

The Problem

Nowadays the people in the public sphere who are most unhappy about *Huckleberry Finn* are African American parents and students who find that the book's established role in the schools creates painful difficulties. The fundamental issue in parents' and children's pain over the classroom prestige of *Huckleberry Finn* has been the 213 uses of the deeply offensive term "nigger." Scholars, following a lead from Ralph Ellison, have been especially concerned with the role of stereotypical minstrel techniques in the representation of Jim. But the core issue may be focused in the phrase with which Robert Penn Warren titled his 1965 volume of exploratory conversations about America in the civil rights era, "Who Speaks for the Negro?" Cold War liberal American culture seemed to find in *Huckleberry Finn* a century-old solution to the race problems that had newly reemerged on the national agenda. Twain's solution would permit an imaginary national first person to trust that, like Huck, in "our" hearts "we" had always been right. In 1944 Gunnar Myrdal's massive study of "The Negro Problem and American Democracy" had defined "the American Dilemma" as "a problem in the heart of the American" (lxix); tragically, Myrdal's perspective made clear that "the" American is white. Many African Americans, inside and outside the academy, have found that answer inadequate, both in the social science scholarship and policy advice following from Myrdal, and in the educational and cultural efforts focused around *Huckleberry Finn*.

Even Ralph Ellison, whose "Fiction and the Black Mask of Humanity" made one of the most powerful affirmations of the greatness of *Huckleberry Finn*, and who was at all times a fiercely committed integrationist, by the later 1960s found it necessary to "insist" that the figure of Jim was "not grounded enough in the reality of Negro American personality" (*Conversations* 171). The reason, Ellison argued, was that Twain's imagined audience was exclusively white:

> I know of no black—Negro—critics (I'm a Negro, by the way) who
> wrote criticisms of Huckleberry Finn when it appeared. It was all
> a dialogue between, a recreation, a collaboration, between a white
> American novelist of good heart, of democratic vision, one dedicated
> to values—I know much of Mark Twain's writing—and white readers,
> primarily. What is going on is that now you have more literate Ne-
> groes, and they are questioning themselves, and questioning every-
> thing which has occurred and been written in the country.

Even as Ellison asserted his unpopular principles—he was a "Negro," he had read and valued a lot of Twain, even black separatists were "American"—he underlined the major thrust of Black Power.

Because "*everybody* reads now" and "*Everybody* is American whether they call themselves separatists, black separatists, secessionists or what not," therefore "everybody is saying, Damn it, tell it like *I* think it is" (172).

Let me spell out the complexity here, for it is still not widely acknowledged. It was only after the Second World War that *Huckleberry Finn* achieved massive canonicity in the schools, as the great spiritual representative of the America that had become the dominant power in the world, and that aimed to embrace alien peoples with the loving innocence that Huck offered Jim; yet these same years were the time that the assertion of African American civil rights, most strongly symbolized in *Brown v. Board of Education* (1954), brought new voices into play concerning the relations of whites and blacks. African Americans increasingly gained the power to assert their rights to define and judge the terms of those relations, but they were also increasingly subjected to agonizing scenes of interracial good intentions. (Of course, I, too, may prove guilty on this count.) *Huckleberry Finn* served a national and global political function as an icon of integration, and the importance of this cultural work overrode the offense the book generated among many of its newly authorized, but also newly obligated, African American readers.

A letter to the *Times* written during a controversy over *Huckleberry Finn* in 1982 looked back to the writer's schooldays in the 1950s:

> I can still recall the anger and pain I felt as my white classmates read aloud the word "nigger." . . . I wanted to sink into my seat. Some of the whites snickered, others giggled. I can recall nothing of the literary merits of this work that you term the "greatest of all American novels." I only recall the sense of relief I felt when I would flip ahead a few pages and see that the word "nigger" would not be read that hour. (Ballard)

When a school board or library attempts to act in response to this pain, out come the authorities to defend the book. The standard pattern is for journalists to draw authority from scholars to dump on parents and children. I am disturbed by the structure of debate I have found, and this book is my response. The character of discussion that is still most prevalent emerges from two examples of what seems to me thoughtlessness on the part of journalists who have earned some claim to be taken seriously.

Christopher Hitchens has been a regular columnist for so diverse a set of journals as the *TLS* (London), *Elle, Vanity Fair,* and the *Nation.* He is a political and cultural commentator whose work I often greatly admire, but I disagree with his attack on those who wish to "remove *Huckleberry Finn* from the curriculum" because they find it racially offensive. He characterized them as "know-nothings and noise-makers" and, in an astonishing swing of medicalizing normativity, "neurotics." It would seem that if you are an African American child who does not like to go to school because some other students feel empowered to talk like the hero of the assigned book and call you "nigger," that is your sickness, not a matter of public concern.

Fred Hechinger, then education editor of the *New York Times,* sounded the same note in drawing from a pamphlet by Justin Kaplan on the troubles of *Huckleberry Finn* over the century since it was published. Kaplan is a scholar most of whose career has been independent of the academy. He was chosen to introduce the 1996 edition of *Huckleberry Finn* (based on the newly discovered first half of the manuscript), and he has long been a public authority. His biographical study *Mr. Clemens and Mark Twain* won the Pulitzer Prize and National Book Award in 1967, and his pamphlet was sponsored by the Library of Congress and the Florida Center for the Book. From the genteel library committees of the nineteenth century to concerned parents and pained students today, Kaplan saw a continuity in attacks on *Huckleberry Finn* by "official or self-appointed guardians of public taste or morality" (*Born* 14). These are not terms of respectful description for parents and children, and in discussing the recent debates, Kaplan could not have been less respectful. "It seems unlikely," he wrote,

> that anyone, of any color, who had actually read *Huckleberry Finn,* instead of merely reading or hearing about it, and who had allowed himself or herself even the barest minimum of intelligent response to its underlying spirit and intention, could accuse it of being "racist" because some of its characters [Kaplan does not say its narrator and hero] use offensive racial epithets. (*Born* 18)

Yet, I would note, no one seeks to ban Frederick Douglass's 1845 *Narrative of the Life of an American Slave, Written by Himself* even though this work uses the term a few times. Douglass makes clear, however, every time the term is used that it is meant as hostile toward African Americans. "One has to be deliberately dense,"

Kaplan added, "to miss the point that Mark Twain is making" (*Born* 19). But what is the point? So any black person who disagrees with Kaplan on this issue is, if not neurotic, at least stubborn and stupid, and probably incapable of "actually" reading. Kaplan used Twain's authority to construct a model of reading in which "the" reader is a white liberal, and a model of race relations that requires blacks to listen to the master-reader's voice, and if you don't take his lesson, it's your fault.

I am not holding Twain solely responsible for such use of his book. For example, ever since *Huckleberry Finn* was first published, readers—not all readers—have referred to Jim as "Nigger Jim," although the book never uses this phrase. Public idolatry of *Huckleberry Finn* lends authority to the continued honorable circulation of this terribly offensive term of racial antagonism. In 1984, to celebrate the centennial of *Huckleberry Finn*, the *New York Times Book Review* commissioned arguably the greatest living American novelist, Norman Mailer, to read *Huckleberry Finn* as if it were a new book, and to write about it not as a monument, but as a piece of living literature. Mailer hymned the book's praises: "The river winds like a fugue through the marrow of the true narrative." What was this true narrative for Mailer? It was "nothing less than the ongoing relation between Huck and the runaway slave, this Nigger Jim whose name embodies the very stuff of the slave system itself—his name is not Jim but Nigger Jim." Rather than refuse to publish Mailer because he had obviously not read the book, the *Times* ran this feature on its front page. Likewise, in a feature article in the Children's Books section of the *Times*, the eminent Czechoslovakian emigré novelist Joseph Skvorecky argued that *Huckleberry Finn* is not racist even though "the second principal character is called Nigger Jim." Evidently no *Times* literary editor recognized the inaccuracy of this statement, because the lesson public authorities wish this book to teach is that even saints say "nigger."

The Word

Now I must go on at some length about the word *nigger.* I start at a historic distance, but then move, as so many Americans have found themselves doing recently, toward Detective Mark Fuhrman's role at the murder trial of O. J. Simpson. You recall that many broadcast media bleeped out Fuhrman's use of the term, and

USA Today would not print the term even in their front-page story revealing the contents of the Fuhrman tapes. So I ask before going on: should people of goodwill unhesitatingly maintain that a word banned from CNN and *USA Today* must be required in the eighth-grade schoolroom?

In 1968 appeared the earliest essay I know on the topic of *Huckleberry Finn* and race by someone still active among senior African American literary scholars. Donald B. Gibson observed a scholarly anomaly. Even though Jim is "frequently referred to by critics as 'Nigger Jim'," actually Jim "is never once called this in *Huckleberry Finn!*" (196).

It is often claimed that Albert Bigelow Paine put this offensive naming into circulation in his authorized biography of Twain (1912). In fact, this pejorative title for Jim was coined in the very first news-paper responses to *Huckleberry Finn,* before its American publi-cation and while excerpts were being published in the *Century* magazine. While the *Louisville Courier-Journal* reprinted the comic account of Jim's misfortunes as a banker, referring to him as "A Col-ored Citizen," both the *Chicago Herald* and *Cleveland Herald* reprinted the touching episode about Jim and his deaf daughter, referring to "Nigger Jim" (Twain, *Huckleberry* [1988] 523). The complexities that have accompanied responses to *Huckleberry Finn* over its history are there from the beginning. The paper from a state only twenty years removed from slavery reprints an episode that contributes to the stereotype of African Americans as incapable of effective citizen-ship in a free economy, while the papers from what had been the "free" states choose one of the most humane representations of Jim but caption it with a name for him that undoes that humanity.

There is little point in detailing the prevalence of this degrading way of referring to Jim during the first half of the twentieth century. It participated in the ethos of segregation that prevailed across the culture. Even Bernard DeVoto used this phrase that Twain never wrote in *Huckleberry Finn* (*Mark* 52, 292). Yet DeVoto emphasized, more than any other scholar for decades before and after, the im-pact of African American cultural practices on the young Sam Clemens, and he intended that his *Mark Twain's America* (1932) should differ from biographical criticism in the wake of Van Wyck Brooks by virtue of devoting scrupulous attention to "what a great man wrote" (xi). Twenty years later, Dixon Wecter, DeVoto's suc-cessor as literary director for the Twain estate, did no better. His posthumously published biographical study, *Sam Clemens of Hannibal* (1952), in tune with polite standards of its time was rather more sensitive than DeVoto had been to the sufferings, and rather less concerned with the cultural contributions, of African Americans in Twain's early milieu. Nonetheless, in proclaiming Jim "Mark Twain's noblest creation" (100), Wecter called him by a name that Twain never used, putting the phrase in quotation marks as if to authenticate it (Wecter also used the phrase without qualification [44]).

The very Sunday after the Supreme Court decision of 17 May 1954 in *Brown vs. Board of Education,* Joseph Wood Krutch wrote in the *New York Times Book Review* in praise of the greatness of *Huckleberry Finn.* He set Twain's accomplishment against the procedures of the "problem novelist" which his Columbia colleague Lionel Trilling had been attacking since the later 1930s. Krutch valued "artistically" even the "intellectual" and "sociological" "points" in *Huckleberry Finn* over the whole tradition from *Uncle Tom's Cabin* to "the complete corpus of recent novels about 'prejudice.'" In referring to *Uncle Tom's Cabin,* Krutch more specifically echoed the argument of James Baldwin's 1949 *Partisan Review* essay, "Everybody's Protest Novel," which had polemically placed Stowe at the beginning of the tradition that led to Richard Wright. Yet Krutch's apparent affiliation with the views of Baldwin, in 1954 an increasingly respected African American writer, did not keep him from naming Jim with the term that continues to mark the American history of racial inequality.

A younger and far more flamboyantly transgressive writer than Krutch, Leslie Fiedler first broached in the 1940s a thesis that has been one of the most productive and controversial lines of thought about American literature and popular culture for nearly fifty years. His 1948 *Partisan Review* essay, "Come Back to the Raft Ag'in, Huck Honey!" (a phrase that embodies Fiedler's thesis but is not actually found in the book), boldly argued that the characteristic American act of imagination involves the deeply affectionate but chaste bond between males of different races. It was part of Fiedler's daring that he linked this historical thesis to current American social practices and tensions around both sexuality and race:

> The situations of the Negro and the homosexual in our society are precisely opposite problems, or at least are problems suggesting precisely

opposite solutions. Our laws on homosexuality and the context of prejudice and feeling they objectify must apparently be changed in accord
with a stubborn social fact, whereas it is the social fact, our overt behavior toward the Negro, that must be modified to accord with our
laws and the, at least official, morality they objectify. (529)

Among the postwar critical works that began the idolatry of *Huckleberry Finn,* Fiedler's is the only one I know that actually brought the
book into relation to the struggle for racial justice. Yet his essay, it
would seem both from intellectual brashness and also to mimic the
ethos of popular culture, continued to name Jim not in Twain's
words but in those of the long American tradition of racial discrimination (530). And in line with Fiedler's wish to remain the bad boy,
even as he became a distinguished senior scholar, holding a chair at
SUNY-Buffalo that he had wished to name after Huckleberry Finn,
his major book *Love and Death in the American Novel* (584) and so recent a work as *What Was Literature* (70), published in 1982, continued to use the term.

In a 1977 essay polemically entitled—contra Fiedler—"Welcome Back from the Raft, Huck Honey!" the neoconservative critic
Kenneth Lynn, who had himself in 1966, as part of his commitment
to the civil rights movement, left Harvard for the University of the
District of Columbia, looked back over the work produced by his
generation of Americanists on *Huckleberry Finn.* Lynn reflected,
"Back in the 1950s . . . literary critics were moved to misread *Huckleberry Finn* for a variety of reasons. Americans in the postwar period
were gradually coming to the conclusion . . . that the ancient pattern of discrimination against Negroes was morally indefensible.
This conclusion precipitated numerous misreadings of *Huckleberry
Finn,*" including Lynn's own. One importance of Lynn's piece is his
acknowledgment that white scholars—not only black parents and
children—may err as readers. He admitted: "Critics like myself
wanted to believe that Huck was renouncing membership in a society that condoned slavery because they did not wish to live in a segregationist nation" (48). Yet misreading continues: Lynn still used
the old misnaming of Jim (42, 48), which is surprising for two reasons. First, the essay appeared in the *American Scholar,* a journal with
famously high standards of editorial care, and second, it formed
part of a series of essays in which Lynn convicted left-oriented
scholarship of tendentious carelessness about documented facts.

But the argument from accuracy is often misused. For example, in the aggressively liberal journal the *Humanist,* June Edwards argued against objections to *Huckleberry Finn* arising in the schools: "*Nigger* is what blacks were commonly called in the South until recent times. It is wrong to censure a novel for historical accuracy. Truth should never be bent to fit an ideology." Edwards's critique of ideologically produced untruth was full of inaccuracy. Her simplified linguistic history may be faulted in at least three dimensions. It erased decades of struggle against the term by many Southern liberals; it forgot that the term was also "commonly" used in the North; and it pretended that in "recent times" the term has ceased to be common. But historiographic debate aside, Edwards was inaccurate in a fourth dimension. For throughout her essay Edwards called Jim by a title that does not appear in the book she was talking about.

What is more surprising and disturbing than Lynn's error in the 1977 *American Scholar,* or—amazingly—twenty years later once more, in 1996 in the *TLS* (London) ("Huckleberry" 4), is that in his own earlier scholarly work, despite its now-acknowledged commitment to a civil rights agenda, he did not allow his wish for racial equality and justice to correct his mistitling of Jim ("You" 409). Even in a textbook that he edited in 1961 for use at quite an introductory stage of literary study, Lynn suggested the following topics for papers: "Nigger Jim: minstrel-show clown, Black Christ, or human being?" and "Compare the description of Uncle Dan'l in *Mark Twain's Autobiography* to Nigger Jim" (*Huckleberry* 217). So the authoritative scholar's pedagogical guidance required students to perpetuate this wounding error. In fact, one motive for John Wallace's 1982 protest was the experience of Rosa Harper: "My child comes home . . . concerned that she had to answer a question on a test about the book by using the word 'nigger' to describe a black character in the book" (Moore 6).

Lynn's teacher and longtime senior colleague at Harvard, the most distinguished intellectual historian active in American studies in the twentieth century, Perry Miller, did not set a better example in his posthumously published lectures entitled "An American Language" of which the third of three is devoted to *Huckleberry Finn* (*Nature's* 230, 238, 240). And to this day, a professionally respected senior figure in Twain studies, Tom Quirk, seems to think that by placing the phrase in quotation marks (64), implying that it is Twain's own usage, he can go on writing as if there were really no cause to worry about offensive language. But Quirk's own language is troubling; he writes of racial issues as if there were not complex issues dividing African Americans, such as those of class and gender, but instead only one single person of color who need be thought about, "the Negro" (65).

British scholars are no more immune than American scholars to this offensive carelessness toward the text they are discussing and the readers they are addressing. In a pathbreaking article that in the wake of American Black Power initiatives rethought *Huckleberry Finn* from Jim's perspective, Harold Beaver argued that "white and black throughout had been mutual pawns, utilizing each other, manipulating each other as *objects* of romance or *tools* of escape." For in "a slave-owning republic, where human labour was bought and sold, human relations too were inevitably turned to strategic devices and men to things" (357). In this context, it makes good sense that Beaver used a dehumanizing term in his own title—"Run, Nigger, Run: *Adventures of Huckleberry Finn* as a Fugitive Slave Narrative"—but it makes less good sense to me that he did not distinguish his own usage from that of the society he condemned, for he too titled Jim "Nigger" (339). An even more distinguished critic and novelist, Malcolm Bradbury, wrote on *Huckleberry Finn* for an international, nonspecialized audience of social goodwill. On every page of his article, on the imagined authority of Mark Twain, Jim was defined by a term that I cannot believe would otherwise have been permitted in the *UNESCO Courier*.

It may be a small professional comfort to literary scholars, but it hardly makes one feel better for either critical standards of reading or politics in the United States that the most admired historians are just as damagingly careless. The most important historian of the American South over the last fifty years, and an important activist and publicist on behalf of the civil rights movement, C. Vann Woodward, in a pained and powerful essay of 1967 referred to Jim by a term that I'm not aware he has elsewhere ever allowed himself to write in his own voice in his published works (*Burden* 181). And in a book that explicitly set out to supplement for our time Woodward's classic *Origins of the New South* (1951) and that won the 1992 Pulitzer Prize, Edward Ayers hauled out this old, mistaken term (538).

This maddening survey suggests that even though *Huckleberry Finn* is claimed as a talisman of racially progressive thought and action, one of its major effects is actually to license and authorize the continued honored circulation of a term that is both explosive and degrading.

Recall the debate at the trial of O. J. Simpson. In a story itself scrupulously sparing in the use of what its headline called the "epithet," Kenneth B. Noble reported that Christopher Darden, "a Deputy District Attorney who is black," said that "what he called the 'N-word' was so hideously pejorative that it would inevitably prejudice the mostly black jury" against Detective Fuhrman, if it could be shown that he had used the term. Darden continued, "It's the filthiest, dirtiest, nastiest word in the English language," so powerful that "when you mention that word to this jury, or any African-American, it blinds people. It'll blind the jury. It'll blind the truth. They won't be able to discern what's true and what's not." Johnnie Cochran, counsel for Simpson's defense, did not claim that the term was any less offensive than Darden had, only that African Americans have to bear so much that they can bear this too and keep their "perspective": "African-Americans live with offensive words, offensive looks, offensive treatment every day of their lives."

Although Judge Ito decided in favor of the defense, he powerfully summarized Darden's argument as maintaining that the epithet is "so vile that it operates as a divisive demand that those to whom or about whom it is said take some action and that its use can cloud the operation of good judgment and common sense."

A powerful illustration of the judge's point comes as a climactic moment in *Uncle Tom's Cabin*. George Shelby, the son of Uncle Tom's original Kentucky master, has been seeking to rescue Tom from the horrors into which he has been sold. But when George finally locates Tom on Legree's plantation, it is too late. Tom has already died from Legree's beating, heroically refusing to reveal anything about the other slaves who have escaped. George threatens to charge Legree with murder. "Snapping his fingers, scornfully," Legree dares him to try: "Where you going to get witnesses—how you going to prove it?" George is stymied by the Southern prohibition against testimony by blacks against whites. Legree in triumph gloats, "After all, what a fuss, for a dead nigger!" Stowe writes, "The word was as a spark to a powder magazine," and George knocks Legree flat (592). So, a major point of *Uncle Tom's Cabin* has been to bring good-hearted white folks to realize that "nigger" is a fighting word, just as Judge Ito said a century and a half later.

A more distressing example of Ito's point occurred in late 1995 in San Francisco. Louis Waldron was charged with first-degree murder after an incident in which he hit a man once. The Irish American who died was on his way home from a bar when a traffic incident with Waldron left him "uninjured but angered." He "called Mr. Waldron a 'nigger.'" Waldron, a college student majoring in criminology, responded with a punch: "the single blow knocked Mr. Hourican, a former amateur boxer, to the pavement, fracturing his skull. He died two days later" (Noble, "A Man"). The charge of first-degree murder makes sense only on the presumption that African Americans form a firm intention to kill anyone who insults them with this offensive term. I don't believe this is true, but it is worth noting that a recent feature in the *New York Times* indicates that in New York street talk, "ethnic slurs" nowadays form the "most taboo language" (Goldberg).

In the Simpson and Waldron cases the fates of several individuals, living and dead, were at issue, but can it be asserted with confidence that the fates of many individuals are not at stake in the classroom? Has any public authority ever defended the decision not to teach *Huckleberry Finn* in a particular class with arguments as powerful as Darden used here? In their different ways, both attorneys crafted arguments that showed high respect for the jurors. Have the discussions concerning *Huckleberry Finn* shown a comparable respect for the citizens—parents or children—who find themselves pained, offended, or frightened by the permission *Huckleberry Finn* gives to the circulation of an abusive term in classroom and schoolyard? The difference is clear enough: in one instance it's a murder trial, in the other instance it's just kids' lives.

In summer 1995, as the Simpson trial continued, Michael Jackson's *HIStory* came out. Here the use of abusively anti-Semitic terms was obviously in the context of an artwork, the speech of a character in a lyric genre, yet neither the widely shared confidence that Jackson did not intend to express an anti-Semitic position nor the aesthetic explanations of impersonation or irony were sufficient to calm a level of outrage that quickly produced not only apology but actual changes in the lyrics for future issues. In February 1996, while relaxing in a hotel room prior to giving a lecture on this material, I was astonished to find, on the five o'clock news, reports from Brazil that Michael Jackson was suspected of having sung his original lyrics. Evidently, he is under ongoing surveillance. By contrast,

Twain's greatness not only means that authorities rush to preserve, rather than to urge changing, his words; his greatness also leads authorities to urge that his words be enforced on every schoolchild. How great must artists be before we trust them so much that their words are treated not only as unchangeable but also as obligatory? How much must a slur hurt, and whom, before we decide that it need not be made a compulsory part of what Cochran called the everyday "offensive treatment" that marks the ongoing racial life of the United States?

The fact that *nigger* is widely used in the text of *Huckleberry Finn* has had the effect of encouraging authors, scholars, teachers, and other persons of goodwill to feel that they are doing the right thing when they name Jim in the language of a racism that it is less important to locate in the psyche of individuals—as Myrdal did in *An American Dilemma*—than in the structures of our nation, what since the days of Black Power has been called "institutionalized racism." Over forty years ago, Lionel Trilling praised *Huckleberry Finn* for being a "subversive book," and Hechinger echoed him in his *Times* article, but it seems to me that *Huckleberry Finn* is currently being read and publicly used in support of complacency.

The Arguments

When they are not simply denying the specific experiences and charges of wounded and angry students and parents, the authoritative defenders of *Huckleberry Finn* must use arguments, and they do. The arguments used by the public authorities are an especially interesting case of the relations between professional academic critical discourses and the sphere of public life from which academic work is supposedly isolated.

The major lines of analysis used by the public cultural authorities closely correspond to the major lines of interpretation worked out over the forty years following the challenge posed by Van Wyck Brooks. Brooks's *Ordeal of Mark Twain* argued in 1920 that Twain failed to achieve the greatness of which he was capable because he muted his social criticism in favor of pleasing a large popular readership. Current public analyses draw particularly on the period when academic canonical discourse around *Huckleberry Finn* was most intensely in formation, roughly the 1950s, the years from Trilling's introduction to the appearance of Henry Nash Smith's summational *Mark Twain: The Development of a Writer* in 1962 and Leo Marx's *The Machine in the Garden* in 1964 — the years, I emphasize, of the rise and cresting of the civil rights movement.

Decades of revisionary academic work has been done since then. Only a few years after Trilling's edition, Leo Marx challenged what I call the hypercanonizing principle that "once a work has been admitted to the highest canon of literary reputability," critics then must "find reasons . . . for admiring every bit of it" (*Pilot* 48). Some thirty years ago, James Cox and Richard Poirier developed critical arguments that cut against the terms by which most recent public discussion has praised *Huckleberry Finn*. Cox found that "Huck's revolt" is not very morally impressive, for he is involved in "a subversive project which has the reader's complete approval — the freeing of a slave in the Old South, a world which, by virtue of the Civil War, had been declared morally reprehensible because of the slavery it condoned" (168). He continued, "if this were all there was to it we would have nothing but the blandest sentimental action" (170). Poirier elucidated an important limitation of Twain's method, which helps to explain why the book runs down. *Huckleberry Finn*, he argued, "cannot dramatize the meanings accumulated at the moment of social crisis because the crisis itself reveals the inadequacy of the terms by which understandings can be expressed between the hero and other members of his society. There is no publicly accredited vocabulary which allows Huck to reveal his inner self to others" (177). This inadequacy of vocabulary, which idolaters take as a truth about Huck's America, Poirier instead treated as a limiting artistic feature of the fictional world Twain has constructed.

The thinking of such revisionists, and many others who have followed, has hardly reached the public authorities. The only new academic development since the early 1960s that has begun to reach the public may be dated from the *Mark Twain Journal* 1984 special issue, for the centennial of *Huckleberry Finn*, edited by Thadious Davis, in which black scholars addressed the book. This special issue, expanded as a book in 1992 (Leonard et al.), began the process that made possible both the accomplishment and the attention won by Shelley Fisher Fishkin's *Was Huck Black?* (1993).

Three major categories organize the decades-long pattern of public critical defense of *Huckleberry Finn:* irony, realism, and historicism. At this point, I will say something about irony, deferring the other topics for later chapters. Within the academy both sophisticated theorists and regretful conservatives tend to assume that stable irony has been superseded since the demise of New Criticism and its technique of close reading of the work in itself without regard to biography or history. But the most insistent public claims made for the value of *Huckleberry Finn* involve its moral stance as an achievement of irony. Hitchens took this position against the noisemakers and neurotics. This comes down to claiming that there is a bad kind of discrimination, practiced by white society in the antebellum South of Twain's novel, and a good kind of discrimination, practiced by readers who are sufficiently sophisticated to understand exactly what parts Twain is criticizing of the world he portrays.

But how does a reader know, and who is "the reader"? In 1971 the sitcom *All in the Family* quickly rose to the top of the charts. Norman Lear, its producer, is now very well known as a liberal, and many liberal viewers at the time understood that in representing the bigoted views of Archie Bunker, the show was subjecting them to satiric criticism, just as critical authorities now hold that Huck's racist language is. But the show reached a far larger audience than the liberal intelligentsia. Many viewers were reported as saying that "they identified with [Archie]." As one of them put it to *Life,* in a formulation that has great resonance for the problems of what *Huckleberry Finn* means in the classroom: "You think it, but ole Archie he says it, by damn" (Patterson 740). Twain and Lear alike provoke different responses from different readers. It is offensive for cultural authorities to grant legitimacy to only a single way of reading.

The one certain basis for a necessary irony in reading *Huckleberry Finn* is that Huck does not know, and every reader the book has ever had does know, that American slavery was historically doomed, and it vanished between the time of the book's action (about 1845) and its publication (about 1885). Moreover, the martyrdom of Lincoln established at least through the North a consensus, which had not existed at the beginning of the Civil War or even at the time of the Emancipation Proclamation, that in the Civil War the North intended not only to preserve the Union, but also to extend freedom to slaves. Everyone who has read the book, therefore, knows enough to understand the irony of "All right, then, I'll *go* to hell."

Here I think James Cox is right and Lionel Trilling and Arthur Schlesinger are wrong. The moral lesson of *Huckleberry Finn* is not relativist or subversive but absolute. As the intellectual historian Perry Miller explained:

> Hell in 1885 was still officially a reality. Even so, Mark Twain's readers were not offended; on the contrary, they loved Huck all the more. . . . Mark Twain enlisted the Protestant conscience on the side of the naive Huckleberry Finn because that conscience was long since assured that slavery had been a sin. The most orthodox of churchmen would smile benevolently over Huck's crisis. All could rejoice in this triumph of instinctive benevolence over the ancient formalities of a crude society and a crude theology—and congratulate themselves upon their sophistication. (282)

Only the universally shared assumption by readers that slavery is morally unacceptable defines the moral significance of Huck's decision to go to hell; all readers recognize that Huck will not go to hell because, contrary to his society's beliefs, he is doing the right thing. But where does the book stand on racism as opposed to slavery? Here many readers have disagreed, and yet here is the crux of the pain for contemporary black readers. If Huck has such moral insight that he is willing to go to hell for Jim's sake, why does he not find new ways of saying his new sense of the world? Why not stop using a word that is part of the system he is, we suppose, rejecting?

I have already referred to Frederick Douglass and Harriet Beecher Stowe. Let me add one more text from the time when the action of *Huckleberry Finn* occurs. In a moment of despair, around 1845, Ralph Waldo Emerson wrote in his journal: "What argument, what eloquence can avail against the power of that one word *niggers*? The man of the world annihilates the whole combined force of all the antislavery societies of the world by pronouncing it" (338). Huck may not mean anything bad by the word, but his continuing usage helps keep it alive and ready to be exploited by those who benefit from the way of the world that denigrates blacks.

I find a further problem with the ironic moral stance. What if we apply the analytic mode, favored by ironizing critics, which involves placing various parts of the book in relation to each other to test their potentially contradictory relationship? Huck, we recall, in the early pages of the book has received a certain amount of religious instruction. Miss Watson tells him "all about the bad place." His response? "I said I wished I was there." And when she tells him about her plans to get to "the good place," he "couldn't see no advantage in going where she was going" (3–4). So from the beginning Huck has been ready to go to hell, and in chapter 31, despite the powerfully affecting rhetorical pressure, there is therefore no actual drama in what is generally referred to as his "crisis." In Aristotle's terms, it is strong in thought not plot, just as the ending of the book undermines what has seemed to be its action by revealing that Jim has already been willed free. As Leslie Fiedler suggested, in terms compatible with my own analysis of Huck as a "sensitive spectator" (the crucial type of character in the mode of writing that I call literary narrative), the "ultimate problem" is whether Huck, "whose role is to suffer and evade," can successfully "take a hand in the affairs of the world, make something *happen*" (*Love* 587). The answer is no.

Or take it another way: Ironizing critics tend to agree that a major structural irony of the book is the exposure of various literary and conventional modes of thought, feeling, behavior, of which slavery may be the most consequential and repellent but is by no means the only one. Tom Sawyer is the exemplary character for this pattern, and Tom's renewed dominance in the book's ending has provoked elaborate critical discussions. But what if Huck's great moment before the return of Tom were itself already only another pose? Is Walter Scott chivalry to be condemned only so that a romantic satanism, like that made famous, and conventional, by Scott's younger contemporary Lord Byron, can take its place? The decision to go to hell was not dominant but was nonetheless widespread across nineteenth-century culture. The same principle of superior knowledge that permits a reader to ironize Huck's fears also allows a reader who knows more to ironize his independence. Readers may recognize its conventionality even if he doesn't, just as we recognize the morality of what he believes is immoral.

Both of these problems that might discomfit public ironizers, but have not, are problems that arise from the narrative structure of *Huckleberry Finn;* they arise from readerly attempts to impose a coherent meaning across a range of differentiated repetitions. Winfried Fluck, over twenty years ago, published what remains the most impressive analysis of the critical literature on *Huckleberry Finn;* it is so iconoclastic that it has never been translated from German and has had accordingly little impact. Yet its critique of unifying attempts to define "pattern" and "rhythm" is devastating. Rather than the coolly dispassionate, ironic love of intricate interrelations, I find a different process at work in readers' idolatry of chapter 31, and their generalization from that to the book as a whole. The critical concept of "the sublime" offers resources that may help us hold onto the thrilling power of chapter 31 while understanding, and thereby perhaps resisting, the extravagance of idolatry.

The crucial treatment of the sublime comes from the Greek critic known as Longinus. What he means by the sublime is, most simply, the greatest moments of literary experience, and it is crucial to recognize that only moments concern him. The sublime does not depend on fancy language, and it does not arise from the unity of a work; like a "whirlwind" it tears up any established pattern or texture, so as to stand out from the context or work in which it occurs. The sublime produces, and depends on, a series of identifications, so that the words of a character, at a sublime moment, seem "the echo of a great soul" that is the author's, and in reading the sublime we are "uplifted," "as if we had ourselves produced" what we hear or read (1.4, 9.2, 7.2). The key Greek term here is *ekstasis*, a getting out of one's place, a "transport" into a new state or position. Such an analysis seems to me appropriately to honor the accomplishment of *Huckleberry Finn* without committing criticism to fruitless and ultimately offensive hyperbole about the excellence of the work as a whole, and it seems to me also to underline why the investments made in the work are so great. Here is the motive for idolatry. Because the structure of the sublime joins reader, character, and author in interlinked identifications, it may lead to narcissistically fixed mirrorings rather than "ecstatic" mobility. Readers may then tend to be highly protective of the characters and authors in which they are invested, and at the same time will feel themselves intimately threatened by anything that seems to criticize or diminish either Huck or Twain. When America itself is added to the system of identifications, the stakes are raised immensely by the "quintessential" linkage of character and author and reader to nation.

2

All Right, Then, I'll *Go* to Hell
Historical Contexts for Chapter 31

After irony, the second major category of claims on behalf of *Huckleberry Finn* I call realism. Justin Kaplan's pamphlet attributes to Twain a "truth-telling" that is "realism." Kaplan's notion virtually self-destructs, however, because this realistic world, which Kaplan calls a "faithful," "historical portrait of a slaveholding society" (18), is also, he writes, a "nightmare" of "bigotry, violence, exploitation, greed, ignorance, and a sort of pandemic depravity" (22). Anyone who believes that is "really" the best description of a functioning human society anywhere may feel themselves on the side of right, but I would not trust them to instruct parents and schoolchildren about morals.

A more sophisticated variant of realism holds that *Huckleberry Finn* transforms the materials of everyday life into the dignity of art through the power of its idiomatic, vernacular style, which in turn exercises a critical force against traditionally elevated notions of dignity. In current literary studies, the most powerful arguments on vernacular realism have been developed from the work of the Russian scholar Mikhail Bakhtin. The inspiration for his critical insight came from the fiction of Dostoevski. Despite being himself a devoutly orthodox Christian and politically conservative czarist, Dostoevski provided such vivid speeches to his atheistic and radical characters that many readers have felt they were the heroes. Bakhtin understands a novel's greatness to arise from antagonistic "dialogue" among different ways of speaking—representing different social values—set to work in a novel's prose, and it has seemed tempting to critics to try applying this to Twain (Berthoff; Marx, *Pilot*; Messent; Sewell). I would argue, however, that in

Bakhtin's terms *Huckleberry Finn* has less "dialogue" than we might imagine, that Twain's concern for accuracy in imitating precise dialects does little to ensure that the speakers of those dialects are taken with full seriousness, precisely for the reasons Kaplan's above-quoted words suggest: the bigoted, violent, depraved, greedy speakers are not presented as embodying ways of life that are conceivably valid alternatives to Huck and Jim for any human being we could imagine as decent.

Exploring American Slaveholding Society

Literary categories that claim a close relation between the text and social reality must be brought to the test of historical study, if we are to honor their claims by taking them seriously. Arguments and opinions concerning *Huckleberry Finn* have often relied on Twain's own statements about the world in which he grew up and in which the book is set. In various autobiographical writings about his early years, Twain strongly emphasized what our era would call the "totalitarian" quality of thought, which provided no space for any alternative to arise. In the pages that follow, I will cite, discuss, and reflect on a text in which Twain very influentially established a sense of antebellum reality on which scholars and admirers have relied. This passage delineating a solid and closed society comes from lecture notes for Twain's worldwide reading tour of 1895–96:

> In those old slave-holding days the whole community was agreed as to one thing—the awful sacredness of slave property. To help steal a horse or a cow was a low crime, but to help a hunted slave, or feed him or shelter him, or hide him, or comfort him, in his troubles, his terrors, his despair, or hesitate to promptly betray him to the slave-catcher when opportunity offered was a much baser crime, & carried with it a stain, a moral smirch which nothing could wipe away. That this sentiment should exist among slave-owners is comprehensible—there were good commercial reasons for it—but that it should exist and did exist among the paupers, the loafers, the tag-rag & bobtail of the community, & in a passionate & uncompromising form, is not in our remote day realizable. It seemed natural enough to me then. (*Huckleberry* [1988] 806–7)

This passage carries powerful historical conviction and wisdom. What is now called "hegemony" really does depend on persuading people that they should support a system that does not obviously reward them; hegemony makes it seem "natural" and right that certain things be done that across the gap of a historical epoch, even if only of a few years, seem almost incomprehensibly irrational, so different may be "human nature" and "common sense" in different historical conditions. Yet there are testimonies from slaveholding days that show a considerably more fractured "community" than Twain posits. Some white people did help runaway slaves, some did speak out against the slave system. More fundamentally, the African American people were not "agreed" as to this one thing.

For Twain in this passage, what he calls the "whole community" excludes slaves. Writing three decades after emancipation, this apparently seemed natural to him still. In *The Grandissimes* (1880), a historical novel set in the early nineteenth century, George W. Cable presented the views of a member of the New Orleans establishment explaining himself to a newcomer: "When we say, 'we people,' we *always* mean we white people. The non-mention of color always implies pure white; and whatever is not pure white is to all intents and purposes pure black. When I say 'the whole community', I mean the whole white portion; when I speak of the 'undivided public sentiment', I mean the sentiment of the white population" (59). So Cable exposed the premises of Southern racism's coded language, which Clemens still fell into. Yet neither Christianity nor the founding principles of America shared this premise. When in the late 1850s the Dred Scott decision seemed to make such a position the law of the land and an authoritative interpretation of American history, it marked a fracture so great that war followed quickly. Because Twain chose to represent slaveholding Missouri as so monolithic, Huck's alternatives—to support slavery or go to hell—in the famous sequence of chapter 31 are impoverished. His virtue that does not know its name is miraculous because unaided, pure because inarticulate, able only to misname itself as damnable.

I prefer to understand *Huckleberry Finn* as built from highly selective artistic choices rather than simple reflections of the reality of antebellum America. To gauge Twain's choices requires going behind his own historical claims and memories and placing them in the context of a fuller range of materials. In his evocation of the solid slaveholding ideology and practices of his childhood, Twain makes things much simpler than they were either in his own life or in the life of the United States.

Defining and naming the character of Huck's social background have been focuses for pressure and tension throughout the history of *Huckleberry Finn*. One long-term cultural effect of the Civil War has been to make it seem that the antebellum "South" is identical with the reign of slavery, yet as William Freehling has argued in his massive revisionary synthesis *The Road to Disunion*, precisely the question of what would count as the South, and for what purposes, was an ongoing matter for debate and struggle from the 1830s into the 1860s: "The myth of a monolithic, unchanging Slave South everywhere distorts the history of the slavocracy" (*Reintegration* 158). The famous senators from the slaveholding states of Kentucky and Missouri Henry Clay and Thomas Hart Benton regularly identified themselves as and were understood to be not Southern but Western. Frederick Douglass's Maryland, Uncle Tom's Kentucky, and Jim's Missouri all were Union states when the war came.

Twain's own sense of regional meaning and location is too highly vexed and various to follow in detail, but one point is worth noting. A question that emerges in reading *Life on the Mississippi* might be phrased, "where or what is 'the South'?" In the journey he recounts in this memoir, Twain gets all the way down to Lake Providence, Louisiana, farther than Huck and Jim go, before he finds "the first distinctly southern-looking town" (441), and only at Baton Rouge is he ready to assert, "we were certainly in the south at last" (468).

Yet in our era of hypercanonization, Twain's Missouri was taken as a model for the "South." Such distinguished scholars as Hamlin Hill and Walter Blair, in their textbook edition of *Huckleberry Finn*, explained that the character of Huck's pap displays "the irrational biases of the Southerner" (3) against political or social equality for African Americans. But as a type within the writing of Twain's time, pap is not a Southerner but a "Pike." According to writers of the period, the Pike is "long, lathy, and sallow"; he wears "molasses-colored homespun"; his hair is "frowsy and husky"; and his beard "frowsy and stubbly." "He shambles in his walk. He drawls in his talk. He drinks whiskey by the tank, [and] has little respect for the rights of others" (Brooks, *Times* 76).

As one of "several new types of man" being produced in the United States, this emblem of "all that was ruffianly in the frontier life" was understood to originate in the heartland of the Mississippi, from the two Pike Counties that faced each other across the river, one in free Illinois, the other in slaveholding Missouri. (Recall that Twain defines five of the seven dialects he reproduces in *Huckle-berry Finn* as versions of "Pike-County" speech.) And when pap car-ries off Huck and holds him captive in an isolated cabin, he goes to the Illinois side. So the book does not mark pap as distinctly "Southern." An early experiment in giving some humane dignity to speakers of backcountry "vernacular," the *Pike County Ballads* (1871) by John Hay were the work of a contemporary of Twain's who had grown up in Alton, Illinois. The reviewers of *Huckleberry Finn* char-acterized it as "a vivid picture of Western life" (Perry 289), or as showing "the rough old life of the South-Western States and of the Mississippi Valley" (Matthews 292).

By the 1960s, we have seen, *Huckleberry Finn* was enlisted on the side of civil rights, implicitly defined not as the active, collective "movement" of African Americans, but as the feelings of liberal Northern whites: sympathy toward African Americans and horror toward the South. David Potter, a great Southern historian of the causes of the Civil War, by 1964 was "distressed" to find that "gen-eralized feelings of guilt concerning race discrimination were being channeled into denunciations of the South as a scapegoat for all the nation's failures to live according to its ideals" (*South* 17).

Huckleberry Finn played a role in this ideological process. It there-fore became important for its expositors to identify as "Southern" the fearsome and repulsive features of *Huckleberry Finn,* but many of those features are just simply American. At least two such op-posed critics as Brooks and DeVoto agreed in understanding the dominant influence on the milieu of Twain's youth as the "frontier," differing only in how they specified and evaluated it. Neither of them treated his environment as "Southern" rather than "Ameri-can." Missouri did not secede from the Union and join the Confed-eracy, though it was the scene of dreadful fighting in the Civil War, a reality barely hinted at in Twain's "Private History of a Campaign That Failed." The state was torn by guerrilla warfare and Union reprisals that led, for instance, to the removal of families from their land over the several northwestern counties of the state. In the sum-mary of James McPherson, "more than any other state, Missouri suffered the horrors of internecine warfare and the resulting ha-treds which persisted for decades" after the war ended (292; see also 783–87).

To Frederick Jackson Turner, the most influential historian of the American frontier and analyst of American sectional life in the era in which *Huckleberry Finn* is set, Missouri belonged among "the North Central States," where the national census reports categorized it. But he acknowledged that it was a rough fit. In language that DeVoto expanded a hundredfold, Turner sketched Missouri's place: "Although by slavery it belonged to the South and found the outlet for its product in New Orleans, it was also the metropolis of the upper Mississippi. The fur trade of the Great Plains and Rocky Mountains, together with the caravans to Santa Fe, gave it a Far Western flavor." I would add that at the time Sam Clemens was born, Missouri was the westernmost state, and from 1837 until the annexation of Texas in 1845, the largest. Turner concluded, "In fact, it was the fighting ground for different sections" (*United* 275). This strangely mixed status showed in the election of 1860. Missouri was the only state carried by Stephen Douglas, thus effectively defining its anomalous position as "center of the slaveholding Midwest" (Freehling, *Road* 19).

Sam Clemens was born to a family that owned enslaved African Americans, and he was born at a time that marked an important change in the history of slavery in the United States. The commitment to slavery hardened as the profitability of slave labor increased and opposition to slavery became correspondingly more vehement. In the 1830s, the great boom in cotton that was opening the lands of the "South-West" made human property increasingly more valuable and provided a motive for the original slaveholding states to preserve their commitment to this system. Moreover, many of those who came west to settle Missouri pushed on that far, rather than stopping in southern Indiana or Illinois, precisely because they wanted either to keep or to acquire slaves. South Carolina's attempt to "nullify" federal tariffs set forward the kinds of argument that would eventually be used on behalf of secession. The rebellion of Nat Turner and concomitant emergence of agitational, Garrisonian abolitionism were made the occasion for newly aggressive justifications of slavery, as well as for strengthening laws and practices of informal social control in slaveholding states. And in the North, the 1830s were notable for mob violence against abolitionists, led not by people like Huck's pap but by "gentlemen of property and standing." In the wake of the mob murder of the abolitionist editor Elijah Lovejoy at Alton, Illinois, in 1837, Abraham Lincoln devoted his first memorable speech, in 1838, to the problems caused by mobs and "increasing disregard for law." With his constant concern for the state of feeling as fundamental to social and political life, Lincoln warned that "by the operation of this mobocratic spirit . . . the strongest bulwark of any Government . . . may effectually be broken down . . . I mean the *attachment* of the People." Against this tendency, Lincoln urged that "reverence for the laws . . . become the *political religion* of the nation" (1:29–32). All of this supports Twain's notebook memory of the "sacredness" of slave property.

Nonetheless, even after the 1830s, through the slaveholding states there was more dissent than Twain's notebook account allows for. Clement Eaton summarizes what emerges from his classic and still authoritative *The Freedom-of-Thought Struggle in the Old South:* Southern laws against expressing positions opposed to slavery were enforced so as to suppress Northern agitators, "rather than to suppress the discussions of moderate Southern men" (143). Dissent was not encouraged, but some of the cases Eaton discusses show that what counted as moderate could go quite a ways. In 1839, Lysander Barrett of Virginia was acquitted despite having circulated a petition to abolish slavery in the District of Columbia, which argued that slavery was "a sin against God, a foul stain upon our national character, and contrary to the spirit of our republican institutions." In 1849 Jarvis Bacon of Virginia, a minister, was acquitted despite having maintained that owners had no moral right to property in their slaves: "If I was to go to my neighbor's crib and steal his corn, you would call me a thief," but it was "worse to take a human being and keep him all his life and give him nothing for his labor, except once in a while a whipping or a few stripes." In 1850, Samuel Janney of Virginia went unpunished for his public rebuttal to a lecture that had defended slavery as both good in itself and sanctioned by the Bible. As part of his defense, Janney countercharged that his opponent had "ridiculed the Declaration of Independence" (133–36).

In the 1895–96 notebook reminiscence, Twain echoes a theme dear to apologists for the slave system before and after the war. Kenneth Stampp, whose *The Peculiar Institution* was the most important history of slavery in the United States published between 1930 and 1970, began publication in this area in 1943 with "The Fate of the Southern Antislavery Movement." Stampp was soon thereafter associated with Dwight Macdonald's very independent left journal *Politics,* and so he wrote with a strong feeling for the political importance of not understating the extent of dissent, even in a situation, such as that of the United States during the Second World War, in which consensus was strongly enforced. Stampp emphasized at the beginning of the article that it had been very much in the interest of slaveholders "to encourage the belief that Southern opposition to slavery had disappeared" by the early 1830s (11), and after marshaling his evidence he concluded that "the contention of planter politicians that the South had achieved social and political unity appears, then, to have been the sheerest wishful thinking" (22), as William Freehling's recent study massively demonstrates.

The most admired twentieth-century historian of the South has been C. Vann Woodward. Woodward wrote *The Strange Career of Jim Crow* (1955) as an activist historiographic intervention in support of *Brown vs. Board of Education.* He argued that the twentieth-century system of racial segregation in the South had not existed as immemorial custom but rather had been established by legislative action, mostly in the 1890s and later. He concluded that if laws at one time had established what came, within one lifetime, to feel like "the way things have always been," so might a later change of laws produce a change in custom and sentiment. Continuing to reflect on racism as the product of human choices and practices, rather than as an immutable given, in "The Elusive Mind of the South" (1969) Woodward questioned the powerful and influential work by W. J. Cash, *The Mind of the South* (1940). Woodward argued that Cash's "emphasis on consensus, on 'One South,' the Solid South, ignores a great deal of evidence of disunity and dissent that does not fit his thesis" (273). In a more recent essay, "Southerners against the Southern Establishment," Woodward mentions William Swain, editor of the Greensboro, North Carolina, *Patriot,* whose pages remained open to antislavery views even after laws banning such publications were passed in 1834 (286).

Relatively privileged individuals like ministers and newspaper editors were not the only people who broke ranks to oppose slavery or to question the system that treated slavery as a self-evident good. In Tennessee in 1834 a constitutional convention met and discussed petitions in favor of gradual emancipation, signed by nearly two thousand voters (Eaton 273). In Kentucky in 1849, over ten thousand votes were cast in favor of proemancipation candidates running as representatives to the state convention (Degler 84).

There were even more Huck Finn-like instances that poke above the edge of anonymity in the historical archive. One example shows extremely severe informal methods used to put down deviant opinion, but the report may be read against the grain. It also shows that even where there was a known danger, people were sometimes not afraid. In Columbia, South Carolina, a stonemason named Powell spoke up for the freedom of African Americans. He was seized by a group that included his "fellow workers," carried down to a pond, stripped of his clothing, "well smeared with tar," and then "a pillow-case was opened and he was feathered" (Wyatt-Brown 453).

Despite the structures of legal and extralegal control, there remained individuals who not only questioned or challenged the rightness of slavery, but who acted on behalf of individual slaves who were seeking freedom, as Huck does with Jim. My point, I emphasize, is not to argue against the moral virtue of what Huck does, or of what Twain does in imagining and portraying Huck, but rather to provide some historical context that may make it possible to think more sharply about Twain's retrospective contextualizings of his fiction, and also about some of the claims made in hypercanonizing discussions of *Huckleberry Finn.*

The most important modern histories of slavery in the United States find it important to mention that there were indeed a "few white Southerners" who "gave sanctuary to fugitives or directed them along their routes" (Stampp, *Peculiar* 120), despite the financial incentive offered in every slave state by laws that "required the owner of a fugitive to compensate the captor for his trouble" (212–13). Eugene Genovese summarizes from a body of legal materials and earlier monographs: "Some of the slaves who ran away ran to other white people. In scattered cases they ran to whites who could help them escape. A few white men protected runaway slaves at great personal risk," although a few were "less altruistic" and "took in runaways to ease their own labor shortage" (*Roll* 655).

Genovese's language of "white men" is itself imprecise, because in the rare but real cases of such assistance, it was sometimes white women. The most famous instance now is that of Harriet Jacobs. In a moving case of sisterhood across race, a woman whose husband "held many slaves" and also "bought and sold slaves," a woman who herself "held a number" of slaves, but who "treated them kindly and would never allow any of them to be sold," offered assistance at a crucial point in Harriet's escape, but she asked for a favor in return: "you must solemnly promise that my name shall never be mentioned. If such a thing should become known, it would ruin me and my family" (Jacobs 99). I cite this at some length in order to make clear that this heroic, elderly Southern female slaveholder held exactly the overall beliefs about the social mores of the community that Twain expresses in his notebook, and yet she acted against them. The case is basically like Huck's, but it is face-to-face, not a solitary anguish, and it involves an action, executing a plan of escape, rather than as in Huck's case a failure to perform an action (that is, *not* sending the letter to Miss Watson).

I have drawn materials from a wide range of slaveholding experience in the decades before the Civil War, when Sam Clemens was growing up and when the action of *Huckleberry Finn* is set. What about Missouri? According to Stampp's 1943 article, "Missouri teemed with dissenters, emancipation societies were numerous, and in politics the 'Charcoals' (so branded because of their alleged partiality for the Negro) waged relentless war upon the champions of slavery." Through his newspaper printing office work, such information would have been readily available to Clemens. In the 1840s and 1850s, Missouri gained many German and Irish immigrants, "who poured into the state to build the railroads," and who were vehemently active against slavery (often on grounds that now themselves seem racist). By 1857 the Richmond, Virginia, *South* felt "compelled, however reluctant," to accept as a "fact" that "a large majority of the people [of Missouri] are in favor of the abolition of slavery" (Stampp, "Fate" 18–19).

In *Celia: A Slave*, Melton McLaurin takes materials a few years later than the action of *Huckleberry Finn* and about fifty miles south of Hannibal: the 1855 trial and conviction of an enslaved woman for the murder of her master who had long been sexually abusing her. As part of establishing the milieu in which these events occurred, McLaurin refers to an uprising in 1850, further west in Missouri, in which "some thirty slaves had armed themselves with knives, clubs, and three guns and had attempted to escape," while shortly after Celia had killed her owner, in a nearby county there was apparently a plot involving "an Irish abolitionist named Martin Gallagher and a Methodist minister, W. H. Wylie" (48).

But the historical record brings abolitionism yet closer to home for Mark Twain. An incident that Twain seems never to have mentioned, but that is recorded in Dixon Wecter's biography, is utterly surprising in light of the notebook claim that Sam Clemens had no opportunities in the 1830s and 1840s to hear about anything that might oppose slavery. In September 1841, when Sam was nearly six, his father was part of the jury for the circuit court at Palmyra that sent to prison for twelve years three abolitionists who had been caught trying to lead five slaves to freedom. In a triumph of the system over its own encumbrances, the three were convicted on the basis of the testimony of the slaves they had hoped to rescue, despite laws in Missouri as elsewhere that prohibited African Americans from giving evidence against Euro-Americans. After five years, the three were pardoned by the governor of Missouri, which might have made some stir in the household of a juror, and George Thompson published an extended memoir, *Prison Life and Reflections,* which in its subtitle characterized their "unjust and cruel imprisonment in Missouri penitentiary for attempting to aid some slaves to liberty."

Things get even closer. It is well known that Tom Blankenship, son of the town drunk in Hannibal, provided a major model for the figure of Huck Finn: "He had as good a heart as any boy ever had. His liberties were totally unrestricted. He was the only really independent person—boy or man—in the community, and by consequence was tranquilly and continuously happy, and was envied by all the rest of us" (Twain, *Autobiography* 2:174). It is not so commonly known, although it has been in circulation since Albert Bigelow Paine's 1912 authorized biography, presumably as an oral account from Twain to Paine, that Tom's older brother Ben Blankenship provided a model for assisting a fugitive slave. According to Paine, this experience of Ben's "provided Mark Twain with that immortal episode in the story of Huckleberry Finn—the sheltering of Nigger Jim" (note that for Paine the relation with Jim is simply an "episode," not the center of the book):

> A slave ran off from Monroe County, Missouri, and got across the river into Illinois. Ben used to fish and hunt over there in the swamps and one day found him. It was considered a most worthy act in those days to return a runaway slave; in fact, it was a crime not to do it. Besides, there was for this one a reward of fifty dollars, a fortune to ragged outcast Ben Blankenship. That money and the honor he could acquire must have been tempting to the waif, but it did not outweigh his human sympathy. Instead of giving him up and claiming the reward, Ben kept the runaway over there in the marshes all summer. The negro would fish and Ben would carry him scraps of other food. Then, by and by, it leaked out. Some woodchoppers went on a hunt for the

fugitive, and chased him to what was called the "Bird Slough." There trying to cross a drift he was drowned. (1:63–64)

Paine contrasts Ben's experience with "Huck's struggle." Paine sees Huck as caught "between conscience and the law," but the point of chapter 31 is that conscience and the law are wholly in accord with one another. The law of slavery works together with what Twain, in a famous comment, called Huck's "deformed conscience." They both oppose what Paine's account calls "human sympathy" and what Twain called Huck's "sound heart" (*Huckleberry* [1988] 806). Paine has restored *conscience* to its conventional position as a transcendent arbiter of morality, and has placed *law* as its opponent, standing for the socially conditioned, historically limited views of slaveholding society. But in chapter 31, law is never even mentioned, only religion and social pressure.

Ben Blankenship was an important human example of secret action, but part of Twain's claim in the notebook reminiscence is that there was no public, articulated ideological support for opposition to slavery. Yet only a year or two before that notebook entry, Twain wrote an essay, "A Scrap of Curious History," which gives quite a different sense of what intellectual, and political, resources were available in the Hannibal of his youth. The essay relates an incident that neither Paine nor Wecter documents and that is in certain respects fictionalized, but that apparently draws from the 1884 *History of Marion County, Missouri* (Blair, *Hannibal* 152).

Written in France in 1894, this brief essay responds to the recent assassination of the president of France. Twain compares the political struggles of France in the 1890s, largely around "anarchism," with the "periodical frights, horrors and shudderings" that "we" in the United States had "passed through . . . fifty years ago," that is, in the 1840s. Now an anarchist in France is called a "madman"; then in the United States, anyone who would "proclaim himself an enemy of negro [*sic* for Negro] slavery" was thought mad. Twain's narrative begins with Robert Hardy: "our first *abolitionist*—awful name!" He aided a fugitive slave in an escape in which a constable was killed. Hardy was hanged, and his "martyrdom gilded with notoriety" led four "young light-weights in the village" to declare themselves abolitionists. Twain's description of their "pass-words, grips, and signs," their "initiations" with "gloomy pomps and ceremonies at midnight," makes clear that they are Tom Sawyer types. But they, too, get involved in something that causes one of them in turn to be hanged, which produces, within a month, "twenty new members."

In calling the hangings, in each case, "a mistake," Twain mimics an analysis from the perspective of the slaveholding social order, since the hangings, in his account, fostered antislavery activity. And in describing the hangings as great social events, he is as savage as he ever was in *Huckleberry Finn:* "People came from miles around. . . . They brought cakes and cider, also the women and children, and made a picnic of the matter," with much "lemonade and gingerbread" sold. Twain's manner is so deadpan here, so matter-of-fact, that George Orwell took this account as defining an everyday norm of life as Clemens was growing up (2:373–74). So within a year or two of Twain's notebook reminiscence of the solid antebellum slaveholding "community," he also offers this wholly different reminiscence of a society torn by slavery not only ideologically, but also with deadly violence. There is some truth to each, and it is wrong to rest too much weight on a single perspective.

Twain in his *Autobiography* famously recalls the paradox of his mother's relation to slavery:

> When slavery perished my mother had been in daily touch with it for sixty years. Yet, kind-hearted and compassionate as she was, I think she was not conscious that slavery was a bald, grotesque, and unwarrantable usurpation. She had never heard it assailed in any pulpit, but had heard it defended and sanctified in a thousand; her ears were familiar with Bible texts that approved it, but if there were any that disapproved it they had not been quoted by her pastors; as far as her experience went, the wise and the good and the holy were unanimous in the conviction that slavery was right, righteous, sacred, the peculiar pet of the Deity, and a condition which the slave himself ought to be daily and nightly thankful for. Manifestly, training and association can accomplish strange miracles. (1:123)

This reflection is thoroughly in keeping with the tenor of the notebook entry, but elsewhere in the *Autobiography* a very different picture emerges. In thinking over his brother Orion, Twain reflects: "Born and reared among slaveholders, he was yet an abolitionist from his boyhood to his death" (2:272). Orion's views were at least as hostile to slavery as were Lincoln's, who was no abolitionist but who believed that slavery was immoral and must not endure in a free nation. Mrs. Clemens must have heard this from her son, if from no one else.

Twain's notebook entry participates retrospectively in constructing an Old South, of which his Missouri was a part, as it had not in fact been when he was growing up. This tendency is repeated elsewhere in his writing. In the *Autobiography* he recounts an experience from his time as an apprentice. The apprentices ate in the kitchen, "with the old slave cook and her very handsome and bright and well-behaved young mulatto daughter." One of the young men persisted in "making love to that mulatto girl and distressing the life out of her and worrying the old mother to death." This is a moment of philological uncertainty. The term "making love," so sexualized in later-twentieth-century usage, was the usual nineteenth-century term for courting, or even just flirting, and yet in this context of strong social inequality it might well extend at least to what would now be considered physical sexual harassment. When the mother asked the man to behave, he only persisted. Twain then observes, "to speak truly, the old mother's distress about it was merely a pretense. She quite well understood that by the customs of slaveholding communities it was [his] right to make love to that girl if he wanted to" (2:276–77). Victor Doyno prolongs this perspective of Twain's in the "Textual Addendum" to the 1996 scholarly edition of *Huckleberry Finn*, referring to "the practice of whites' sexual exploitation of slave women, which had been culturally accepted for several generations" (371).

But customs and cultures are never so uniform as such a claim asserts, whether made by Twain or by a modern scholar. Mary Chesnut's memoir shows that women of the slaveholding class were deeply embittered by such exploitation (29–31, 168–69), and Harriet Jacobs's *Incidents in the Life of a Slave Girl* shows that enslaved women did not passively accept it. The case of Jacobs shows clearly that even in the much more compelling instance where it was the master, not merely an apprentice, who was the sexual aggressor, "custom" and the "community" might well operate on the side of the woman. Indeed, according to Jacobs both white and black public opinion together protected her for a long period. Custom, and even law, are matters where the slaveholders' power was never so absolute as their theory claimed, and it is not discounting the brutality and inhumanity and horror of the American system of slavery to insist also that there was negotiating, or fighting, room within it.

In another account from his world tour, Twain has a striking experience. In India he witnesses the brutality of a hotel manager to a "native" servant. The manager first hits the servant and only then tells him what the matter is: "It carried me back to my boyhood, and flashed upon me the forgotten fact that this was the *usual* way of explaining one's desires to a slave." While he could "remember that the method seemed right and natural to me in those days, I being born to it and unaware that there were other methods," he could also remember that such practices "made me sorry for the victim and ashamed for the punisher." After some thoughts about his father, Twain then moves to a dreadful memory:

> When I was ten years old I saw a man fling a lump of iron-ore at a slave-man in anger, for merely doing something awkwardly—as if that were a crime. It bounded from the man's skull, and the man fell and never spoke again. He was dead in an hour. I knew the man had the right to kill his slave if he wanted to. . . . Nobody in the village approved of that murder, but of course no one said much about it. (*Following* 351–52)

The community may have forborne, but the law, even in slave states, did not give the right of dealing casual death, as Eugene Genovese makes clear in a powerful discussion of the complexities of law and slavery. Indeed, there was legal provision even for slaves to act in self-defense if their life was endangered, and slaves were acquitted in such cases (more likely when an overseer, not an owner, had been killed) (*Roll* 34–35). A remarkable incident in Missouri never came to law: a slave's owner refused to have a slave punished for having blinded a member of the owner's family who had wantonly killed a slave child for crying (37). Whites were brought to law and punished for murdering slaves, though more frequently small-fry than "gentlemen of standing" (38–39).

Because of the rhetorical authority of Twain's very powerful notebook passage about the agreement of the "whole community" concerning the "sacredness" of slavery, and because it has figured in important interpretations of *Huckleberry Finn,* I have devoted a great deal of detail to thinking through the historical plausibility of its claims. But it should also be remembered that this notebook entry was part of the planning for Twain's platform performance during his around-the-world reading tour. His standard act was his "Morals Lecture," and however deep, incisive, and insightful, it was also comic. It relied on exaggeration, overemphasis, and all the other rhetorical devices that can make great art but that cannot always produce a literally credible result. For example, in a newspaper account of the lecture there occurs a battle with conscience very much like that of chapter 31 of *Huckleberry Finn*. It is not about anything so important as slavery, or the loyalty of one human being to another. It is presented as part of a plan of "inoculation." To avoid future sins, you must commit each and every one that you might be guilty of, and thereby become immunized against it. In this case, as a boy, Twain recounts, he stole a watermelon that turned out to be unripe, and the comic point of the inoculation is that he has never again committed the sin of stealing an unripe melon. In a sequence that is baldly humorous because of its insistence that the sin at issue is defined by the *kind* of melon, and no more is at stake, the rhetoric of mock repentance closely approaches that of chapter 31, where after drafting the letter to Miss Watson, Huck "felt good and all washed clean of sin":

> I began to reflect and I said to myself, I have done wrong; it was wrong in me to steal that watermelon—that kind of watermelon. And I said to myself: now what would a right-minded and right-intentioned boy do, who found that he had done wrong—stolen a watermelon like this. What would he do, what must he do; do right; restitution make restitution. He must restore that property to its owner, and I resolved to do that and the moment I made that good resolution I felt that electrical moral uplift which becomes a victory over wrong doing. (Lorch 324)

The Key Passage

According to Twain's notebook entry, the purpose of which was to introduce to his audience, and to prepare for the maximal effect in reading aloud, a passage from *Huckleberry Finn*, there was no dialogue over slavery in his childhood time and place. Nonetheless, in *Huckleberry Finn* itself, in Bakhtin's terms, there is considerable dialogism between voices in the sequence of chapter 31, on which I shall now focus closely (268–71). Huck hears in his mind the voice of the schoolmarm, given a twist by his own dialect and by a wavering in personal pronouns: "There was the Sunday School, you could a gone to it; and if you'd a done it they'd a learnt you, there, that people that acts as I'd been acting about that nigger goes to everlasting fire." Huck's imperfect impersonation causes the voice of authority to condemn itself out of its own mouth ("as I'd been acting"), rather than condemning him. Moreover, it is both comic and true to social reality that even though he hasn't gone to Sunday school, he knows what he would have learned if he had. Huck next assumes as the form for his own self-report the rapid repetitive rhythms of preacherly exhortation: "It was because my heart warn't right; it was because I warn't square; it was because I was playing double." And one of his most famous lines still seems part of the preaching voice: "You can't pray a lie." After he has written the letter, Huck takes on the voice of revival testimony for his mock climax: "I felt good and all washed clean of sin for the first time."

The sequence begins with a mangled thunderclap, as Huck turns into indirect discourse in his own speech what should be a dreadful and elaborate warning:

> And at last, when it hit me all of a sudden that here was the plain hand
> of Providence slapping me in the face and letting me know my wicked-
> ness was being watched all the time from up there in heaven, whilst
> I was stealing a poor old woman's nigger that hadn't ever done me no
> harm, and now was showing me there's One that's always on the look-
> out, and ain't agoing to allow no such miserable doings to go on only
> just so fur and no further, I most dropped in my tracks I was so scared.

What we might call the "syntax of another" suspends his identity and transports him into this space of moral debate, which is resolved only when, as is usually claimed, Huck finds again his own language (though note the exceedingly artful rhetorical balance of overlapping doublets and triplets): "I see Jim before me, all the time, in the day, and in the night-time, sometimes moonlight, sometimes storms, and we a floating along, talking, and singing, and laughing." As this string of memories unrolls, the language in which the decision is finally put gains force from its sudden snap back to a discarded idiom, "All right, then, I'll *go* to hell." The syntax has the direct simplicity of the memories of Jim, but the key word, deferred to the end, returns to the religious language that is alien to Huck's own human sympathy.

I find the sequence much more powerful for making hell a joke than for the bravery of the boy believing he is facing hell. I cannot agree with Toni Morrison that this is "Huck's ultimate act of love, in which he accepts the endangerment of his soul" (Introduction xxxvi). In 1879, Mark Twain defined "the most malignant form of Presbyterianism" as "that sort which considers the saving of one's own paltry soul the first and supreme end and object of life" (Smith and Gibson 1:256). I make this judgment that the religious satire outweighs the experiential pathos because Huck has displayed, right in this sequence, perhaps more than anywhere else in the book, a mind, a style, open to the voices of others. But if other voices can sound through his, why so limited a repertory? What were the social alternatives, even within slave society, that Twain excludes from this scene because they might diminish the comic miracle of Huck's decision? Once we acknowledge that indeed there was talk against slavery, even in slaveholding states, what intellectual and ideological resources could antislavery talk draw on? These questions, I think, are what it means to take seriously Bakhtin's idea of a "dialogue" among socially antagonistic languages as the basis for the form and accomplishment of *Huckleberry Finn*.

Every source, from antebellum slave narratives to current scholarship, agrees that there were two primary resources. As he was growing up enslaved in Baltimore, Frederick Douglass found that the working-class "white boys" with whom he spoke readily expressed a "bitter condemnation of slavery, that springs from nature, unseared and unperverted." He never "met with a *boy* . . . who defended the slave system." Instead, "they believed *I* had as good a right to be free as *they* had," and "they did not believe God ever made any one to be a slave." (This passage first appeared in *My Bondage and My Freedom* and is retained in *Life and Times;* see *Autobiographies* 224, 531–32.) That is, these real-life Hucks consoled him with hopes drawn from American religion (God) and politics (right). William Craft in the very first words of his account of his and his wife's escape from slavery names the Bible and the Declaration of Independence as the authorities from which they had heard, even as slaves, the principles of human equality that motivated them to resist their status as "chattels." A few years later, Senator Charles Sumner of Massachusetts, a leader in Radical Reconstruction, based the arguments for his civil rights bill less on the Constitution than on "the Declaration of Independence and the Sermon on the Mount" (Foner, *Reconstruction* 504).

For besides the language of damnation that preoccupies Huck in chapter 31, Christianity also includes a language of love. Huck has early in the book been told about praying for "spiritual gifts": "I must help other people, and do everything I could for other people, and look out for them all the time, and never think about myself" (13). But he "couldn't see no advantage about it" and so puts it from mind. Yet it is just such Sunday school altruism in this sequence for Huck to sacrifice his own salvation so as to save Jim. So, too, the United States was not only a slaveholding society but also a society founded on principles of liberty and independence. Although the discourse of civic equality among slaveholders was always apt ground for ironists, it did provide an alternative, culturally authoritative resource, with which even Southerners might— and some did—argue against slavery. Twain steers as clear as he can of this language. The season was right for it—Huck and Jim come off Jackson's Island on the June rises, and Twain even proposed in his notes for the book that Huck run into a Fourth of July speech. But the "Declaration of Independence"is mentioned only in Huck's comically confused characterization of the antics of Henry VIII, and the only person in the book to use the language of "rights" is pap in his poisonous claims that his rights are violated by a "govment" that lets a man of color vote.

To elaborate what is at stake for Twain in omitting treatment of the Fourth of July from *Huckleberry Finn*, a wide array of materials will help, ranging from the minutely biographical to the broadly cultural and historical. In Twain's working notes for *Huckleberry Finn*, written probably in 1883 while he was completing the book (*Huckleberry* [1988] 736), occurs the following entry:

> Takes history class among the niggers?
> Join Sunday school before 4th July
>   Teaches Jim to read and write (*Huckleberry* [1988] 753)

The entry about the Fourth of July appears to be a later interpolation, as I read the MS in photocopy (*Huckleberry* [1988] 741). By the practices of Hannibal in the 1840s, Huck might join an organization before the Fourth so as to be eligible to march with it in the procession (Wecter 150–52). So the possibility of a Fourth of July scene was in Twain's mind, and the thought of that scene arose as he reread notes about activities involving, however humorously, the intellectual and cultural uplift of enslaved African Americans.

Twain's association between the Fourth of July and improved

conditions for African Americans is also suggested by a late speech, which he gave in London on 4 July 1907. After graciously emphasizing that the original Declaration of Independence was an act performed by "Englishmen," since there was not yet an American nation, Twain asserted that Americans have a later "Fourth of July"

> which is absolutely our own, and that is that great proclamation issued forty years ago by . . . Abraham Lincoln. Lincoln's proclamation, which not only set the black slaves free, but set the white man free also. The owner was set free from the burden and offense, that sad condition of things where he was in so many instances a master and owner of slaves when he did not want to be. (*Collected* 2:821–22)

The very inaccuracies and tendentiousness of Twain's rhetorical gesture are important. He here echoed the New South ideological position that most slaveholders "did not want" their human property but held their slaves only out of responsibility to school and civilize this human "burden" passed on to them by their ancestors, and he still associated the Fourth of July with the freeing of slaves, completely forgetting both the actual date of the Emancipation Proclamation (1 January 1863) and the notorious fact that it did not actually free any slaves, since Emancipation applied only in areas that the Union did not control.

Likewise in Twain's autobiographical dictations, the sense that the Fourth of July ought to mean freedom also for slaves provides the irony in an otherwise nostalgic reflection about the Hannibal of his youth: "It was a little democracy which was full of liberty, equality, and Fourth of July, and sincerely so, too; yet you perceived that the aristocratic taint was there. . . . I suppose that this state of things was mainly due to the circumstances that the town's population had come from the slave states and still had the institutions of slavery" (1:120).

Twain's particular sense of the Fourth of July takes its place in a larger set of national and regional meanings and practices, both at the time of the action of *Huckleberry Finn* and at the time of its writing. Americans quickly became aware of a national tendency to inflate their ritual commemoration, and the Fourth therefore had a long tradition as an object of humor. As early as 1807, Washington Irving mocked a speaker who "thunders with peculiar emphasis and pompous enunciation, in the true style of a fourth of July orator" (272), and in 1857 the *North American Review*, an organ of high culture and conservative politics, defined a "Fourth of July oration" as the usual synonym for "bombast and mere rhetorical patrio- tism," including "sentiment, pyrotechnic flashes . . . arrests, burst- ing cannon, draggled flags, steamboats, the disgust of the educated and the uproar of the multitude" (Boorstin 482). In his 1869 *Story of a Bad Boy*, one of the generic models for *Huckleberry Finn*, Thomas Bailey Aldrich devoted some thirty pages (more than a tenth of the whole book) to the incidents of a Fourth. Fully as much as Shake- spearean bombast, camp-meeting hypocrisy, and the "soul-butter" of funeral "orgies," this was a part of American life fit both for Twain's satire and for his reflection.

The Fourth was always excessive, but the historian Michael Kammen suggests that the type of excess changed over time. For some fifty years, into the 1820s, the Fourth was likely to be a "solemn ceremonial," usually "accompanied by church services" (54). Begin- ning in the Jacksonian period, and predominating by the 1840s— that is, in Huck's time—came the food and firecrackers that won censure from the *North American Review* and that still define the holiday. Even a remote Tennessee village might put on a grand mar- tial display of its militia with hundreds of people present (Franklin, *Militant* 203–5), and in Hannibal in 1849 lions, tigers, leopards, and cougars were part of the scene (Wecter 192).

Against this increasingly thoughtless assertion of a national pur- pose of freedom, contradicted by the facts of life in the United States, Frederick Douglass asked, pointedly on the *fifth* of July 1852, "What, to the Negro, Is the Fourth of July?" And indeed, in the North, many free blacks preferred to celebrate the first of August, the date of West Indies emancipation, looking back to England as a reproach to America (Davis 124f.). According to Kammen, already by the 1840s "free Negroes refused to participate" in celebrations that they considered to be "hypocritical sham" (53). In the slave- holding parts of the country, Eugene Genovese notes an increasing tendency for slaveholders to warn each other "to keep the blacks away from 4th of July orations" (*Rebellion* 126). For, as Twain him- self recorded in his 1884 notes "Villagers of 1840–43" (Blair, *Hanni- bal* 37), an essential part of all such orations was always the reading of the Declaration of Independence, which proclaims that "all men are created equal." In the 1930s WPA interviews with people who had been enslaved, "Some . . . recalled the 4th of July as a big holi- day but added that they heard no political speeches. Many others did report having heard them, as worried slavery stalwarts constantly insisted" (Genovese, *Rebellion* 128). Winthrop Jordan notes an uprising by slaves in Camden, South Carolina, planned for 4 July 1816 (153); the fears of a slave uprising on 4 July 1835 precipitated much preemptive bloodshed in Mississippi (Freehling, *Road* 110); Nat Turner intended his rebellion to start on 4 July 1831; and David Walker ended his 1829 abolitionist *Appeal,* even after fierce critique of Jefferson: "See your declaration, Americans!! Do you understand your own language?" (85).

After the Civil War and Emancipation, the two major festivals for African American fraternal and social organizations were 1 January, in commemoration of the Emancipation Proclamation, and 4 July. In a reaction equal and opposite to that of free blacks before the war, on these days "Southern whites generally remained indoors" or stayed at work (Foner, *Reconstruction* 95, 289). Kammen confirms that during Reconstruction, the Fourth "became an exclusively Negro festival in the South" (58). (In his classic 1937 study of how the North and South came once again to feel united, Paul Buck claimed that during Reconstruction the Fourth "was silently ignored" by the "South" [33], which he thereby defined as excluding African Americans.)

In the state conventions to reconstruct the political system, the language of the Declaration of Independence figured prominently. One prominent participant observed that "the colored people . . . had read the Declaration until it had become part of their natures" (Foner, *Reconstruction* 114). Precisely because of the radical power of the Declaration and the Fourth in the antebellum agitation against slavery and in the consequent social and political transformations, when Reconstruction was halted a new language began to prevail. Beginning from the centennial observations of 1876, there was a very strong tendency for the "nation . . . to shift its attention and emphasis" (Kammen 61) from the Declaration to the Constitution, which is a document not of revolutionary mobilization but of consolidating compromise.

Twain's 1907 speech linked the Fourth with Lincoln, and Lincoln is indeed the nineteenth-century national political figure whose meaning seems most closely bound to the principles of freedom and equality. Lincoln's emergence as a compelling national voice began with his response to the Kansas-Nebraska Act of 1854. Lincoln's standard autobiographical account, indeed, indicates that he had given up politics for his legal practice until he was galvanized by this crisis. By undoing the Missouri Compromise, the act released slavery from the geographical limits that Lincoln had believed would assure its ultimate end. In thus fostering the growth of slavery, the act seemed to him fundamentally inhumane. Lincoln's 1854 awakening resembles that of Harriet Beecher Stowe in 1850, in response to the newly rigorous fugitive slave legislation. Both began their nationally transformative work from the basis of fellow feeling, the sentiment of sympathy. Lincoln argued in his Peoria speech of 1854 on the Kansas-Nebraska Act:

> The great majority, south as well as north, have human sympathies, of which they can no more divest themselves than they can of their sensibility to physical pain. These sympathies in the bosoms of the southern people, manifest in many ways, their sense of the wrong of slavery, and the consciousness that, after all, there is humanity in the negro. (1:326; *sic* for Negro)

With the logic that was always inseparable from his sentiment, Lincoln went on to argue, from the premise of "humanity in the negro": "If the negro is a *man,* why then my ancient faith teaches me that 'all men are created equal.'" Therefore, "there can be no moral right in connection with one man's making a slave of another" (328). By this logic, Lincoln defined the essence of the Kansas-Nebraska position as that expressed by one of its supporters, who "called the Declaration of Independence a 'self-evident lie'" (339). And indeed, in the 1840s the editor of the *Richmond Examiner* had been even more explicit: "Negroes are not *men,* in the sense in which that term is used by the Declaration of Independence. Were the slaves men, we should be unable to disagree with [the abolitionist] Wendell Phillips" (Frederickson, *Black* 86).

In 1855, as political debate, and bloodshed in Kansas, continued, Lincoln wrote to a friend:

> Experience has demonstrated, I think, that there is no peaceful extinction of slavery in prospect for us. The signal failure of Henry Clay, and other good and great men, in 1849, to effect anything in favor of gradual emancipation in Kentucky, together with a thousand other signs, extinguishes that hope utterly. On the question of liberty, as a principle, we are not what we have been. When we were the political slaves of King George, and wanted to be free, we called the maxim that "all men are created equal" a self evident truth; but now when we have grown

fat, and have lost all dread of being slaves ourselves, we have become so greedy to be *masters* that we call the same maxim a "self-evident lie." The Fourth of July has not quite dwindled away; it is still a great day—*for burning fire-crackers!!!* (1:359)

The debasement of the Fourth of July celebration climaxed and epitomized the failure of American political morality. By failing to carry through into reality for others the freedom that the nation's founding ideology claimed as a natural right for all human beings, American political morality became only a sparkling show, a lot of noise with no substance—a sitting duck, one imagines, for the satire of *Huckleberry Finn.*

Lincoln tried to restore that morale. In 1857, speaking against the Dred Scott decision of the Supreme Court, Lincoln summarized Chief Justice Taney's opinion as holding that "negroes were no part of the people who made, or for whom was made, the Declaration of Independence" (1:395), and in a special message to Congress in 1861, on the occasion of his first Fourth of July in office, Lincoln inveighed against the documents by which the Confederacy had founded itself. The Confederate rebels were caught in a bind, because they could not simply reiterate the founding principles of the United States without once again opening the ironies of what the historian Edmund Morgan has formulated as "American Slavery, American Freedom." Lincoln pointed out that the Southerners "have adopted some [state] Declarations of Independence," but that in them "they omit the words 'all men are created equal'" (2:259).

Lincoln's Gettysburg Address not only stylistically achieved a prose as simply "of the people" as Twain's would be; it also, Garry Wills has argued, politically reincorporated the Declaration into American national identity. Like so many other accomplishments of the Civil War and Reconstruction period, however, this reincorporation was not permanent and has had to be repeatedly renewed. In the time that *Huckleberry Finn* was being written, the principle that "all men are created equal" was being written out of the national consensus; the United States, having quashed the Southern rebellion, was rapidly distancing itself from revolutionary principles and sympathies (Frederickson, *Inner* 187). By showing Huck groping unassisted toward the sentiments, what Lincoln called the "human sympathies," on which such a political premise would arise, Twain defined a place in human nature that could remain a basis for resistance in bad times. Yet in wholly omitting from his representation of Huck's America any of the rhetorical, political, or more broadly social resources that supported resistance to the slave power in Huck's time and to Bourbon restoration in Twain's own time, *Huckleberry Finn* defines no place that citizens can work together in resistance. This is not the worst possible compromise, but it is a great diminishment for the possibilities of freedom, and it has rarely been acknowledged as one of the costs of Twain's achievement.

Huck's "crisis" is like that of a Christian in the wilderness, not like that of a citizen in debate; his moment of judgment is not a courtroom scene, and even his anxieties about stealing someone else's slave never involve legal penalties, only damnation and social ostracism. Twain excludes the category of law because even in the debased form of slave law, the law rests on a claim to justice, and the notion of justice is a culturally valued abstraction that could support Huck in his moment of need, just as earlier Judge Thatcher offered the legal form to protect Huck's money from Pap.

I have argued that to keep pure a reader's sense of Huck's individual autonomy, Twain had to purge from Huck's consciousness the available alternative languages of value in post-Jacksonian America. Since, as I have shown, these languages figure in the book, however minimally, it was indeed Twain's artistic choice to exclude them from this scene. This is an honorable and powerful literary strategy, but its effect is to disconnect Huck not only from his own time, but also from the time Twain was writing in, for these discourses still carried considerable weight in Twain's 1880s. The effect now of idolizing a passage that depends on such a technique is to remove consideration of *Huckleberry Finn* from the actualities of our time too. To combine Bakhtin with Lionel Trilling: Twain does far less than Dostoevski to activate within his work the whole "dialectic" of his culture's struggles with itself, then or now.

The years after Lionel Trilling's 1948 essay, when academic hypercanonization set the terms for public idolatry, were also the years of the American civil rights movement. The most inspiring and influential figure of this movement was the Reverend Martin Luther King, Jr. King's oratory and argument alike built from the Bible and the basic American premise of human equality, and on this basis the movement brought many individuals together in collective action against what, at the time they began, seemed a "whole community" devoted to the "sacredness" of segregation. The model of chapter 31, as circulated through critical discussions of *Huckle-berry Finn* in these years, offers no insight into how such a thing could happen, whether a Civil War in Twain's life or civic transfor-mation in ours. Indeed, Shelley Fisher Fishkin, who is the most ac-tive current scholarly advocate for the continuing hypercanoni-zation of *Huckleberry Finn*, summarizes the book's lesson: "Mark Twain knew that there was nothing, absolutely *nothing*, a black man could do . . . that would make white society see beyond the color of his skin" (*Lighting* 6). No wonder some readers challenge the book's authority.

Twain's great skill achieved tremendous rhetorical power. Many readers can gain moral self-satisfaction in articulating the values Huck couldn't, and in knowing the ruin of the slave system that dominated the terms of his meditation in chapter 31. Huck had no voice to hear, no person to talk with who could appreciate his moral decision, but readers fill that lack. The dominant public tradition of reading *Huckleberry Finn* has made it a talisman of self-flattering American virtue. The utopia of loving, comradely relations between whites and blacks has frequently been described as the myth of the book, the ideal abstraction from human life by which life it-self may be further shaped and oriented. However, in the domi-nant public tradition that I find around us, the effective myth is rather the dream of a young, white, male naiveté fed by innocent impulses and validated absolutely by the higher authority of pos-terity. Through refusing to acknowledge the limitations in Twain's achievement, both as a novelist and as a moralist, current public criticism fosters rather than fights free from the still significant in-volvement in racism that informs even *Huckleberry Finn,* and we make of Twain's supposed transcendence a defensive alibi for our own failures to overcome the historical conditions with which we still struggle.

3

Forty Years of Controversy, 1957–1996

This chapter further excavates the history, up to the present, of *Huckleberry Finn* in the national press, especially the *New York Times* and *Washington Post*. When I began this book in the later 1980s, the record seemed monolithic. In the last few years, however, while I have been completing my work, things have changed a bit. This history, then, falls into three parts. I begin with the first discussion that displayed the structure of idolatry, in which cultural authorities defended the book's greatness. This occurred in 1957 in New York. Next, I examine the case of "idol and target" that set the tenor for most of the last two decades—the controversy provoked by John Wallace in 1982 when he declared *Huckleberry Finn* "racist trash" and in 1984, the centennial year, when he published an adaptation that removed the words *nigger* and *hell*. Finally, I gauge the changes in discussions during 1995–96, ending with the outright attack on *Huckleberry Finn* by the novelist Jane Smiley.

A Strange Preview

The first discussion I know of in the public press concerning the racial offensiveness of *Huckleberry Finn* took place in New York City in September 1957. The controversy remains somewhat puzzling. The first news account (Buder) cried out on the front page, " 'Huck Finn' Barred as Textbook by City." The story explained that *Huckleberry Finn* "has been criticized by some Negroes as racially offensive" (1), but the school official interviewed denied that the decision (not to bar *Huckleberry Finn* but to remove a particular edition from a list of approved texts) had anything to do with any objections, and the NAACP, Urban League, and Anti-Defamation League of B'nai B'rith all said that they were unaware of any protests (29). The only source citing racial objections was the publisher whose previously approved edition had been dropped. He "added that the company was bringing out a new version that would meet the criticisms" (29). The criticisms make the whole affair rather farcical: "the edition, an adaptation of the original, did not capitalize the words 'Negro' and 'Negroes'" (29) (Blair *Mark Twain* [390 n. 5] says that the editor was Verne B. Brown). But in the book that Mark Twain wrote, the word *Negro* never appears, with or without capitalization! So the whole discussion concerns an "adaptation" of the text that has altered Twain's words, and consequently, a correspondent observed a week later, was "fit for nobody to read" (Rogers). (Twain's publishers, Harper and Brothers, had already in 1931 produced an "expurgated" edition for use in junior high schools [Brown 84].)

Even though its own information made clear the irrelevance of discussing the actual text of Twain's book, the *New York Times* in both this initial article and a later editorial ("Huck Finn's Friend Jim") accurately quoted the phrase with which Jim is introduced to the reader: "Miss Watson's big nigger, named Jim." I highlight this quotation, because over the next three decades the *Times* seems to have forgotten Twain's actual words, and regularly allowed writers in its pages to treat as Jim's name an offensive phrase that Twain never used, "Nigger Jim."

While *Huckleberry Finn* was being discussed in New York, national attention focused on the early days of Southern school integration. In September 1957, Governor Orville Faubus of Arkansas called out the National Guard to preserve order by preventing African American students from attending Central High School in Little Rock. President Eisenhower responded with the first use of federal troops in the South since Reconstruction, sending in some thousand troops of the 101st Airborne Division and nationalizing the Arkansas National Guard, in order to oversee integration. Along with the first story about *Huckleberry Finn*, the *Times* also printed stories about resistance to integration in the once-rebel state of Arkansas and the once-Union state of Kentucky, with cross burnings and death threats, and on the next day a story from North Carolina headed "Lone Negro Quits Charlotte School."

The discussion in the *Times* linked the controversy over *Huckleberry Finn* in New York with the events in Little Rock. In a letter, Hoxie N. Fairchild, an English professor at Hunter College, contrasted the "juvenile delinquents of Little Rock" to *Huckleberry Finn*, a "great document in the progress of human tolerance and understanding." And he introduced one of the topics that keeps coming back in subsequent exchanges: "At all events one thing is certain: whatever his skin pigmentation, any adult who objects to this enlightened work because Huck calls Jim a 'nigger' rather than a 'Negro' simply does not know how to read a great book." The next day the *Times* editorial asserted: "The truth is that *Huckleberry Finn* is one of the deadliest satires ever written on some of the nonsense that goes with the inequality of races." Since in the book, "the mean and foolish people are not Negroes" but whites, "One might go so far as to say that *Huckleberry Finn* is not fair to white people." And therefore, the *Times* concluded, though the book certainly should be available in New York City schools, "One is not so certain about the Central High School of Little Rock, Ark."

As I understand this coy wit, the *Times* meant that white people in New York were broad-minded enough to love a masterpiece even though it represents white people as mean and foolish, but the white people of Little Rock, as shown by their dreadful response to their African American fellow citizens who wished to go to school with them, were too small-minded to accept such a work. The *Times* did not mention what the editorialist may have further had in mind, namely, that in *Huckleberry Finn* Arkansas is very specifically represented as backward and violent. The *Times* exemplifies here the Northern liberal smugness that was inseparable from the process of hypercanonization and that continued to feed discussions of *Huckleberry Finn* long after it became evident—in my schematic chronology, since 1964—that the North, too, has little to be proud of and much to answer for.

The comparison between New York and Little Rock offers a specific invidious comparison between whites. But what is the implicit point about African Americans? Insofar as the *Times* believed (although never established) that protests by New York African Americans caused the book's removal, then those black New Yorkers were as bigoted as the Arkansas whites. At this historical distance, it seems clear enough that in the South African Americans were struggling to integrate schools, and in the North African

Americans were (at least imagined to be) attempting to make their voices heard in already integrated schools. In both cases this African American self-assertion caused trouble to the white establishment, which responded with defensive hostility. Governor Faubus made clear what was going on, while it's not clear that the *Times* ever understood what was at issue in its response, any more than Fairchild, or his successors in denouncing the failure really to read, acknowledged that there may be differences about what really reading means, that an "enlightened" book does not actually cast a light by which it may "simply" be read.

What New York students were really reading, in 1957, was a textbook adaptation that bowdlerized Twain's language, but the *Times* never picked up this issue. Further, the school system did not remove *Huckleberry Finn* from the high schools. The change affected only elementary and junior high schools (Buder 1). And finally, there is an obscure dimension of bureaucratese that the *Times* never untangled for its readers, but which may mean that absolutely nothing at all was really at stake, except an opportunity for the newspaper to strike preemptively against possible African American challenges. For the superintendent of schools explained that the Verne Brown edition had been dropped from the approved textbook list not because *Huckleberry Finn* was considered offensive to Negroes, but only because "it was not considered a textbook" (*New York Times*, "Nominees"). This same technical emphasis was made in a subsequent story reporting the mayor's support for the Board of Education's decision. So perhaps by removing *Huckleberry Finn* from the "textbook" category, the board made it possible for students to read the book Twain had written rather than a bowdlerized adaptation.

A curious coda to this controversy came a few months later in a speech by ex-president Harry Truman, who asserted his Missouri roots in challenging "those who would edit Mark Twain's . . . 'Huckleberry Finn.'" He pointed out that there would be a terrible "distortion of history" if it were possible for "each succeeding generation . . . to edit what was set down by others in the past," and in this vein he concluded by imagining how the Communists might rewrite the Bible (*New York Times*, "Truman"). The structure of Truman's comparisons makes Mark Twain's work the equivalent for Americans of what the Bible is for Christians, and makes those who would tamper with Twain as un-American as Communists were thought to be or, I would add, as un-American as J. Edgar Hoover thought civil rights activists were.

There were only occasional incidents in the news between 1957 and 1982. One seems to promise much. It was datelined Boston in 1966, and the cluster of stories on the page with it powerfully evokes an era: "Berkeley Students Vote to Suspend Strike after Losing Support"; "Coed 'Slave' Sale on L. I. Protested by Negro Women" at SUNY-Stony Brook. The incident itself occurred at the University of Massachusetts: "Negro Students Protest Reading 'Huckleberry Finn'" (*New York Times*, 7 December 1966). The event, however, seems much less than the headline promises. The protest involved "two Negro girls" who "walked out of a sophomore English class recently." Their reason for walking out was not, it turns out, any objection to reading the novel. Rather, they left "when the character Nigger Jim was mentioned." The evidence suggested, although the story did not acknowledge, that they were protesting a class in which a racially offensive misnaming was permitted to circulate, since Twain's character does not bear the name the article mentions, a fact the *Times* knew a decade earlier but had apparently forgotten by this time. So the news story treated "Nigger Jim" as part of the canonical idol. Both in 1957 and in this instance, the actuality seems more ambiguous than the headlines suggest.

John Wallace's Provocation

There can be no doubt about the protest, however, in the current phase of controversy over *Huckleberry Finn* in the schools, which dates only from 1982. John H. Wallace, exploiting the visibility of his serving at the Mark Twain Intermediate School in Fairfax County, Virginia, gained a great deal of attention for his arguments that the book should be withdrawn from use there because it was "racist trash" (Moore 1). He then prepared an edition to cope with this problem by removing the word *nigger* and also the word *hell*—in other words, bringing things back to the Verne Brown edition which it had seemed so important for the *Times* to defend back in 1957. To this day little has been published that seriously engages the practical classroom issues for which Wallace's charge is a polemical shorthand. (The best discussions are by my student Peaches Henry and Allen Carey-Webb.)

The responses to Wallace, renewed in the centennial period of

1984–85, were extremely varied and continue to this day. Whether blaming bad teachers, bad students, or weak administrators, whether claiming from scholars the support of history, of ironic subtlety, or of deep meaning, all of these responses presume, and build from, the sacred status of *Huckleberry Finn*.

The responses that seem to me most bizarrely offensive came from the famous civil libertarian Nat Hentoff and from Michael Patrick Hearn, editor of *The Annotated "Huckleberry Finn."* Each was responding to the point that often teachers do not do a very good job of teaching the book, so that whatever the virtues of Twain's work in itself, it occasions very nasty classroom experiences. In February 1985, in a unit titled "Literature or Racist Trash" that was aired to coincide with the Chicago opening of *Big River*, Hentoff was on *Nightline* with Ted Koppel. At one moment, Hentoff attempted to forge a bond with his adversary, John H. Wallace, by responding, "Now, that teacher should have been fired on the spot? You're absolutely right" (Champion 153). But Wallace did not favor removing the teacher from the classroom, but the book; and I imagine if Hentoff actually learned of a teacher who had been fired on the spot for failing to adhere to a particular interpretation of a literary text, his memories of the First Amendment might revive. Hearn, a few months later in the *Nation*, defended the novel over which he had editorially labored by insisting, "The problem is the teaching, not the novel. . . . Should any class fail to discuss the humanity of Mark Twain's novel, then the school board should keep *Huckleberry Finn* and chuck the teacher." Why the *Nation* chose to publish this rhetorical outburst from someone who, on the evidence of his words, does not himself favor free speech, I cannot readily imagine, except that hypercanonization licenses any foolishness so long as it is in Twain's favor.

Less bizarre, but just as offensive, are the responses that rehearse the charge that those who disagree with them really cannot read. Hearn, the editor of *The Annotated "Huckleberry Finn,"* hurled this charge, but then displayed his own limitations as a reader. He found in current controversy "a perfect example of how one can read a book and not really *read* the book." According to Hearn, Twain "was a reformed Southerner." (As recently as the 1980s, in a national leftist journal, the assumption continued of Northern virtue and Southern guilt.) In *Huckleberry Finn*, therefore, "he expressed his shame for the way his race had treated another." To support this claim, Hearn quoted a famous line from the book, "Human beings *can* be awful cruel to one another" (290).

Hearn quoted correctly, just as did his opponents who found the word *nigger* in *Huckleberry Finn*, but he quoted this sentiment to substantiate his claim that Twain was making good in *Huckleberry Finn* his regret for the history of the treatment of African Americans in the South. Huck, however, speaks the line to sum up his feelings after he has seen the king and duke tarred and feathered and run out of town on a rail, a savage and brutal and possibly fatal punishment. The vigilantes have located them through information given by Jim (289), just as the duke had feared (273), and contrary to Huck's wish (275) and even his attempt (289). So Huck's line refers to the result of the revenge of an African American on the white men who had kept him chained and then sold him. This is a perfectly human response, but it does not show what Hearn claimed. Hearn's adaptation of Huck's line nicely exemplifies the point of John H. Wallace's very sensible insistence that "black students do not see the same thing in this book that a white teacher sees" (Champion 144).

Journalistic writers, quite properly, do not generally point by name to the academic authorities whose arguments underlie positions the media may take, but the fact of academic authority in itself sometimes proves important. For example, the *New York Times* editorial of 1 January 1984 commented on *Huckleberry Finn* as it began its centennial year. The problem of racism brought forward by John Wallace was evident "on the surface" of the book in the usage of *nigger*, but "volumes have been written about the book's deeper significance" ("Think"). "Deep" academic interpretations are routinely mocked by the *Times* as foolishly arcane and bejargoned, but their collective mass protects the book from being taken simply as it is.

Yet the editorial itself got caught in a problem of interpretation. To justify its assertion that "Twain was no racist," the editorial offered this evidence: "Twain dramatizes Jim's humanity, making him not so bright as Huck but innately stronger in heart and conscience." The *Times*'s logic is simple: If Twain shows Jim as good, he can't be a racist. Someone might object that to show an African American (in this book, *the* African American) as weak-headed but strong-hearted is itself racist stereotyping. The *Times* might reply that this objection, by ignoring the obvious goodwill in the characterization, rejects the book's surface intention. But the *Times* itself, only a few lines earlier, had abandoned the troubling "surface" for the deeps.

Along with the authority of "volumes" and key terms from Trilling, important claims about history are also made to serve the arguments of hypercanonization in the press. During the 1982 controversy, the *Washington Post* paired opposing views on *Huckleberry Finn*. Against John Wallace's "*Huckleberry Finn* Is Offensive" stood Robert Nadeau's "*Huckleberry Finn* Is a Moral Story." Nadeau invoked the principle of history. One may justify features of the text by reference to the world of the 1840s, when the book is set. If something was there in the world the text represents, then it is good for it to exist in the text. So he faced the problem of racially offensive language:

> *Nigger* is, of course, a terribly offensive word in our own time and should definitely not be used by anyone who respects the rights and integrities of others. But it might help to explain to those students who might continue to study the book at the intermediate school that in slave states the word was merely the ordinary colloquial term for a slave, and not necessarily abusive. (Champion 141)

Before I discuss Nadeau's claim, it is proper to emphasize that on this deeply troubling issue the academic authorities had given very little guidance. In their college text editions of *Huckleberry Finn* such outstanding critics and scholars as Lionel Trilling (1948), Henry Nash Smith (1958), Kenneth Lynn (1961), and Hamlin Hill and Walter Blair (1962) had nothing whatever to say linguistically, historically, or pedagogically about this problem, nor did the Norton Critical Edition (1961, 1977). The one prestigious text edition I know that did offer advice was Leo Marx's 1967 Bobbs-Merrill edition.

Here is what Marx said in a footnote at the first appearance of the word:

> In the South before the Civil War, "nigger" was the universal term for a slave. Today, of course, the word is considered abusive and certain opponents of racial intolerance have attacked Clemens for using it. (As recently as 1957 the book was removed from an approved textbook list in New York City, allegedly for this reason.) Criticism of the book on this ground is irrelevant not only because it is inconceivable that

Huck would have used another word but, even more important, because Clemens' point of view throughout is plainly sympathetic to
Jim and critical of the slavery system. (13)

The *Norton Anthology of American Literature* slightly differed from
Marx, and the two together seem to be the authority for what
Nadeau claimed. Here is the Norton: "Huck appropriately speaks
the colloquial word used in the South to describe black slaves; it is
not used derisively or contemptuously" (2:28).

The *Norton* usefully corrected Marx in one respect: the term was
indeed colloquial rather than universal; *servant* was the usual genteel and polite term. In using it, slave owners dignified their own
position as well as euphemizing that of their chattel, for it is honorable to be served by retainers, but degrading to be surrounded, like
a tyrant, by slaves. And by not reflecting on our contemporary concerns over the word, the *Norton* avoided some of Marx's confusions.
In his awareness of current racial issues, Marx was quite scrupulous
about the 1957 New York incident, but he still missed something
important. That incident was not the residual *end* of something, as
Marx's phrasing suggests, but a place of emergence, and therefore it
was precisely *relevant*. Especially in 1967, "irrelevant" was a strange
word for Marx to use, where *anachronistic* (or as people now say,
ahistorical) seems more what he meant.

Marx's concluding judgment blurred several issues. As many defenders of *Huckleberry Finn* in recent decades have done, he con-
flated the problem of slavery with the problem of race. Paul Berman
put it most succinctly in his review of *Big River*: "A friend of the
slaves can hardly be racist." There is no doubt that in *Huckleberry
Finn* Twain criticized the slavery system; in 1885, it would have
been hard to find any public defenders of that system. As the
United States has found ever since emancipation, however, there
are still racial problems after slavery is gone. Moreover, it seems
wrong for Marx to deny people their right to choose their friends or
allies in a current fight. Marx might as well have forbidden African
Americans the derogatory use of "Uncle Tom" on the—perfectly
true—grounds that Stowe was sympathetic to Tom and critical of
slavery, a much rarer and braver position in 1852 than in 1885. If
readers judge that however "sympathetic" to Jim, Twain is conde-
scending or unthoughtful, this forms legitimate grounds for criticism: even if it was written to defuse the offensive term, the book
did not succeed in doing so.

Most important, I think, neither Marx nor the *Norton* acknowledged that even a good-hearted lad may nonetheless actively participate in an organized system of racial domination that operates in part through the "universal" circulation of a term that is treated as if it were merely descriptive, but which is actually pejorative. Individually, one may not intend contempt, yet one may use a term, or otherwise participate, in a system that is socially structured to convey contempt. Twain's novel quickly exposes the literal inadequacy of attempts to defuse the term. Within a few chapters of its first usage, the term clearly refers to a person who is not a slave. In pap's tirade against the "govment," he refers to a "free nigger," who was "most white as a white man" (33)—in other words, socially "black" but not legally enslaved. Clearly the term here does not specify condition of servitude but rather what we call "race."

Nadeau's defense of the term is caught in similar shiftings. Shortly after defending the term as the ordinary word for slave, he also adduced chapter 31 ("All right, then, I'll *go* to hell"). This chapter he found especially valuable in freeing children who are "subjected . . . to a religious education in which the interpreters of spiritual verities seek to sanction the view of black people as innately inferior." But for the scene to work as he wished, it requires readers to grasp that *nigger* does not simply mean slave, for that has no bite on life today, but must also refer to any and all African Americans—just what he had begun by denying.

Moreover, Nadeau, Marx, and the *Norton* all chose to ignore what I expect my readers know and in any case the *OED* makes clear: the term *slave* is not itself neutral. Contrary to Roger Sutton, who in *School Library Journal* criticized John Wallace's adaptation of *Huckleberry Finn* for replacing an "ugly word" with *slave,* the term *slave* is not at all "only descriptive, carrying no value judgment or emotional freight." Slavery is understood to be a shameful situation; to call someone a *slave* is to offer an insult. The Harvard historian of American immigrant groups Oscar Handlin analyzed the history behind the term as it came to function in the American colonies. In the 1600s, as the first enslaved Africans were brought to Virginia, they were still called "servants," for "the word 'slave' had no meaning in English law." *Slave* did possess "a significant colloquial usage," however, as "a general term of derogation," which "served to express contempt" (7).

The whole founding impulse of the United States was to escape the "slavery" to the Crown inflicted by British colonial rule, as Lincoln observed in his reflection on the Fourth of July. In Mark Twain's writings about politics in the 1880s, no term is more frequently used to denounce the failure of freethinking "independence" than the term "slave" or its variants. In Twain's 1884 "Mock Oration on the Dead Partisan," a major contribution to his bold Mugwump commitment to political independence, he describes the deceased party man: "He was a slave. . . . He had no mind of his own, no opinion of his own; body and soul was the property of that master. . . . And the desire of his heart was to make of a nation of freemen a nation of slaves like himself" (*Collected* 1:852). In the same period, Twain was developing the line of thought posthumously published as *What Is Man?* and as part of his argument for the wholly determining power of circumstance he cites "the tyranny of party . . . which turns voters into chattels, slaves, rabbits." To highlight the "contradiction" between the false belief in freedom and the actual state of things, Twain links the current rhetorical "rubbish" about "liberty, independence, freedom of opinion, freedom of speech" to the conditions a "generation earlier," that is, before the war, when "their fathers and the churches shouted the same blasphemies"—that is, claims for freedom—"when they were closing their doors against the hunted slave, beating his handful of human defenders with Bible-texts and billies, and pocketing the insults and licking the shoes of the southern Master" (*Collected* 1:854–56).

Evidently Twain's own painful and difficult experience of standing against very strong peer pressure to stay loyal to the Republican Party became his model of the larger difficulty, hyperbolized as impossibility, of human agency: "When a man leaves a political party, he is treated as if the party owned him—as if he were its bond slave . . . and had stolen himself, gone off with what was not his own" (*Collected* 1:855–57). So to say that *nigger* just means *slave* and therefore should not be taken badly is to see things from the perspective of one who can never imagine enslavement as "relevant."

John Wallace achieved an effective riposte in dialogue with Ted Koppel on *Nightline,* when Koppel invoked the criterion of fidelity to a past milieu. Koppel put forward a claim that we have seen has considerable academic support: "when we're talking about Twain, we're talking about nineteenth-century America, not twentieth-century America. And those terms, the fact that the term was used in nineteenth-century America is a fact of life." Wallace all but interrupted Koppel to reply, "Well, Ted, it is a fact of life that it is used today. So . . . what are you saying?" (Champion 154).

Beyond historical claims that rely on the antebellum nineteenth century to justify the book's representation of that world, historical arguments may also be made that refer to the relation of *Huckleberry Finn* to the world it was written in, the 1880s. In a 1985 centennial homage, George Will combined historicism with name-calling. According to Will, "charging Huck with racism is cuckoo." Why? Because the response when Twain's book was first published shows that "the passage where Huck's conscience is nagging him" in chapter 31 is "what caused some nineteenth-century moralists to say that Huck should be kept from the tender eyes of children." Will was apparently echoing a retrospective, polemical claim from Twain's *Autobiography* (2:333) that is not supported by other sources. Beyond the analysis of the overall religious situation by Perry Miller, cited in the previous chapter, the material presented in Victor Fischer's unsurpassed article on the reception of *Huckleberry Finn* from 1885 to 1897 shows that the negative response to *Huckleberry Finn* by some purist readers and librarians was based on an overall distaste for the social milieu and language represented. Their negative view was not especially focused on "I'll *go* to hell!" let alone on the morality of assisting a fugitive slave.

In fact, chapter 31 won praise from the book's first appearance. The thoroughly highbrow Thomas Sergeant Perry, usually a reviewer of new French and German books, reviewed *Huckleberry Finn* in the flagship of the genteel tradition, the *Century* magazine, in which excerpts from *Huckleberry Finn* had recently appeared. His next-to-last paragraph focused on the book's "humor," of which he found an "admirable instance" in Huck's "mixed feelings about rescuing Jim . . . from slavery": "His perverted views regarding the unholiness of his actions are most instructive and amusing." The terms of praise differ from those used since hypercanonization took effect. Perry saw not exemplary heroism but a humorous instance of good-hearted ignorance. Only in 1901 did William Dean Howells first morally elevate this chapter by seeing in it Huck's "spiritual struggle" (Cady 342). Nonetheless, chapter 31 was valued as a high point from the first responses.

In contrast to Will, who presented *Huckleberry Finn* as boldly challenging prevailing standards of its time, the *Washington Post*

(8 April 1982) was somewhat more accurate in presenting *Huckleberry Finn* as broadly allied with liberal opinion of its time: "when the book was published . . . it was considered progressive for the way it portrayed the injustice of racial prejudice." But this is still overstated. Fischer does not cite any reviews or other responses that either praised or blamed *Huckleberry Finn* for its views of racial prejudice. Indeed, no response at the time seems to have remarked even the possible relevance of *Huckleberry Finn* to the racial issues of the 1880s.

One of the major senior Twain scholars, Louis J. Budd of Duke University, has been concerned since the 1950s with the bearing of *Huckleberry Finn* on issues related to the South in Twain's time. In *Mark Twain: Social Philosopher* (1962), Budd developed a powerful historicist interpretation of *Huckleberry Finn*. He expertly mapped *Huckleberry Finn* in relation to three literary landmarks of the 1880s. Thomas Nelson Page wrote nostalgic evocations of the Old South, which by showing slavery as a benign human relationship implied that after the war free African Americans would be well cared for by Southern whites if they relied on whites' goodwill and stayed in subordinate positions. The powerful historical novel *The Grandissimes* (1880) was written by the Louisiana-born, ex-Confederate soldier George W. Cable, who also wrote important essays that strongly criticized the South's refusal after the Civil War to grant full legal rights to African Americans. In *A Fool's Errand* (1879) and other works, the carpetbagger judge Albion W. Tourgée offered fictionalized accounts of the struggles over Reconstruction. Budd then proposed that a reader of the time would have experienced *Huckleberry Finn* not only as excelling within the field defined by these three contemporaries, but as going beyond them to face the world after Reconstruction, after the deal struck in 1877 that withdrew federal troops from the South, leaving to the South alone the (non)enforcement of postwar guarantees of civil rights for African Americans:

> Readers of the 1880s saw the immediate use of implying that the Confederacy had deserved to lose and saw that to question the myth of the happy slave is to cast suspicion, by a weak but common linkage, on any later move the Deep South makes concerning the Negro. Those who believed Page's "Marse Chan" could stop worrying about the freedman; those who believed *The Grandissimes* would oppose abandoning him to the Redemptionists' custody. More forcefully than Cable's fiction and more expertly than Tourgée's, *Huckleberry Finn*

gave a timely answer to Page. . . . However, it did much more than oppose the glamorizing of the Old South. Gracefully moving in and out
of the antebellum context to suit the purpose right at hand, it managed
also to judge the South's conduct after being paroled to its own conscience by the compromise of 1877. (95)

Budd provided no account of any actual "readers of the 1880s" who
had seen in *Huckleberry Finn* what he did, and since Budd understood his work as historical, this evidently troubled him. It has not
troubled subsequent commentators, who claim a "growing consensus" that the ending provides "direct commentary" on racial politics after Reconstruction, or even that the book as a whole is "prin-
cipally" about Twain's own time (Fishkin, *Lighting* 197; Doyno,
Afterword 7; Jehlen 97).

Against this current, Budd has importantly revised his earlier as-
sertions, although without stating that he has done so. In his first
book, he claimed confidently, "In 1885 [*Huckleberry Finn*] unmistak-
ably read as a commentary on the Southern question; to believe this
was accidental is to be naïve" (*Social* 106). But in his 1983 study of
Mark Twain's "public personality," Budd was much more circum-
spect about the relation of *Huckleberry Finn* to its contemporary
readership: "Despite close study . . . we know little about how
Twain hoped it would strike the hodgepodge of publics he was ac-
quiring" (88). Note Budd's scrupulous point that Twain wrote for a
plurality of publics. In his introduction to a 1985 volume, *New Essays on "Huckleberry Finn,"* Budd took a further step, apparently
now more careful to clarify what we do not know: "Because Jim
emerges so appealingly through his comradeship with Huck, we
can overrate [the novel's] relevance, planned or effectual, for the situation of the freed slaves in the 1880s" (10). It is necessary to add a
caveat here. I admire Budd's concern, as a mature scholar, to make
his claims more precise in the light of changing knowledge, but
there is one respect in which this sentence of his is not at all careful.
By 1885, a whole generation of African Americans was coming to
maturity all of whose members had been born in freedom; the issue
was not only the "freed slaves."

Budd by 1985 had come to doubt the premises of his earlier work,
for he proposed that whether they "help" or "hurt" the reputation
of *Huckleberry Finn*, those who argue on the basis of "historical accuracy or impact" do so "misleadingly." He asked, rhetorically expecting an answer of *no*, "Does Jim essentially challenge the pater-

nalism that Uncle Remus is happy to accept from Joel Chandler Harris, who admired the novel heartily?" Even old Marxist critics "accepted" the novel's "reputation for scorning racism," but that truism was now attacked by "some of Jim's descendants" (13). Budd here, for all his scruple, fell into the rhetorical trap set by the logic of representative genealogy, the other side of historicism. If the book represents America ("quintessentially"), and Huck is the great exemplar of the American character, then Jim, as "the Negro," must be the ancestor of all African Americans. Of course Budd cannot really believe this, but talking about *Huckleberry Finn* has made many smart people say foolish things. In any case, it is clear that journalists who make historical excuses for what is offensive in *Huckleberry Finn*, or historical boasts of its accuracy and impact, need to pay closer attention to the actual scholarship on which they rely.

Recent Changes

When I first began the work that led to this book, in the middle 1980s, it seemed that *Huckleberry Finn* had achieved an immovable place in the American curricular canon, as well as in the larger culture. My interest was to explore how it had come to such a position, and what the reasons were for its successfully maintaining its place. Over the decade I have been paying attention to *Huckleberry Finn*, there have been changes, especially noticeable in 1995–96, as I have been completing and revising my work, which have brought significant new elements into the public press discussions. There are three main clusters I will focus on: pedagogical discussions, especially those provoked by curricular decisions at the National Cathedral School in Washington, D.C.; discussions occasioned by publication of new material from the long-lost manuscript of the novel's first half; and a polemic by the novelist Jane Smiley.

One new feature in the classroom debate was that the *Washington Post* allowed high-school English teachers the opportunity to explain themselves at lucid length. The contributions by Rhoda M. Troboff, chair of English at National Cathedral School, and Kevin J. Barr, chair of English at Georgetown Day School, showed good pedagogical and curricular sense. Responses aroused by the news about this curricular revision showed the continuing gap between the painful experience of African American students and the idolatry of *Huckleberry Finn* by public pundits. Just as had happened in 1982 in New York, a correspondent wrote to report her own painful classroom experience: "Years ago I sat in a NCS classroom as the only black student in the class, and I remember feeling invisible while 'Huckleberry Finn' was being taught" (Bellinger).

Some things change very slowly, as evidenced in the piece by Nat Hentoff, the best-known usual suspect when there is controversy over *Huckleberry Finn*. Long years after his novel *The Day They Came to Arrest the Book* and his TV debate with John Wallace, Nat Hentoff once again blamed school authorities and parents, while ignoring the thoughtful deliberations of the teachers. His defense of *Huckleberry Finn* failed to engage with the documented arguments by the teachers, instead accusing "objecting parents and fearful administrators." In their fixation on a troubling word, such readers "overlook—or ignore—the story." Here is Hentoff's account of the story: Huck is "reared in seas of bigotry by whites who used 'nigger' as the commonest of debasing words," but he "transcends all his previous learning when he finally finds a decent, caring adult, Jim." So, in Hentoff's reading, even though Huck continues to use the word to the very end, the therapeutic power of Jim's care for him has purged it of its debasing force. This is the romance of interracial good intentions in almost its purest form, differing from the 1993 Disney film only by acknowledging the offensive word, which the screenwriters simply removed. I can see why some people might find it desirable to force students to read and admire a work that teaches that the loving care of a decent, middle-aged black man can cure white boys of racism, but I can also see why some might find it less compelling.

Hentoff, at least, acknowledged the debasing power of a word that Jonathan Yardley, in his *Washington Post* column on the National Cathedral School controversy, preferred to dismiss with the historical excuse that "it was common white usage a century ago and no one thought twice about it." When he refers, loosely, to "a century ago," he means in the time of Twain's writing (1876–1884) rather than in the time of the book's action (1835–45). But Sam Clemens participated in a widespread linguistic shift. According to Eric Foner, by the early 1870s a "striking change" came over the rhetoric and platform of the Democratic Party: its "veterans of racial politics abandoned the term 'nigger' in favor of 'negro' or 'colored person'" (*Reconstruction* 506). Likewise, by 1868, when he began

courting Olivia Langdon, whose family had been strong abolitionists, Twain in his writing and recorded speech did not use the term
casually (Leonard et al. 7–8). Huck speaks quite a different language from that of the everyday adult life of Sam Clemens or Mark
Twain. And in the period when *Huckleberry Finn* appeared, there is
clear evidence that the use of *nigger* was not a casual matter among
people of racial goodwill in the 1880s, and there were such people:
it was not a matter of "no one" caring.

Twain undertook a reading tour with George W. Cable, who was
in process of being driven from the South by resentment against his
advocacy of civil rights for African Americans. In their correspondence, Cable invited Twain to think twice about the word. Cable
proposed a change in the flyer listing their evening's performances:
use the title "How come a Frenchman doan' talk like a man?" instead of what Twain had originally proposed, a different phrase
from the same episode from *Huckleberry Finn*, "Can't learn a nigger
to argue" (98). Cable, who was a serious Christian and at times an-
noyed Twain by his churchgoing, abstinence from alcohol, and refusal of profanity, explained his preference in self-deprecatory
terms, but the point is very clear: "When we consider that the pro-
gramme is advertised & becomes cold-blooded newspaper reading
I think we should avoid any risk of appearing—even to the most
thin-skinned and super-sensitive [*sic*] and hyper-critical matrons
and misses—the faintest bit gross" (Cardwell 105). Cable emphasized the importance of context: he had no objection to the word in
the book or as part of the performance from the book, only as it
stood free and unexplained in the public eye.

Further evidence exists that the term *nigger* was not politely ac-
ceptable, even in the heart of the South. A writer who, however
deeply sensitive to African American culture, was in no way a
bleeding heart, Joel Chandler Harris, published in 1892 *On the Plantation*, a fictionalized memoir of his experiences as a noncombatant
teenager in the Civil War. The term *nigger* is used only by the characters—black and white alike—quoted as speaking in the 1860s;
the retrospective narrative voice, even right after a passage in which
quoted speakers have used "nigger," always uses "negro."

The African American writer Anna Julia Cooper, in *A Voice from
the South* (1892), commented on the use of *nigger* as extremely socially significant. Southern whites who resented the possible emergence of some form of equality, signaled by the use of the term *Negro*, might still be warmly gracious to an obviously socially inferior

African American. As Cooper summarized this: "A Southern white man's regard for his black friend varies in inverse ratio to the real distance between them in education and refinement." She made her point with a quotation from the comic magazine *Puck:* "I can get on a great deal better with a nigger than I can with a Negro" (218).

The term *nigger,* then, was clearly understood to form part of a strategy of enforcing African American subordination. In his Pulitzer Prize-winning history of Southern "life after Reconstruction," Edward Ayers quotes this etiquette lesson from a memoir to illustrate the ethos of the later nineteenth century. When a young man referred to a respected black man as "Mr. Jones," his aunt quickly corrected him: "No, son. Robert Jones is a nigger. You don't say 'mister' when you speak of a nigger. You don't say 'Mr. Jones,' you say 'nigger Jones'" (Ayers 132). If the term was not in those days a fighting word, it was not because no one cared, but because white supremacy minimized the chances of a fight.

In claiming, against the sort of readily available evidence I have just cited, that no one a century ago cared about the term *nigger,* Yardley was just reiterating a point he had made in 1982, in response to John Wallace's initial provocation. In 1995, however, Yardley also offered a new emphasis on *Huckleberry Finn's* "essential being as literature." His arguments here show how extreme are the positions to which defenders may feel driven in order to preserve hypercanonization. Schools must offer students "the revelatory experience of reading it purely as such." Yardley opposed not only the choice not to teach *Huckleberry Finn,* but also the choice to teach *Huckleberry Finn* in any way that involved "the dissemination of convictions and 'values.'" Such teaching, he asserted, is "most suitably undertaken . . . in the discussion of ethics and morality rather than in the teaching of literature." Yardley's position is quite remarkable. Apparently he favors the dissemination of convictions and values in ethics classes (which some would consider to be a dubious imposition on freedom of discussion and inquiry), but he believes that convictions and values have nothing to do with literature "as such," "in its essential being."

Yardley's proclaimed defense of literature actually strives to deny the viewpoint defined by the most influential Anglo-American public defenders of literature, from Matthew Arnold in the mid-nineteenth century to Lionel Trilling in the mid-twentieth. Arnold, who insisted that it is the task of criticism to "see the object as in itself it really is," also defined literature as fundamentally "a criticism of life" (234, 343), and for Trilling what made literature interesting enough to care about was the moral energy of its imaginings. Not only did Trilling praise *Huckleberry Finn* for its "subversive" moral energy (*Liberal* 108). He argued, in his next book, *The Opposing Self*, that in fiction and poetry of the last two centuries, the "modern imagination" of "selves conceived in opposition to the general culture" makes a "new idea in the world." This idea, he emphasized, "is an idea in the world, not in literature alone" (xiv–xv).

For Yardley, however, only a "utilitarian view" concerns itself with politics or culture, with "racial issues, or critique of gentility." An appropriately literary view, at once "more expansive and more accurate," instead invokes the authority of Mencken and Hemingway to see *Huckleberry Finn* as "the greatest of all American novels, the wellspring from which all else flows." As Yardley reaches his conclusion, he flows from treating *Huckleberry Finn* as literary to asserting its pure participation in the identity of the nation—in contrast to other ways of taking the book, which Yardley calls utilitarian, which quarrel with the book's relation to the nation: "Precisely because it is so quintessentially American, 'Huckleberry Finn' has always discomforted those who . . . prefer to see American reality depicted through [tinted] glasses." But, "like the great river . . . it just keeps rolling along." That is, "literary" readers accept the identity of book and nation.

Yardley's defense of pure "literature," which so readily, but uncritically, transforms into a nationalist position, proves, in its context, simply an attempt to deny any value in reading *Huckleberry Finn* together with works by African Americans. For no one ever intended that it not be taught. Despite headlines proclaiming *Huckleberry Finn* "Bounced from Class Again" and Valerie Strauss's story asserting that National Cathedral School was "the latest area school to pull . . . Huckleberry Finn from its curriculum," despite Yardley's own accusation that the school was the latest to "stop teaching" *Huckleberry Finn* and his denunciation of its "removal" from the curriculum, all that was at issue was the shift of *Huckleberry Finn* from a tenth-grade course to an upperclass course. As Rhoda Troboff explained: *Huckleberry Finn* was no longer appropriate in the required tenth-grade course because that course had been changed to one studying masterpieces of British literature (not an obviously antiliterary or merely utilitarian topic); and it was hoped that the upperclass course would enrich the study of *Huckleberry Finn* by teaching it along with works by African Americans.

Yardley was afraid, though he stated it as a certainty rather than a fear, that this meant that "'Huckleberry Finn' remains in the curriculum not as a work of literature but as a cautionary tale about American race relations" (rather than as the triumphal tale that Hentoff still saw in it?). Yardley imagined, though he again stated it as a necessity rather than as a possibility, that if *Huckleberry Finn* were taught "in conjunction with works by African American authors," then it would become "a backdrop against which to contrast the works of Zora Neale Hurston and W. E. B. Du Bois" and would be reduced to "merely a sociological document or a benchmark against which we can measure our subsequent progress"—just the way it has long been taught, except with no reference to African American writings! So when Yardley proposed purely literary reading, it was a specific defense against what he saw as the important new issue: not banning the book so much as reducing its power by making it no longer the unique wellspring but instead only one among a range of differing voices representing racial experiences in the United States.

Yardley's position seems an unpromising line of defense for those who wish to resist the effective integration not now of the classroom but of the syllabus. For even as he invoked Mencken and Hemingway as authorities for the founding role of *Huckleberry Finn* in American fiction, he actually abandoned the ground on which they had based that claim. In the teens and twenties, and into the period of hypercanonization, Twain's stylistic example had seemed to offer pure colloquial, "vernacular" American speech against the overformal modes stigmatized as the "genteel tradition."

Yardley, however, for all the aesthetic revelation he ascribed to *Huckleberry Finn*, saw its language as an obstacle, not its great strength. Valerie Strauss's news story had begun this topic, characterizing *Huckleberry Finn* as "written in a dialect that has long since disappeared," an assertion never to my knowledge made before in a news article about the book. In his opinion piece the next day, Yardley amplified. He recalled that back in 1982, at the time of Wallace's protest, he had reread the book, and he "was struck by how many of the words were dated and how many of the idioms needed annotation" (I assume this means he was reading it in an annotated edition, rather than that he was reading along, just wishing that he knew what Huck was talking about). He concluded: "Mark Twain may be as much a puzzlement to the student of the 1990s as Geoffrey Chaucer was to the student of the 1950s." This is incredible! Not even Shakespeare, somewhat dated but still effectively readable, but Chaucer, writing in what linguists treat as actually a different language from modern English? But if Yardley meant what he said, and if he spoke for current educated nonacademic opinion makers, then *Huckleberry Finn* will soon go the way of what was once in the United States the canon of British literature: known only to a few, and talked about by a few more who do not actually read it.

In contrast to the writers of the *Washington Post*, Bobbie Ann Mason in the *New Yorker*, in summer 1995, took a much less bookish and metropolitan view, finding the language of *Huckleberry Finn* still effectively that of local speech: "Mark Twain's original boyhood language, the deepest source of his artistic energy, is the language of my grandparents and parents, and it is still spoken throughout the mid-south, from the Appalachians through the Ozarks." The most authoritative article on the dialects of *Huckleberry Finn*, by David Carkeet (himself based in St. Louis), confirms her sense of the language's currency.

Mason's was one of five brief pieces in the *New Yorker*, commissioned in summer 1995 to accompany the first publication of materials from the newly rediscovered manuscript portion. Three of the pieces reflected on racial questions in ways new to prestigious public discussion of *Huckleberry Finn:* by E. L. Doctorow, whose *Billy Bathgate* is a much-noted recent successor to Huck's narrative voice; William Styron, whose *The Confessions of Nat Turner* (1967) suffered the exemplary fate of Southern white liberalism in the late sixties, winning a Pulitzer Prize and then being torn apart in a volume in which ten black writers responded; and David Bradley, whose *The Chaneysville Incident* (1981) is an intricate and powerful fictional inquiry into African American history and how it continues to shape the present of African Americans. This group of responses is unparalleled in my reading of the public press materials on *Huckleberry Finn* over many years. All three pieces were really thoughtful, and they ended up with quite different emphases, while all agreeing on many essentials.

Doctorow worked through complex turns of argument to reach a judgment: The ending of *Huckleberry Finn* means that "one vision prevails, and it is the wrong one." The depiction of Jim "made Twain blow his greatest work." Huck "struggles against the white mores of his time to help the black man, Jim, escape from slavery, but it is Huck's progenitor who portrays Jim, in minstrelese, as a gullible black child-man led by white children." Doctorow recognized that in his description of *Huckleberry Finn* we might hear echoes of the New Testament, paradoxically overturning old habits and structures to bring in a new world of salvation, but in his last sentence Doctorow fiercely though not absolutely resisted this implication: "The irony may not be redemptive."

Styron concluded by invoking the controversies over *Huckleberry Finn*, which he suspected would never end, because Huck and Jim stand as "symbols of our own racial confusion." And he showed that confusion in his own account of the debates. He judged John Wallace's edition of *Huckleberry Finn* an "all-time curiosity" for removing "every use of the word 'nigger,'" but he seemed wholly unaware that until 1957 the New York City school system had been using exactly such an edition. Despite the excellent explanations offered by the teachers, he considered that the National Cathedral School could have made its curricular change only as the result of "panic." Styron drew on his own feel for Southern speech, and also his extensive documentary research for *The Confessions of Nat Turner*, to offer a new clarification about Twain's vocabulary in *Huckleberry Finn*: "a twelve-year-old Missourian would have had scant familiarity with the word 'slave'—a term that was generally confined to government proclamations, religious discussions, and legal documents." Therefore he took Huck's language as "innocent vernacular usage," but only a few sentences earlier, Styron had emphasized that "'nigger' remains our most powerful secular blasphemy." Is it then so odd that it provokes distress? And is it inconceivable that it may never have been "innocent" to use it? Huck's pap after all sets an example of usage within the family that no one would call innocent.

David Bradley's piece also focused on this troubling word from beginning to end. He started, "The first time I was called a nigger was on the playground on my first day of school." He moved from his playground experiences to his private reading. Right in the middle of the essay, he reported the discovery that made him a great admirer of *Huckleberry Finn:* Huck "says 'nigger' often but means nothing by it." And when (in chapter 15) Huck humbles himself to Jim after his nasty trick, Bradley had a further epiphany: "not all poor white trash are bigots." The point of this for him was that through this reading experience he began to "judge intent by action rather than rhetoric." Bradley wished that experiences like his might be shared widely in classrooms, but despite all that his essay faced, and it faced a great deal, it did not discuss whether teachers can successfully require children to have the experience that he discovered for himself. (And of course Twain's book makes Huck's greatest moment solitary and sets it explicitly against his society's pedagogic values.) All of us who are teachers build our autobiographies deeply into our classrooms and curricula, but I have little hope for this kind of universalization. Precisely because, as Bradley emphasized, "'nigger' is offensive not because it was said by literary characters in 1845 but because it is *meant* by literal Americans in 1995," he wished for children to face the word in a book rather than somewhere where noses get bloodied. Yet in a classroom, as opposed to a private reading experience, what literary characters say is wholly embroiled with what literal people mean. So I differ pedagogically from Bradley, even while completely agreeing with his cry of anguish: "America ought to be a place where 'nigger' has only a historical meaning."

We still lack sufficient material on the strengths and weaknesses of differing classroom approaches to *Huckleberry Finn.* One attempt to develop such materials has recently been made by the National Council of Teachers of English (NCTE) in a volume commissioned to demonstrate the way classrooms might put into practice the recently promulgated set of national standards. In *Standards in Practice Grades 9–12,* Peter Smagorinsky devoted the second of his four chapters to "Perspectives on *Huckleberry Finn,*" using as his focus the experience of a teacher in a junior-year American literature class in a northeastern suburban high school with a multiracial student body and considerable social tensions. The overall story of the chapter is the teacher's decision to change his mode of teaching in order to make a major focus of the work on *Huckleberry Finn* the development of students' capacities to ask questions of a text and of each other. This shift opened the possibility of students' drawing from their involvement with the book. The teacher's previous relation to his teaching was summarized as follows:

Because he had never been called "nigger" himself, Mr. Gorin could read the language of the novel and distance himself from the abusive term. Over the years his African American students had complained about having to read a novel where the term "nigger" was used so frequently, but Mr. Gorin was convinced that they needed to get beyond their hurt feelings and take a more detached academic approach to the novel. *Huckleberry Finn* was clearly a masterpiece of American letters, thought Mr. Gorin, and Twain's use of the word "nigger" was ironic. For many years he told his black students that they needed to transcend their initial emotional response to the term and achieve the proper distance to see Twain's larger purpose. That most African American students failed to do so, Mr. Gorin attributed to their lack of maturity as both students and individuals. (25)

Familiar as this view is, the explicitness with which it is spelled out makes more evident what too many in the debates have ignored. Contrary to Mr. Gorin's initial view, what hinders "proper" reading of *Huckleberry Finn,* as of most difficult literary works, is not lack of distance but lack of sympathy, that is, a failure to get close. The success of his new teaching technique, which depends on students' involvement, underlines the fallacy of his old view, which is still widely shared in journalistic discussion. The racially abusive term acts as a barrier to intimacy between many students and Huck, and without that intimacy no "understanding of the literary conventions of irony," which the teacher wished, will actually do any good. If the reader feels only, "To hell with you," then "All right, then, I'll *go* to hell" can bring at best the response, "About time," rather than a thrilling sense of transformation. In order to read Twain's irony, one must first be engaged by Huck's narrative.

The deep problems with the notion of irony that continue to haunt this well-meaning pedagogical account may be seen in its summary of what students should get from studying *Huckleberry Finn:* "they need to try to recognize both the ironic structure of the text and the emotional impact that irony can have on people whose negative experiences are being satirized." This is, I think, confused. What is "being satirized," we believe, is white racism, but by that reading, then, the people of whom one should be especially solicitous in discussing *Huckleberry Finn* are white racists. But I take it from the chapter as a whole that black readers are the objects of solicitude, so what is really meant by "negative experiences" is the pain of slavery. But that's not being satirized! What I read from this muddle is a sorry subtext, that it's the negative experiences, as readers, of black students that are satirized by a book that again and again is invoked to show that black people really can't read in the authorized way. When even teachers who will be accused by many of political correctness get themselves into such tangles trying to make the case for *Huckleberry Finn,* it is easy to see why some might just rather forget about the problem.

Such a teacher might be gripped by *Harper's* January 1996 issue, in which the noted novelist Jane Smiley went a long step beyond the summer 1995 *New Yorker* pieces. As suggested by her title, "Say It Ain't So, Huck: Second Thoughts on Mark Twain's 'Masterpiece,'" she expressed not simply complex ambivalence but real hostility. Her animus was not against Huck the character, but rather the author: "The villain here is Mark Twain." Because Jim is "never autonomous" but always "subordinate" to Huck, therefore the "claims that are routinely made for the book's humanitarian power are, in the end, simply absurd."

Smiley wished to go beyond the question of the word "nigger" to what she called "the deeper racism of the novel," namely, "the way Tom and Huck use Jim." She argued that to value so highly "Huck's paltry good intentions" is to fall into "meretricious reasoning." For "white Americans always think racism is a feeling," but racism is better understood by "black Americans" as "a way of structuring" American culture, politics, and economics. In contrast to this structural understanding, the tradition has embraced Huck because he "*feels* positive toward Jim, and *loves* him, and *thinks* of him as a man," even though Huck "doesn't actually have to act in accordance with his feelings." Here Smiley joined work by the sociologist Stephen Steinberg and the cultural critic Benjamin DeMott that appeared at about the same time as her essay, and I wholly support all three in their critique of what might be called "the antiracism of good feelings."

My views are not nearly so hostile to Mark Twain and *Huckleberry Finn,* but I agree with many of Smiley's points. We both focus on the years after 1948; what I have called the moment of hyper-canonization, she named the "Propaganda Era." Her view agrees with the premise of this book, that "there is more to be learned" about the United States "*from*" the canonization of *Huckleberry Finn* than "*through*" its canonization." She saw the "universal inclusion of the book in school curriculums" as following from the proclamation of its greatness by the Propaganda Era critics. She emphasized that this was "clearly a political act," which set very low terms for the discussion of racism and American history, and which formed a nationalist basis by which "American literature can be found different from and maybe better than Russian or French or English literature."

Smiley followed important feminist arguments by Nina Baym on the process of canonization, and she argued that *Huckleberry Finn* has come to its place through the suppression of *Uncle Tom's Cabin* from the canon. She echoed Hemingway, against the grain, to propose an alternative genealogy for American literature: it would have been better if all American literature had grown from *Uncle Tom's Cabin* and its "portrayal of an array of thoughtful, autonomous, and passionate black characters." Even though Smiley said that Twain, not Huck, is the problem, she contrasted the narrative voice of Stowe to that of Huck. Stowe's voice is "courageously public," while Huck's is "secretive." Valuing Twain over Stowe makes racism "f[a]ll out of the public world and into the private one, where whites think it really is but blacks know it really isn't." I agree with Smiley's contrast between public and private, but I am acutely unhappy with her level of generalization, and with her own rhetorical positioning, in which she named both "whites" and "blacks" as monolithic groups and placed herself beyond both.

For the purposes of literary criticism, a crucial claim of Smiley's is that *Huckleberry Finn* is weakened by virtue of Twain's necessary and evident conflicts over racial issues, while Stowe's work is strengthened by "her lack of conflict," which makes for "the clarity of both the style and the substance of the novel." Here is where Smiley ran most sharply against the powerful critical premises of the "Propaganda Era," and she failed to recognize several features of the encounter. First, the critics of this period whom she was challenging included not only those she named as "Lionel Trilling, Leslie Fiedler, T. S. Eliot, Joseph Wood Krutch, and some lesser lights." The period also included James Baldwin (powerfully negative on Stowe) and Ralph Ellison (powerfully positive on Twain), so that her distinction between what whites think and what blacks think falls aground. Second, the related distinctions she made between public and private, between conflict and its absence, map onto founding premises of the most admired American criticism from the 1940s to the present, namely, that a work of literature will be greater for containing, rather than excluding, conflict. (This is what New Critics called "paradox" and Bakhtin the dialogic; for Trilling it was the internally contained dialectic, the yes and no of a culture. In the instance of race, it was precisely Myrdal's "American Dilemma.")

A work of literature, in this line of thought, enhances its chance for achieving a valuable complexity precisely by its privacy, by its freedom from direct politics, from what might be called propaganda (the critics of the "Propaganda Era" strongly reprobated anything they recognized as propaganda), but what was most specifically called the "protest novel." In my next two chapters, I will be exploring these issues—by surveying the relations between *Uncle Tom's Cabin* and *Huckleberry Finn* over the course of their coexistence and by explaining the position in favor of internal conflict and against protest fiction that Lionel Trilling built his major work from, and that James Baldwin memorably encapsulated in "Everybody's Protest Novel."

4 ⎯⎯⎯⎯⎯⎯⎯⎯⎯

Uncle Tom's Cabin vs. *Huckleberry Finn*

The Historians and the Critics

In setting *Uncle Tom's Cabin* and *Huckleberry Finn* as opposites, Jane Smiley repeated a well-established gesture of what she called the "Propaganda Era," except that by preferring *Uncle Tom's Cabin* she reversed the established evaluation. In its broadest terms, the distinction between *Uncle Tom's Cabin* and *Huckleberry Finn* is the difference I have mentioned earlier between "national" and "literary" narratives. In the middle third of the twentieth century, this issue was phrased as a literary critique of "protest" fiction.

Lionel Trilling's praise of *Huckleberry Finn* gained force from Trilling's campaign, begun in the later 1930s and continuing even beyond the publication of *The Liberal Imagination,* against the widespread conventions shaping current fiction of social protest. Trilling was often in sympathy with the political goals of such novels, but he found them weak as literature, and, he argued, their weak sense of what human beings were like was itself politically damaging. *Stalinism* was the strongest name he gave to this tendency to reduce individual complexity on behalf of a collective cause. Appearing in *Partisan Review* in 1949, the year after Trilling had joined its masthead, James Baldwin's "Everybody's Protest Novel" took Trilling's critique an important step further, for Baldwin gave special attention to American protest fiction on racial issues.

Although Baldwin's central pages were devoted to the genre as a whole, the two works he attacked in detail were *Uncle Tom's Cabin,* with which he began, and Richard Wright's *Native Son* (1940), with which he ended. Baldwin's first sentence laid *Uncle Tom's Cabin* as the "cornerstone of American social protest fiction." The fundamental vice of this genre, for him, is "sentimentality," which he characterized in a bravura passage: "Sentimentality, the ostentatious parading of excessive and spurious emotion, is the mark of dishonesty, the inability to feel; the wet eyes of the sentimentalist betray his aversion to experience, his fear of life, his arid heart; and it is always, therefore, the signal of secret and violent inhumanity, the mask of cruelty." Stowe's inability to produce honest feeling, experience, and life comes from her being "not so much a novelist as an impassioned pamphleteer" (326–27).

As a pamphleteer, she is devoted to a "Cause," rather than to "truth." For Baldwin, truth means "devotion to the human being, his freedom and fulfillment; freedom which cannot be legislated, fulfillment which cannot be charted." In contrast to the unchartedness of "human being," the Cause is all chart and legislation and science in the name of "Humanity," the abstraction rather than the concrete, the general instead of the specific. This inhumanity in the name of Humanity means that "Causes, as we know, are notoriously bloodthirsty." In the late 1940s the memory of the Nazis and the pressure of the Cold War assured this identification of Causes with mass murder. Baldwin named the crucial quality of human being in the same terms that New Criticism was at this time developing to describe literature: "complexity," "ambiguity, paradox" (327). Despite its "good intentions," protest fiction uses simplifying "categories" instead of inventing complicated human beings, but categorization must fail because "literature and sociology are not the same" (329–30). Current defenders of *Huckleberry Finn* still use these terms that emerged after World War II.

Baldwin brilliantly portrayed the self-deluded goodwill he found at the core of the problem. He said "an American liberal" once told him that "as long as such [protest] books are being published . . . everything will be all right" (330). That is, the continuing production of such works replaces the never-attained solution of the problems they decry. The deadpan vernacular narration of *Huckleberry Finn,* in this postwar system of values shared by Baldwin and Trilling, stands for its honest engagement with life. Yet the liberal slogan Baldwin mocked just as well fits the current responses by public authorities to objections made against *Huckleberry Finn* in the schools: "As long as this book is being taught, everything will be all right." And to turn the specific "human being" Huck into a national exemplar, as the hypercanonic critics do, is to reestablish "categories" in a way that I call "nationalizing literary narrative" and discuss more fully in chapter 6.

The conjunction of Trilling's praise of *Huckleberry Finn* and Baldwin's demolition of *Uncle Tom's Cabin* offers a point of departure for thinking more widely about the relation of these two novels, which in the last few years have begun to be sympathetically discussed together, but which for most of this century, when paired, were seen as opposites—as was still the case not only in Smiley's essay, but in the letters *Harper's* published in response, almost all of which took for granted a view of *Uncle Tom's Cabin* much like Baldwin's.

Starting from the 1920s—that is, after the deaths of Twain, Howells, and almost everyone else who had known as adults the days of slavery—it became common to compare *Uncle Tom's Cabin* and *Huckleberry Finn*, to the detriment of *Uncle Tom's Cabin*. One of the modes by which the hypercanonization of *Huckleberry Finn* proceeded was by competitively draining the prestige of Stowe's work, which increasingly became a novel that everyone knew had been famous, but no one any longer read. For the only time in its history, *Uncle Tom's Cabin* went out of print for a few years in the 1940s. In one of the first issues of the new *Saturday Review of Literature*, in 1924, its editor, Henry Seidel Canby (b. 1878), a generation later an editor of the *Literary History of the United States*, in reviewing Twain's *Autobiography*, observed, "The final condemnation of slavery is not in the abolitionist 'Uncle Tom's Cabin' but in the experiences of that convinced Southerner, 'Huckleberry Finn.'" In his 1950 introduction to *Huckleberry Finn*, the mid-century's leading man of letters, T. S. Eliot, winner of the 1948 Nobel Prize, with characteristic emphasis on technique as the key to moral effect, claimed that "The *style* of the book, which is the style of Huck, is what makes it a far more convincing indictment of slavery than the sensationalist propaganda of *Uncle Tom's Cabin*" (330). Despite Edmund Wilson's extended positive exploration of Stowe in *Patriotic Gore* (1962) and Ellen Moers's strong praise in *Literary Women* (1976), this pattern began to change only in the 1980s, and it has not yet ended.

I became aware of this pattern in the late 1970s, when I began to introduce *Uncle Tom's Cabin* into the syllabus of courses on antebellum American literature. In conversation with students at the opening meeting, in which I discussed with them the reading list, I found that even though none or very few of them had read *Uncle Tom's Cabin*, they believed that they knew it had been a work of propaganda of no literary interest once slavery had been abolished, and that because *Huckleberry Finn* was not propaganda but instead a work of art, it was actually a far more powerful attack on slavery. The students were not acquainted with Baldwin's essay or Eliot's introduction, and the comparison to *Huckleberry Finn* was not something that I brought up. I found that many of the students most eager to make this comparison did not conceive that it means something very different for each of the two novels to speak of it as condemning or indicting slavery. Even though I could go through chronological exercises that showed the students knew that the Civil War had brought about the end of slavery in the United States, and that *Huckleberry Finn* was written after the Civil War, it held a place in their minds as a work with the same contemporary relation to American slavery as that of *Uncle Tom's Cabin*, which appeared as a book in 1852. This mythicization of history, by which *Huckleberry Finn* gained the prestige of abolitionism despite its having been written at a time when slavery did not exist and was defended by no one, helped provoke me to this book.

Twain and Stowe for many years were close neighbors in Connecticut, with warm personal relations. Yet during Twain's lifetime their works were not thought of together. While *Huckleberry Finn* was predominantly thought of as a boy's book, *Uncle Tom's Cabin* continued to hold an important place in critical consciousness of American literary history through Stowe's long lifetime (she died only in 1896) and on into the earlier twentieth century. The example of Thomas Dixon (1864–1946) illustrates the continuing prestige and currency of *Uncle Tom's Cabin*. Dixon's racist and anti-Reconstruction works of fiction began with *The Leopard's Spots: A Romance of the White Man's Burden, 1865–1900* (1902), written quite explicitly as a response, after fifty years, to Stowe. Stowe's Simon Legree reappears as the villain in Dixon's novel: "Rumors of his death proved a mistake. He had quit drink, and set his mind on greater vices"—that is, as an opportunistic carpetbagger (84). Dixon himself went on to greater things too. *The Clansman* (1905) became the basis for the film *The Birth of a Nation*, which Dixon's friend Woodrow Wilson screened in the White House and which in turn sparked the renewal of the KKK in the United States, spreading, for the first time, to the North. More broadly, Kenneth Warren has

shown that in the later nineteenth century *Uncle Tom's Cabin* provoked critical reflections on the category of the "sentimental" (still
working in strange ways in Baldwin's 1949 essay), which formed
the basis for a new ideology of "discrimination." As I shall go on to
show, those astute enough to distinguish realistic from sentimental
fiction were also, it seemed, skilled at making social distinctions
that would prevent the mingling of races or cultures.

A *Literary History of America* (1900) by Barrett Wendell (b. 1855)
was mocked from its first appearance for excessive focus on New
England. Nonetheless, Wendell found *Huckleberry Finn* worth mention and praise. In discussing New England abolitionists of the
1830s and their concern with the dehumanizing effects of slavery, he
quoted, as the briefest possible example of this dehumanization,
Huck's famous lie to Aunt Sally about the steamboat explosion:

> "Good gracious!" she exclaims, "anybody hurt?"
> "No, 'm. Killed a nigger."
> "Well, it's lucky; because sometimes people do get hurt." (Wendell 342)

In a vein that I expect will horrify anyone reading my pages,
Wendell explained that "seventy years ago" New Englanders might
have been distressed at the callousness Huck enacts, but "modern
ethnology" taught that "Africans . . . linger far behind the social
stage" achieved by Americans. The unenlightened "philanthropic
people in 1830," however, believed that any "distinction between
Caucasians and Africans" was no more than "a matter of complex-
ion." Readers in the late twentieth century typically recognize in
Uncle Tom's Cabin quite substantial differences between the races,
characterized by George Frederickson as a "romantic racialism,"
his term for distinctions—such as Stowe's belief that people of
African descent are more readily open to the message of Christianity—that are not meant as pejorative, even though to modern readers they seem so. Like Wendell, however, Charles Francis Adams—
grandson of John Quincy Adams, son of Lincoln's minister to Great
Britain, and himself a combat soldier in the Civil War—by the early
years of the twentieth century had come to see Stowe as a deluded
racial egalitarian. In a much-repeated oration on the centennial of
Robert E. Lee (1907), Adams criticized Stowe's "female and sentimentalist" view that "the only difference between the Ethiopian
and the Caucasian is epidermal" (Silber 178).

Wendell, in any case, had cited *Huckleberry Finn* not as an example of abolitionism, but only for its accurate representation of a particular way of feeling, once common only in the slave South, but now shared in cultivated New England. Wendell also mentioned *Huckleberry Finn* as the "masterpiece" among attempts "to reproduce the native dialects of the American people" and as thereby showing a rigorous "artistic conscience" (477). This "amazing Odyssey of the Mississippi" was not only an important "picture of the Middle West" of an earlier era, but "in certain moods one is disposed for all its eccentricity to call [it] the most admirable work of literary art yet produced on this continent" (503).

Wendell's praise of Twain, strong as it was, did not fundamentally shape his book. I have quoted almost in full the three very brief and scattered mentions of *Huckleberry Finn*. And despite his inclination to the new national culture of white supremacy, he still accorded Stowe and *Uncle Tom's Cabin* an important place in his account, some five pages in a book of less than six hundred pages. *Uncle Tom's Cabin*, even though it was "written carelessly" and is "full of crudities," nonetheless, "even after forty-eight years," still seems "a remarkable piece of fiction." And Wendell emphasized that the "great popular success" of *Uncle Tom's Cabin* and its relation to the "changing public opinion of her day" are no grounds to doubt Stowe's "power" as a writer, whether in the "pervasive vitality" of her characters, her "faithful" descriptions, or her "strong and vivid" style (354).

William Dean Howells (b. 1837), the most important American-based reviewer during the years of Twain's adulthood, was deeply angered by Wendell's history, especially by its dismissive attitude toward abolitionism. In contrast to Wendell's emphasis on how much historical distance separated his readers of 1900 from the antebellum period, Howells, in challenging particular interpretations of Wendell's, discussed details from the 1850s as if they were of the utmost contemporary significance and vividness (Cady 375). Howells, far more deeply than Wendell, held both Stowe and Twain in the highest esteem. In an 1897 essay, "My Favorite Novelist and His Best Book," in which he discussed many favorites, Howells made a claim that must seem outrageous now to readers schooled on Hawthorne and Melville, but that closely echoed the earlier judgment of the Civil War hero and realist novelist J. W. De Forest in his 1868 *Nation* article "The Great American Novel": "Until after the war we had no real novels in this country, except *Uncle Tom's*

Cabin." But it was not just outstanding in an impoverished field: *Uncle Tom's Cabin* is "one of the great novels of the world, and of all time." History has not diminished its appeal: "The fact that slavery was done away with does not matter; the interest in *Uncle Tom's Cabin* will never pass, because the book is really . . . true to human nature" (Cady 275).

Despite Howells's close friendship with Twain and his strong commitment to social justice for people of all classes and races, which led him not only to call himself a socialist but also to participate in founding the NAACP in 1909, despite Howells's confidence that Twain was "entirely satisfied with the results of the Civil War" and "eager to have its facts and meanings brought out" ("My Mark Twain" 696), and even despite his admiration for Huck's "spiritual struggle" in chapter 31 (Cady 342), I know no grounds for believing that Howells thought of *Huckleberry Finn* as doing cultural work comparable to Stowe's with regard to racial issues of the 1880s and beyond.

Perhaps the clearest instance of Howells's evident separation of *Huckleberry Finn* into a sector of his mind unrelated to *Uncle Tom's Cabin* occurred in one of his monthly *Harper's* "Editor's Study" columns (September 1886). Howells discussed Dostoevski's *Crime and Punishment,* contrasting the terrible social circumstances of czarist Russia to the better conditions of the United States. Notoriously, Howells concluded that American writers should not undertake Dostoevskian themes but "concern themselves with the more smiling aspects of life," because those are the "more American" (Cady 94). Howells had not yet come to his socialist position, and so he argued that because in the United States the "wrong from class to class" is "almost inappreciable," therefore American writers should seek the "universal" (the highest and proper goal of art) not in "social interests," as might be appropriate for European writers, but rather in "the individual."

This theoretical position perfectly anticipated that adopted by a wide spectrum of major writers—Lionel Trilling, James Baldwin, Ralph Ellison, Robert Penn Warren—in the 1940s as a response to the vogue of "protest fiction" associated with broadly socialist sympathies, often polemically construed as Communist or Stalinist. Nonetheless, at the time in the 1940s when this position was triumphant, Howells himself was largely put down as part of the "genteel tradition" that in so many ways he not only stood outside but fought against. One might explain this misunderstanding by the fact that the writers of the 1940s saw the focus on the individual as the means to achieving "tragedy," while Howells had associated it with the "smiling aspects."

In the same *Harper's* column in which he made this notorious argument, Howells also reconsidered the matter. The "Editor's Study" was meant to be reflective, a "space for thought," not merely journalism, and yet it was also a review column, in which new books would be mentioned and discussed, as with Howells's reporting on the newly available French translation of Dostoevski, who was still scarcely known in English. In the same column he also took notice of Sarah Bradford's biographical study of Harriet Tubman, the African American heroine who had become known as the "Moses of Her People" for her nineteen trips back into slaveholding territory, after her own escape, to lead out others. This part of the column was omitted in Howells's *Criticism and Fiction* (1891), the revised compilation in which most later readers have had access to the Editor's Study pieces.

Howells turned to Bradford and Tubman by reflecting, "It is only now and then, when some dark shadow of our shameful past appears, that we can ever believe there was a tragic element in our prosperity." Even in this case, though, such a book "Affects us like a tale 'Of old, unhappy, far-off things, / And battles long ago'" (quoting from Wordsworth's poem "The Highland Reaper" the speaker's response to hearing the reaping woman sing in Gaelic, a language he does not understand). Howells emphasized: "we cannot realize that most of the men and women now living were once commanded by the law of the land to turn and hunt . . . fugitives back into slavery; that those who abetted such outlaws were sometimes mulcted to the last dollar of their substance in fines." Howells concluded, "We can hardly imagine such things for the purposes of fiction" (95). This from the man who just two years earlier had done his friend Mark Twain the favor of scrupulously proofreading *Huckleberry Finn*!

Evidently *Huckleberry Finn* for Howells was simply not part of the literature of slavery, and so he didn't think of it even where to readers a century later the history Howells evoked of antebellum social and legal support for slavery seems exactly what *Huckleberry Finn* is about. So long, then, as abolitionism remained a still powerful and valued concern of recent history, readers could prize both

Uncle Tom's Cabin and *Huckleberry Finn* without thinking of them as rivals for mastery over the same literary terrain. As those who had lived through the Civil War yielded to a new generation, distinctions once very important blurred, and new alignments of literature took shape, in which from the 1920s into the 1940s, *Uncle Tom's Cabin* suffered both from its association with progressive racial views (however much many more recently have denied that!) and from its "feminine" technique of sentiment. Because of its masculinist system of characters and its deadpan narrative mode, *Huckleberry Finn* was preserved, it seemed, from the taint of sentiment (although it has recently become possible to revise that view), and so could be praised safely as a racial exemplar when that once again became a good.

In the later nineteenth century, *Uncle Tom's Cabin* was not discussed exclusively within literary circles. Major historians who wrote about the antebellum period treated Stowe's work as a historical force. It is significant that, to my knowledge, no (nonliterary) historian has ever considered *Huckleberry Finn* worth the kind of attention that *Uncle Tom's Cabin* long received, and to a lesser extent still does. The examples I will be discussing all come from 1892, a notable year in the history of blacks and whites in the United States, because it was the year in which Homer Plessy tested the Louisiana law prohibiting whites and people of color from traveling in the same railway cars. When the Supreme Court upheld this law in *Plessy vs. Ferguson* (1896), it laid the basis for six decades of segregation on the basis of "separate but equal."

James Ford Rhodes, in the first volume (1892) of his massive history of the United States from the Compromise of 1850 through Reconstruction, made an extended comparison between *Uncle Tom's Cabin* and *La Nouvelle Héloïse* (1761) by Jean-Jacques Rousseau. He found them alike not only for their immediate impact in their cultures, extending far more deeply than mere popularity, but also for their slower but decisive political impact (278–85). In his chapter on conditions in the South, Rhodes asserted the accuracy of *Uncle Tom's Cabin*, citing testimony from Frederick Douglass (a valued source drawn on frequently by Rhodes) concerning an African American he had known personally who equaled "Mrs. Stowe's Christian hero" (363-65). Rhodes emphasized too the way in which Stowe's work entered the political process even though much of its impact was on women, who could not vote and generally were excluded from political debate: "The cruelty of separating families . . . especially awakened the sympathy of Northern women, who counted for much in educating and influencing voters in a way that finally brought about the abolition of slavery" (318). The links between women's feelings, sentimental fiction, and political change seemed obvious to him.

Rhodes (b. 1848) was from Ohio; his family ties included abolitionists; and although his history won tremendous acclaim, he was not a professional historian but a retired businessman who turned to history after he had made his fortune. Woodrow Wilson (b. 1856), in contrast, was Southern by birth and connections, and he was one of the first to receive a Ph.D. in history from Johns Hopkins, the first American university to grant the research doctorate. Nonetheless, in *Division and Reunion* (1892), a survey of American history since 1829, published the same year as Rhodes's first volume, Wilson wrote of *Uncle Tom's Cabin* with admiration for its "moving imaginative portrayal of the pathos, the humor, the tragedy, the terror of the slavery system" (154). However, because of the professionalization of history, as well as perhaps his more Southern perspective, he took quite a different view than Rhodes did of the accuracy of *Uncle Tom's Cabin*. Although Wilson acknowledged that it "unquestionably showed what *might* come out of the system" (my emphasis), its actual substance was "built upon wholly exceptional incidents." Because it "was a product of the sympathetic imagination," rather than of reliable and specific documentation, therefore "the historian must reject [it] as quite misleading" (154).

Wilson's *Division and Reunion* was one of the first major histories of the United States distinctly oriented to Southern concerns, but as part of what is both a professional neutrality and a political aim of sectional reconciliation, Wilson was far more concerned to exculpate the South from guilt than to launch an attack on the North, of either the past or the present. Indeed, he held an interesting understanding of what a historian's professional neutrality meant. In a discussion of Southern history at an 1896 meeting of the American Historical Association, he was reported as claiming, "A man might as well quarrel with his own nature and that of his ancestors as for the true historian to find fault with the people he attempts to describe" (Veysey 78).

Among the writers of the 1880s whose work brought a newly

nostalgic view of the slave South, one of the most important was the Virginian Thomas Nelson Page (b. 1853), whose short stories appeared in the *Century* magazine in the same period in which it excerpted *Huckleberry Finn*. As long ago as 1937, in a Pulitzer Prize-winning book that shared in the renewed national support for the South that began in the post-Reconstruction period, the Harvard historian Paul Buck contrasted Page and Stowe in terms that are suggestive for Twain too. Buck observed that in Stowe, "the sympathy of the reader is directed to the lowly slave"; in contrast, the postwar fiction about the slave South makes "the overthrown gentry" into the "recipients of a forgiving pity." But in both cases, he astutely noted, "the Negro was primarily a device by which a white philosophy of race relations was advanced" (210). *Huckleberry Finn* differs from Page's book by making no appeal for readers' sympathy to be extended to the slaveholders; and yet Jim, too, has been mostly read as a figure to make whites think in certain ways about racial issues.

Page also wrote full-length fiction and influential nonfiction. His collection of essays *The Old South* (1892) took virtually the same attitude toward the institution and practices of slavery as Wilson, but Page was much more critical of the prewar North, even as he sought an alliance in the present between white men South and North to minimize social change that might otherwise arise from the activity of a free population of African Americans.

Page rated very highly the political significance of culture. He went so far as to claim that the reason the South lost the Civil War was the "lack of a literature" (50) with which to make its concerns and way of life compellingly known to outsiders. In contrast, the North had the power of literature on its side. As Page understood the course of history, "by arousing the general sentiment of the world against slavery," *Uncle Tom's Cabin* successfully "overruled the Supreme Court, and abrogated the Constitution," both of which had offered protection to the way of life of the slave South (303). For Page, "literature" included all valued forms of writing, so history, essays, and fiction were all part of what he was thinking of. In the absence of any extended and respected history that truly set forth the South, "by the world at large we are held to have been . . . ignorant, illiterate, semi-barbarous . . . sunk in brutality and vice . . . a race of slave-drivers" (254). Any fair-minded person must agree, I think, that even if one detests the practice of slavery, life cannot have been like this for all people everywhere in the South, yet pretty much what Page described here is the image that many admiring readers of *Huckleberry Finn* have proclaimed as its view of "the" South or "the" Southerner.

The power of the position for which Page spoke may be seen in a passage that is still remarkably relevant to debates going on now in the United States. He put forward what he considered "today the most portentous as the most dangerous problem which confronts the American people" (280). And he noted that one sign of its danger and portent is that "even the terminology for it in the two sections varies irreconcilably." In the North it is simply understood as "the question of the civil equality of all citizens before the law." But the South calls it "the question of negro domination." The even more ideologically charged term by which this issue had been framed during Reconstruction was "Africanization." Page proposed to diminish the split between sections by giving the problem a name by which it could be known "more accurately": "it should be termed the race question."

Page was not solely responsible for transforming the terms of debate and understanding. For example, the conservative French novelist Paul Bourget reported on his trip to the United States in 1894. One of the constant themes of this work is the importance of "the idea of Race" (4); race is the reality, while in the United States "class struggle is . . . only an appearance" (216). As part, then, of a prestigious, intellectually advanced, international development of social Darwinism, Page's work helped push along a shift of the utmost consequence.

Page got away from "lawyer's facts," lest the North challenge on constitutional grounds, including the newly established grounds of the Reconstruction amendments, the Southern restoration of white domination. If the North could be made to agree that it is a "race problem" rather than a problem of law or fairness or human rights, then long-existing, and deepening, cultural practices of racism could be brought to bear on the Southern white side, as Barrett Wendell's literary history demonstrated. Page was right on the mark when he argued in his appeal to the North for understanding and shared commitment on this issue, "the only thing that stands to-day between the people of the North and the negro [*sic* for Negro] is the people of the South" (284). Within Page's lifetime the First World War brought the first great migration of some half million African Americans from the South, and by the 1940s the "race problem" was fully national.

Like Wilson, Page argued against sentiment, but he went beyond Wilson in the role he accorded to race. Page asserted: "whatever a sentimental philanthropy may say; whatever a modern and mis-guided humanitarianism may declare, there underlies the whole matter the indubitable, potent, and mysterious principle of race quality" (313). *Quality* is historical, mysterious, organic, intuitive, as opposed to the simplistically self-evident *equality* of Enlightenment documents such as the Declaration of Independence. And now-adays, a century after Page, American national consensus does agree that it is a "race problem," and that this means that it is a mat-ter of complex feelings, rather than of simple justice. Speaking for the self-renewing Southern ruling class of his day, which was suc-cessfully putting forward the terms that would become hegemonic throughout the United States, Page urged, "get politics out of it, and the problem will be more than half solved" (343). At the same time as Page was putting forward this view, Booker T. Washington— who praised Twain's "deep sympathy" for Jim, but misremembered Jim as "a poor, ignorant negro boy who accompanies the heroes of the story, Huckleberry Finn and Tom Sawyer, on a long journey down the Mississippi on a raft"—was putting forward its African American complement. So long as the race problem could remain out of politics, it would be in the sphere of sentiment, and in that sphere the South had seen the need to rearm, and it carried the day. One use for *Huckleberry Finn,* then, when civil rights began to return to the national agenda, was that it does effectively operate in the realm of sympathy, but without the overtly sentimental rhetoric that had been discredited in Stowe.

Huckleberry Finn is far more polemically hostile toward the South than is *Uncle Tom's Cabin,* yet it fit better the worldview that Page and Wilson were helping to form, because it changes the model of action Stowe put forward in *Uncle Tom's Cabin.* Although Tom's death comes through his nonviolent resistance rather than in armed battle, he is nonetheless an activist (though since the "New Negro" movement of the 1920s, many African Americans have devalued this personalistic, rather than political, mode of action). Through-out his protracted torture, he keeps information from Legree and assists the escape of fellow slaves. In his mode of Christian love, he is active, never just a spectator, and never represented clownishly. For both Huck and Jim, however, all the power of what they do is in their feelings, whether their powerful affection and loyalty toward each other, or Huck's alienation from the system of slavery. The self-undoing plot of the novel prevents either Jim or Huck from effective action, and the mise-en-scène and language of the book carefully shield it from politics. Consequently, it was never understood to be competing with Stowe during the time that abolitionism maintained any prestige in the culture.

In the earlier twentieth century historiography ceased to emphasize slavery as shaping the history of the United States. The "progressive" history of Turner, Beard, and Parrington put economic issues in the center, and an offshoot from this analysis enabled the "revisionist" interpretation of the Civil War, which demonized rather than ignored abolitionism. This is the context in which *Huckleberry Finn* came to be understood as preferable to *Uncle Tom's Cabin* as a critique of slavery.

T. S. Eliot's introduction powerfully stated the key terms: "Huck is passive and impassive, apparently always the victim of events; and yet, in his acceptance of the world, and what it does to him and them, he is more powerful than his world, because he is more *aware* than any other person in it" (330). Even as Eliot wrote of Twain's "indictment" of slavery, his emphasis on passivity rehearsed an important motif in the racist turn away from the Civil War. It is by now well known that some 180,000 African Americans fought as soldiers in the Union Army, some fifteen percent of the total Union force, many of them once-enslaved men, some of whom had made their way to Union lines as "contrabands," others who were part of the population in rebel areas overrun by Union troops. The eagerness of these black men to fight, and their successful record in combat, played a crucial part in moving Lincoln, and the American people more broadly, toward acknowledging the necessity of full emancipation by the war's end. But as part of the reaction against the war, a constant motif of Southern apologists was to emphasize the helplessness of (ex-)slaves who had, passively, been freed.

In 1901 the *Atlantic Monthly*, from its founding closely associated with support for abolitionism and then Reconstruction, commissioned a set of articles to reassess Reconstruction twenty-five years after it had ended. In the spirit of achieved reconciliation, the authors included Northerners and Southerners, and not only whites, for W. E. B. Du Bois also contributed his important essay on the history of the Freedmen's Bureau. The essays by those with Southern sympathies very clearly demonstrated this emphasis on African American passivity. In the lead essay, Woodrow Wilson asserted, "the slaves had been freed by the force of arms" ("Reconstruction" 17), but with no mention that the arms had significantly included their own. Hilary A. Herbert had long served in Congress representing Alabama and then became secretary of the navy for Grover Cleveland. Herbert wrote, "Not in all the imaginings of the Arabian nights is there any concept so startling as the sudden manumission of four million of slaves, left unshackled to shift for themselves" (35). The way in which Herbert defended laws restricting or forbidding African Americans use of firearms is astonishing. He explained that "recollections of the negro insurrection headed by Nat Turner," as well as "predictions long ago made by Mr. Calhoun and frequently by others," had produced in the South "a very general fear that . . . the suddenly emancipated slaves might attempt to repeat the massacres of San Domingo" (referring to the insurrection in the 1790s by which Haiti, in the spirit of the French Revolution, won its freedom from colonial rule to become the second independent state in the Western Hemisphere). Looking back to define a continuity with the distant 1790s and 1830s, Herbert omitted the fact that in the rather more recent 1860s many African American men in the South had served as Union combat soldiers, displaying discipline, training, and skill rather than murderous irrationality. However nightmarish it may have seemed to the Southerners, this record was hardly something that the North could disavow, if it were recalled to memory.

This context of national discussion suggests an alternative political allegory for *Huckleberry Finn*. Some critics now understand *Huckleberry Finn* as criticizing the failure of Reconstruction, in its flawed attempt to win freedom for African Americans who were, by law, already free. But one might also link *Huckleberry Finn* to a long-persisting inability to recognize the agency of African Americans in regard to their liberation and advancement. Mark Twain's letter committing himself financially to assist an African American student at Yale Law School has often been cited in the last dozen years as evidence for his racially progressive views. Yet in the letter, Twain asserted that whites owe blacks a debt of reparation because "we have ground the manhood out of them" (McDowell). A century after Twain's wish to aid the helpless, Ronald Reagan remembered and honored *Huckleberry Finn* in similar terms. In a 1985 *Washington*

Post article, subcaptioned "The President Defends the Values of an American Classic," Reagan's inaccurate summary of the book is, "Huck works hard to keep Jim free, and in the end he succeeds" (Champion 156–57).

One way of evading the problem of African Americans' activity in armed self-liberation was by playing down the importance of slavery and its consequences and turning the attention of historians to other issues. Frederick Jackson Turner (b. 1861) was the historian most responsible for an understanding of American history that achieved this effect. Woodrow Wilson and Turner were close friends as young historians at Johns Hopkins, but Turner already offered quite a different view from Wilson's of the overall shape of American history. In "Problems in American History" (1892), Turner named the "fundamental, dominating fact of United States history": it is "the expansion of the United States from the Alleghenies to the Pacific." Excessive "attention to slavery" may obscure this truth by overemphasizing what is, however important, still only an "incident." What Turner defined as the "real lines of American development" are found "in the history of westward expansion." This shift of attention away from slavery was associated for Turner with a larger geographical reorientation: "the true point of view in the history of this nation is not the Atlantic coast; it is the Mississippi Valley" (*Frontier* 28–29).

This piece was preamble to Turner's "The Significance of the Frontier in American History" (1893), which for many decades shaped the whole understanding of American history from colonial times into the twentieth century, precisely by giving it a new point of view. Turner criticized Rhodes for treating only as "incidental to the slavery struggle" the legislation that was "called out by the western advance." Turner flatly rebutted Rhodes: "This is a wrong perspective" (*Frontier* 52). In contrast to the "sectional" character of slavery, in the Mississippi Valley, "on the tide of the Father of Waters," Americans lost their sectional character: "North and South met and mingled into a nation" (*Frontier* 56). Turner's concern with expansion as the action and the Mississippi Valley as its scene defined the understanding of American history by which Bernard DeVoto made Twain into America's most fully representative writer. (Though *Uncle Tom's Cabin* is also a novel of the Mississippi Valley.)

One need not impute base motives to Turner to find that his

shifting of the perspective of American history away from the question of slavery to the question of continental expansion effectively responded to a widely shared wish that these terribly vexed and painful questions would go away, a wish to believe that some things had at last been resolved if not solved. At the moment in 1877 when federal troops were withdrawn from the South, thus ending Reconstruction, the *Nation* editorialized, "The Negro . . . will disappear from the field of national politics." Punning on the title of the journal, the *Nation* concluded, "Henceforth, the nation, as a nation, will have nothing more to do with him" (Foner, *Reconstruction* 582). A cartoon by Thomas Nast in *Harper's Weekly* from 1885, the year *Huckleberry Finn* was published, was entitled "A Dead Issue," and it shows a dignified yeoman plowman representing the "South" putting off a bent and greasy-looking representative of the Northern press: "I should like to oblige you by killing a few Negroes, Mr. Tribune, but I am too busy." Other issues seized national attention. In 1877, the end of Reconstruction, there were bloody confrontations between labor and property, and Foner directly links this turn in national politics to the abandonment of civil rights in the South, for the federal government built armories to house troops "not in the South to protect black citizens, but in the major cities of the North" (582), so as never again to be caught short-handed if industrial owners should feel threatened.

Huckleberry Finn occupied a curious position. Insofar as slavery was past and the race issue in current politics was "dead," then Twain's novel could function as a distraction. As in other forms of fiction popular in the decades after the Civil War among a wide, nonelite readership, such as the dime novel (Saxton 330), the book's conflicts are cast in "the ideological dimensions of the 1830s and 1840s." This is less a question of slavery as such than of what many modern critics have seen as the broader issue of "conflicts between fraternal egalitarianism on the one hand and social hierarchy and defence on the other"—that is, the authenticity and closeness of Huck and Jim, against the fraudulent claims of superiority by the King and Duke. Twain's foregrounding of their transatlantic social and cultural pretensions, along with Tom Sawyer's "evasion," places *Huckleberry Finn* squarely in the Jacksonian rhetoric of American equality struggling against "vestiges of the feudal past or alien intrusions."

Yet this structure of values looked back to a vanished social and

cultural order, and it distracted attention from "class divisions arising out of industrialization." *Huckleberry Finn's* America of WASPs
and slaves could appear a welcome simplification compared with
an America of the 1880s, in which immigration, increasingly of
Catholics from southern, central, and eastern Europe, was becoming a politically sensitive concern. As Woodrow Wilson put it in his
1892 *Division and Reunion,* by the 1880s immigration "had long since
become a threat instead of a source of increased wealth and material
strength" to the United States, for it brought "the pauperized and
the discontented and disheartened of all lands" rather than the
"hopeful and the sturdy classes of former days" (243). Of course,
even in those former days, the issue had been hot. With German
and Irish immigrants coming in large numbers into Missouri in the
1840s, and as we have seen, involving themselves in abolitionist activity, it becomes of some interest that Twain wrote to Kemble, the
illustrator for *Huckleberry Finn,* not to make Huck look too "Irishy"
(*Huckleberry* [1988] 450).

Another major new social and political concern at the period
Twain was writing *Huckleberry Finn* was the figure known as the
"tramp," a sometimes pitied and more often feared image of men as
migrant, casual labor or out of work, and with no home, newly
filling the landscape and changing the self-understanding of the
United States for both property owners and workers (Denning
149–57). To the extent that Huck and Jim matched this contemporary type, they were a source of discomfort to genteel opinion, but
for many more readers they presented a pair of mobile males of
working age, but without work, whose adventures could be followed with far less anxiety than those of their current counterparts.

Huckleberry Finn, then, was read largely as a boy's book during
the first three or four decades of its existence, when, despite its concern with an escaped slave and the vacillations of a white boy's feelings about helping that slave, the novel was not understood as existing in the same cultural space as *Uncle Tom's Cabin.* Since then, it
has been read as an alternative to Stowe's work, which it is, insofar
as both works make an appeal to the power of sentiment, but Stowe
meant to change readers' feeling about slavery, while Twain relies
on their already condemning it.

5 _____

Lionel Trilling
The Key Text in Context

In 1948 the number of veterans in college on GI Bill benefits equaled the total number of all American college students in 1940. The year 1948—when Lionel Trilling's introduction to the Rinehart College Edition launched *Huckleberry Finn* into academic hypercanonization, and thereby changed a book, once felt as a nationally shared yet personal possession, into assigned reading— marked much more than the democratic transformation of American higher education. Even a few years after 1948, it was already evident to Norman Podhoretz, an intellectual of a new generation, that the literary culture of the earlier twentieth century had turned into something else, as the world itself had changed: "The 'modern' world of which Faulkner, Hemingway, and Dos Passos were the most penetrating interpreters, the world of the 20's and 30's whose articulate consciousness they were, froze to death in 1948" (*Doings* 23).

Lionel Trilling has been widely recognized as the exemplary American cultural intellectual of the Cold War. The stark postwar emergence of the conflict between the United States and the Soviet Union as the dominant fact of contemporary history made Trilling's fifteen years' experience as an "anti-Stalinist" relevant far beyond the limited circles of New York City factions. To understand the context of his critical redefinition of *Huckleberry Finn*, it is necessary to understand the place of racially liberal politics in the emerging Cold War era. In 1947 Walter Lippmann had popularized the phrase *Cold War*, the year after Winston Churchill had made the "Iron Curtain" an unavoidable part of the era's mental landscape. In 1949,

Mao's Communist revolution took charge of China, the Soviet Union exploded its first atomic bomb, and NATO was formed. In 1948, the Organization of American States, the first of the U.S. Cold War defense alliances, was set up; months of airlift kept supplies coming to the Western-occupied portions of Berlin after the USSR had cut off land access to the city; and the Marshall Plan was put into effect in Western Europe, after the Soviet Union had refused to participate in its being implemented in the East as well. This new situation was both dangerous and promising for the political fight against racism in America, which had, in the 1930s and into the 1940s, been strongly linked with leftist groups, including the Communist Party.

The Second World War had shown that "prejudice" and "discrimination" were neither harmless nor beneficial but so murderous as almost to defy description and outrun imagination. The term *racism*, so familiar now, was coined only in the 1930s, to describe Nazi policies and practices. As the Civil War and the First World War had done before, once again space opened for African Americans. Their participation was needed in the war effort, and both experience and opposition to Nazi ideology diminished the authority of once "scientific" systems of racial thought—the sort of thing Barrett Wendell praised Yankees for achieving against Stowe's sentimentalism—that had dominated much Western thinking for nearly a century. Yet there was also renewed pressure to keep blacks in their place, just as there had been in earlier periods of progress in racial equality at the end of Reconstruction (marked by the emergence of the KKK in the South) and in the aftermath of the First World War (marked by riots of whites against blacks in the North). John Egerton's massive study of "the generation before the civil rights movement" documents a wave of terrorism across the South directed especially against returning African American veterans, but more broadly against any who challenged the segregationist system that had defined their place for some fifty years (362–74).

One of the ways African Americans resisted being made to stay in their place was by leaving. In the 1940s, spurred by the end of the sharecropper system, which had been established in the years after the Civil War and was ended by the invention of a machine that could pick fifty handworkers' worth of cotton (Lemann 5–6), some 1.6 million African Americans moved north, more than in any decade before or since (Steinberg 182). Although large numbers of black emigrés from the South had begun to settle in Chicago, Detroit, and New York in the 1920s and 1930s, it was only after the Second World War that the demographic pattern was established that has for the second half of the twentieth century made "black" and "urban" synonymous in the consciousness of the United States and that in recent decades has made the North more than the South the focus of problems and policies related to race.

Harry Truman, president of the United States by succession to Franklin Roosevelt, came from northwest Missouri country that had been slaveholding and sympathetic to the Confederacy, and in personal life he was careless in his terms for peoples of colors, nationalities, and religions different from his own. He was chosen for the vice-presidency partly because of his relative neutrality on issues related to race: he was trusted by the powerful Southern conservative Democrats, but he had not offended the Northern liberals. It turned out, however, that issues of racial equality became an outstanding feature of his presidency as in 1948 he campaigned for an election that everyone believed he could not win.

Roosevelt's third-term vice-president, Henry Wallace, displaced by Truman in 1944, had already set out on a third-party presidential candidacy, and by the Democratic Convention yet a fourth party emerged. Strom Thurmond, then the Democratic governor of South Carolina, led protestors against the Democratic platform out into a convention of their own, from which he emerged as a candidate. At the Democratic Convention, Hubert H. Humphrey, mayor of Minneapolis, later a leading liberal in the Senate of the 1950s and 1960s and Lyndon Johnson's vice-president, spoke the message that drove out the Dixiecrats. It was time for the Democratic Party "to get out of the shadow of states' rights and walk forthrightly in the bright sunshine of human rights" (Egerton 496). Henry Wallace was breaking new paths in his campaigning in the South. Not only did his positions attack "segregation, one-party politics, and the denial of civil rights," but he refused to "address segregated audiences or patronize segregated hotels or restaurants" (Egerton 504). In contrast, Truman's campaign hardly entered the South at all. Nonetheless, both as president and in his campaign, Truman took extremely important steps.

In 1947, Truman was the first president of the United States ever to address the NAACP, doing so from the steps of the Lincoln Memorial. His actual speech was judged by Walter White, head of the NAACP, as "even more courageous" than Lincoln for its "specific condemnation of evils based upon race prejudice . . . and its call for immediate actions against them" (McCullough 569). In his campaign, Truman was the first Democrat or Republican presidential candidate ever to speak in Harlem, and for his speech at "Rebel Stadium" in Dallas the stands were desegregated for the first time. Truman's 1949 inauguration was the first time that African Americans were welcomed at the main events, and therefore able to stay in Washington hotels that had long been segregated (McCullough 677, 702, 724). Already in 1947 Truman had convened the President's Committee on Civil Rights, which had called for the "elimination" from "American life" of "segregation, based on race, color, creed, or national origin" (Franklin, *Race* 147). In 1948 he asked Congress to establish a permanent Fair Employment Practices Commission, and he issued executive orders undertaking to end segregation in the military and civil service.

In his symbolic and practical steps toward equality for African Americans, Truman was carrying forward what in the 1930s had been initiatives of the left, whether CIO labor activity or cultural work of the Popular Front, but in the years after the war, as sympathetic involvement with the concerns of African Americans became a relatively more mainstream commitment, it took on, both politically and culturally, associations shaped in complex ways by the refraction of the thirties through first hot and then cold war.

In the 1930s, the genre of the "protest novel" had been widely practiced as a means of cultural support for progressive political causes, but the message of populist idealism conveyed through the conventions of naturalistic fiction came under the ban of anti-Communism. Against a faith in the "people" came insistence that "man," the "individual," was the most important focus; the techniques of modernism became more widely available as conventions; and an emphasis on the goodness or innocence of "the people," corrupted or endangered by the forces of prejudice or the hunger for profit, yielded to insistence on the "fallen" nature of "man," the necessary ambivalence of the individual. So as opposed to the polarized tendencies of romanticism (bad) and liberalism (good) that organized V. L. Parrington's *Main Currents in American Thought,* a guiding work of the 1930s, Lionel Trilling insisted in his position-defining essay "Reality in America," introducing *The*

Liberal Imagination, that the most important writers will contain *within themselves* the polarities of their culture, the yes and no in inner "dialectic."

This was the version of Huck that Trilling developed in his introduction. Like George Orwell in Trilling's definitive essay-portrait of 1952, Huck is a truth teller. For the 1930s, the book *Huckleberry Finn* represented the American experience in Bernard DeVoto's nationalist celebration of the empire of democracy. Trilling's focus was far more on the character of Huck than on the variousness of America represented by the book, and this version of Huck lent national-popular credibility to a figure shaped on the lineaments of the isolated, alienated intellectual. Is it any surprise that English teachers and other intellectuals should find the greatest moment of American literature one in which a solitary writer struggles over drafting and revising a text, as Huck does with his letter to Miss Watson in chapter 31?

One of the American writers in whom Trilling found the dialectic was William Faulkner, who in 1948 published *Intruder in the Dust,* his last major work prior to winning the Nobel Prize in 1950. This novel involves an elderly African American who is wrongly accused of murder and is vindicated by several members of the white community, spurred by a teenager. It is not as complexly structured as Faulkner's great works of the 1930s, but it reached a larger public than they had, perhaps in part because it curiously embodied the dialectic by being an anti-protest-novel protest novel. Even while treating the subject of race and the law in the South, a subject of much concern to liberal opinion and beginning to surface on the national agenda for the first time since Reconstruction, Faulkner's novel speaks against Northern, liberal interference in matters that it presents as private business among Southerners, white and black.

The most respected literary critic in the United States, Edmund Wilson, titled his *New Yorker* review of *Intruder in the Dust,* "William Faulkner's Reply to the Civil Rights Program." Although the timing of writing and publication made it factually improbable, Wilson explicitly read the novel as Faulkner's "counterblast" to such developments of 1948 as "the anti-lynching bill and the civil-rights plank in the Democratic platform" (*Classics* 465). Yet while sensitive to its antiliberal ideological message, Wilson found in the novel's fictional mode something strangely familiar. Its "exhilarating" happy-ending climax recalled fictional feelings most typical of the left,

whether "the triumph of Communist-led workers in the early Soviet films" or the Popular Front "emotion that one got from some of
the better dramatizations of the career of Abraham Lincoln" (469).

In selecting his quotations from Faulkner, Wilson showed a profoundly important ideological characteristic of the later 1940s, the
emergence of the notion of the "totalitarian" as a category linking
Nazi fascism and Soviet Communism, a notion given persuasive
polemical form in Hannah Arendt's *The Origins of Totalitarianism*
(1951), but already available earlier, as seen in the recently published draft from 1950 of *American Civilization* by the black, radical
organizer and intellectual C. L. R. James. Wilson quoted Faulkner
on the dreadful result that will follow from Northern pressure on
the South. If the more humane individuals of the South are not left
free to do their good, their antagonism to Northern meddling will
force them into alliance with the bad. They will thus be put into
"the position of the German after 1933, who had no alternative between being either a Nazi or a Jew, or the present Russian (European, too, for that matter) who hasn't even that, but must be either a
Communist or dead." As part of a dramatic speech by a character,
these comparisons are crudely sketched, but they nonetheless accurately register major contours of thought of 1948. The emerging national concerns with civil rights brought the South into a frame of
thought defined by the great current and recent issues of world history and politics.

The way of thinking that joined the American South by analogy
to Nazi Germany or the Soviet Union played an important part in
the writings of American historians in the immediate postwar
years. Allan Nevins published in 1947 the first two volumes of *The
Ordeal of the Union,* a six-volume series on the causes and course of
the Civil War, finally completed only in 1960. In considerable agreement with the "revisionist" interpretation of the Civil War developed in the 1930s, Nevins explicitly argued that just as proper Allied policy toward Germany after the First World War might have
made the Second World War unnecessary, so the Civil War would
have been preventable by more skilled statecraft.

In the *Saturday Review*, Arthur M. Schlesinger, Jr., came out
swinging. Schlesinger was closely associated with liberal, anti-
Communist Democratic party politics, for which he provided a
manifesto with *The Vital Center* (1949). In this title, drawn from the
epilogue to *Moby-Dick,* Schlesinger not only polemically claimed

the center, the high middle ground between the Communists and the conservatives; he also signaled the new appreciation by liberals for complex, highly literary fiction committed to "paradox" and complication. In a further life complication, the teacher with whom Schlesinger had studied *Moby-Dick*, F. O. Matthiessen, found that his continuing leftist sympathies and deep engagement with the campaign of Henry Wallace excluded him from the new center. Matthiessen's suicide in 1950 is one of the most painful marks of the Cold War within American literary studies.

Schlesinger in his review elucidated his opposition to the revisionist position by turning against Nevins the analogy between the politics of the Civil War and the politics of the twentieth century. Schlesinger imagined, in the spirit he attributed to Nevins, that a "future historian" might say that "the primary task of statesmanship in the 1930s was to furnish a workable adjustment between the U.S.A. and Germany, while offering strong inducements to the German people to abandon the police state, and equal persuasion to the Americans to help the Nazis rather than scold them." So far, the point is fairly simple: Nevins's sense that the North could have eased the South out of its commitment to slavery is as foolish as we now see "appeasement" was as a policy for dealing with Hitler. Writing in 1947, with his eye toward the 1948 presidential election that many at that time did not think Truman could even be nominated for, Schlesinger gave a further twist to his comparison, turning from the recent past to the very moment: "In essence, this [that is, the equivalent of appeasement] is Mr. Wallace's current thesis about the Russians" ("Failure" 10). And yet, if soft on Communism, Wallace was strong on race matters. Almost every one of the white historians who from the mid-fifties into the seventies helped to make the field of African American history one of the most intellectually dynamic areas of research had in their teens or twenties been involved in the Wallace campaign (Meier and Rudwick, passim).

In 1949 Schlesinger developed his review of Nevins into a full-scale article against revisionist historiography ("The Causes of the Civil War: A Note on Historical Sentimentalism") published in *Partisan Review*, the major intellectual organ of liberal anti-Communism. By 1949, Wallace was safely in the past, but the basic point remained. To say that there "should" have been no abolitionists in the antebellum United States, as the revisionists did, was, according to Schlesinger, "about as sensible as to say that there 'should' have been no anti-Nazis in the 1930's or that there 'should' be no anti-Communists today" (318).

In this larger essay, Schlesinger defined, within recent American culture, an important context for revisionism. He treated it as equivalent, within the intellectual world of history writing, to other ideologically conservative literature of the 1930s sympathetic to the Old South: in mass culture *Gone with the Wind* (1936), and in high culture the "agrarian" manifesto whose contributors included a number of major poets, *I'll Take My Stand* (1930). Just as Schlesinger's opponents of the late forties were called "soft on Communism," so these Southern works were soft on slavery.

This theme of softness seems the link by which Schlesinger brought into play the notion of sentimentalism, which in ordinary usage hardly fits the stance of either Margaret Mitchell or the often hard-edged reactionary polemic of *I'll Take My Stand*. Schlesinger connected revisionism to "the modern tendency to seek in optimistic sentimentalism an escape from the severe demands of moral decision" (320). The imagination that Schlesinger called sentimental (not at all like Stowe's) believes that objectivity and progress will by the natural course of the world triumph over prejudice and conservatism. This mechanistic view of history fools itself into believing that it is modern and up to date, even scientific, which is why Schlesinger's charge of sentimentalism has such power to wound. Schlesinger is attacking the view of life that Lionel Trilling would criticize as the liberal imagination, which paradoxically imagines itself not to need imagination. So despite his use of analogies both to Germany in the thirties and to the current USSR, Schlesinger was clearly aiming his polemic against the American left.

Schlesinger turned another screw against revisionists: their sense of the world was not only sentimental rather than scientific, it was sentimental in a way that made it a weak kind of religion. Contrary to their view, "history is not a redeemer, promising to solve all human problems in time; nor is man capable of transcending the limitations of his being" (325). Further defining his understanding of "man," Schlesinger explained that "man" is "entangled in insoluble problems; history is consequently a tragedy in which we are all involved, whose keynote is anxiety and frustration, not progress and fulfillment" (325).

It is marvelous that such grimness should have fueled activism on behalf of interventionist government, but the paradox of this moment was the liberal belief that optimism bred inertia, pessimism bred struggle. The authority for this view of human nature was the theologian and activist Reinhold Niebuhr, who made a conservative, "neo-orthodox" theology the ground for his progressive commitments of the 1930s and liberal anti-communism in the 1940s. Niebuhr's penetrating analysis of the possibilities for Negro liberation struggle in *Moral Man and Immoral Society* (1932), in which he argued that given the balance of actual force, nonviolent resistance would be the only path that might win enough support to lead to victory, played an electrifying role in the development of Martin Luther King when he read it in 1950 (Branch 82).

African Americans joined directly in the rethinking of nineteenth-century American racial history in relation to the events of the middle twentieth century. John Hope Franklin, a few years older than Schlesinger but not so well established, had just completed what remains the standard history of blacks in America (*From Slavery to Freedom* [1947]) when he published a polemical review. Just as Schlesinger was provoked by Nevins, so Franklin was responding to a volume in the prestigious *History of the South* series by a senior historian, eminent enough to be co-editor of the series. Merton G. Coulter's *The South during Reconstruction* (1947) had already won almost universal praise at the time Franklin took on its demolition. In revisionist spirit, Coulter treated the Civil War as a breach in the continuity of American history, but for Franklin the Civil War fit right into the "basic ideology" of the "American concept of freedom"; it was a war as necessary to fight as the wars of "1775, 1917, or 1941" (*Race* 28). Despite Coulter's avowed principle of studying the past as it was in itself, rather than invoking "present day standards," Franklin found that Coulter violated this principle, for in the imposition of Reconstruction on the South Coulter saw a "glimmering resemblance to the later cults of Fascism and Nazism" (38).

Given his opening, Franklin made his move: it is the antebellum South itself that resembles Nazi Germany: "an oppressed race; the great and continuing drive for *Lebensraum*; the annihilation of almost every vestige of free thought and free speech; and the enthusiastic glorification of the martial spirit." Franklin concluded, "Perhaps, then, the north, enjoying a more favorable ideological position, may be regarded as accomplishing an overthrow of 'nazism'" (38). I have highlighted only the particular ideological analogy of this review-essay, but it also brought forward ample scholarly ground for challenging Coulter's view. Franklin sent out five hundred copies of his review to historians, expecting that most members of the profession would not be reading the *Journal of Negro Education*, where it appeared. Responses were warm, even when not wholly in agreement (Novick 349).

Franklin aimed to be "a historian without regard to race" (Meier and Rudwick 117), but he has never failed to register in the strongest terms his criticism of the patterns of discrimination in the United States in his lifetime. The comparison to Nazi Germany was not limited to an early stage of Franklin's career for a particular polemic purpose. In an essay of 1963, he reflected on his experiences a few years earlier in the "segregated Atlanta train station." The "barbaric treatment" of "Negro passengers" by "railway officials and city policemen" so deeply "mortified and touched" Franklin that he wrote a piece called "DP's in Atlanta," in which he compared the treatment of these African Americans to the "treatment of displaced refugees in Nazi-occupied countries during world war 2" (*Race* 306). The special force of the comparison comes from the fact that the bureaucratic term "displaced person," and its even more antiseptic abbreviation, refer to those dwellers in lands conquered by the Nazis imported into the Reich to work as slave laborers, so the parallel to African Americans is shockingly close. Even in 1988, when he was invited by the American Council of Learned Societies to speak in an annual distinguished lecture series, in which eminent humanists reflect on their lives and careers, Franklin felt it important to recall his own humiliations in trying to volunteer for honorable service in World War II, and then to buy a home in Brooklyn in 1956. He concluded in a weighty present tense: "The high cost of racial discrimination is not merely a claim of the radical left. It is as real as the rebuffs, the indignities, or the discriminations that many black people suffer" (289–90).

The year 1948 can stand for the starting point from which such a view might begin to gain wide public credibility. This year began the process, as I have shown, that led to the Civil Rights Act of 1964, and the hypercanonization of *Huckleberry Finn* drew energy from accompanying this national transformation, which coincided as well with the solidification of the Cold War. By the years after World War II, literature of overt group protest had lost respect in favor of protest internalized within a complex individual self, and the movement toward racial integration became less associated with the political left while the left itself was demonized as Stalinist. Lionel Trilling linked these two emergent national concerns through his essay on *Huckleberry Finn.*

"Huckleberry Finn" I

Lionel Trilling's 1948 introduction to the Rinehart College Edition of *Huckleberry Finn* was collected in 1950 in *The Liberal Imagination* as *"Huckleberry Finn."* Through its circulation in both these venues, it is widely recognized as marking a decisive turn in discussion of Twain's novel, yet an important book on Trilling characterized it, without further discussion, as "one of the least ambitious and least moving essays" collected in *The Liberal Imagination* (Chace 95), and it is wholly unmentioned in the fullest book-length treatment of Trilling (O'Hara) and in the most recent authoritative overview of his career (Teres). There are interesting reasons specialists on Trilling might overlook this piece, which nonetheless gained wider circulation, and arguably had greater effect, than any other single piece he wrote.

Among the sixteen essays in *The Liberal Imagination,* *"Huckleberry Finn"* is one of three written originally to introduce a book. The other essays either grew from reviews, or were written for journals or for invited lectures. The three introductions come in sequence in the first half of the book, numbers 4 through 6. They were written for very different audiences. The essay immediately preceding *"Huckleberry Finn"* is "The Function of the Little Magazine" (1946, fifth in the volume), a piece deeply implicated in Trilling's sense of himself and his audience. Written to introduce *The Partisan Reader,* a selection from the first decade of the *Partisan Review,* this exploration and defense of the idea and practice of high, minority culture in the United States stands between the *Huckleberry Finn* essay and the introduction written for another 1948 reprinting of a classic American work of the 1880s, Henry James's *The Princess Casamassima* (fourth in the volume). But the James essay, widely acknowledged as a standout, was written for a trade reprint, not for the freshman classroom. James was for Trilling an extremely important case. American liberals judged James harshly, yet James is the kind of writer who, Trilling believed, has the most to offer liberalism. James can awaken the imaginations of well-meaning people who are otherwise too ready to believe—unrealistically yet also unimaginatively—in the efficacy of mechanistic social solutions. Because of its different audience and occasion, *"Huckleberry Finn"* is far less overtly "dialectical," reflective and ironic, than the Trilling signature note. For example, in *"Huckleberry Finn,"* Trilling scarcely used the first-person plural forms "we" and "our." The overall linguistic decorum of the piece does not presume that the introducer and the student being introduced have anything much in common—except for American vernacular speech, a topic I discuss in later chapters.

"Huckleberry Finn" follows closely the piece on Henry James, and it comes immediately before the essay on Rudyard Kipling (seventh in the volume). The essay takes part in the complex movements between positive and negative evaluations of well-known literary figures that helped to make *The Liberal Imagination* so influential. The negatives are Kipling and three Americans: Sherwood Anderson, Theodore Dreiser, and the historian V. L. Parrington. The positives are Freud and another three Americans: James, Twain, and Scott Fitzgerald. The most striking feature of this array is the generational dynamic they map. All four negative critiques attack authors born between 1865 (Kipling) and 1874 (Anderson), that is, thirty to forty years the senior of Trilling (born 1905). Three of the positive essays praise far more senior figures, born between 1835 (Twain) and 1856 (Freud), while Fitzgerald was born in 1896. Trilling had written many pieces on contemporary American writers of his and Fitzgerald's generation fully as severe as his treatments of the older generation, but he did not choose to reprint them in *The Liberal Imagination*. In other words, the book displays an evident pattern of condemning false fathers, while valuing grandfathers and brothers.

These authors are made intimate parts of Trilling's own recounted life as a reader, and he reaches out to the common experience of those who read him. *Huckleberry Finn* is as American as a tree planted in youth that stays with its planter throughout life, and as prestigious as the *Odyssey*, the childhood reading of an Athenian boy. Contrast the opening words of the essay immediately following *"Huckleberry Finn"*: "Kipling belongs irrevocably to our past." He is no longer current, but he is "fixed deep in childhood feeling," and therefore "for liberals of a certain age he must always be an interesting figure." Kipling is so early an experience that "for many of us our rejection of him was our first literary-political decision" (114). And Sherwood Anderson is no less a figure of the past.

Trilling had two brief personal encounters with Anderson, once "when he was at the height of his fame" and already then his power was less than "a few years before when anything that Anderson wrote had seemed a sort of revelation." The second time, about two years before his death, "he had by then not figured in my own thought about literature for many years" (20). Anderson's "greatest influence" is placed in "adolescence": "the age when we find the books we give up but do not get over" (22). Anderson's "easy populism" contrasts to Huck's awareness of being *"wicked."*

"*Huckleberry Finn*" is structured in four parts: a brief biographical contextualization of the book's composition; an exploration of the book's special excellence; a brief contextualization of the book in relation to the America in which it was written; and a brief discussion of the "form and style," that is, structure and language. The three parts I have called brief together make up nearly half of the essay; the exploration of its excellence takes up more than half. Leo Marx's important and influential challenge to Trilling's defense of the book's ending (discussed in chapter 7), then, took up Trilling only at a relatively minor point of his own argument. Marx scrupulously acknowledged that Trilling was primarily a "moralist," not a formalist, and, indeed, the bulk of Trilling's essay defines the greatness of *Huckleberry Finn* in moral terms.

The exposition of the greatness of *Huckleberry Finn* begins from its "power of telling the truth" (101). Trilling compared *Huckleberry Finn* to *Tom Sawyer*. In a phrase that surely puzzled most freshmen who encountered it, Trilling characterized the truth of *Tom Sawyer* as merely the "truth of honesty." In contrast, the truth of *Huckleberry Finn* is "more intense . . . fiercer and more complex" (101). It is the "truth of moral passion," which "deals directly with the virtue and depravity of man's heart" (102). In moving the weight of truth from the outer world to the human heart, Trilling echoed the argument of Nathaniel Hawthorne, who in his preface to *The House of the Seven Gables* contrasted the "romance" he wrote to other writers' "novels," which were faithful to externals. From moral passion, Trilling moved rapidly to a phrase that is a keynote of *The Liberal Imagination* as a whole, the "moral imagination" (103). This moral imagination is the agency of what Trilling most valued, "moral realism."

Trilling's rhetorical and conceptual task in this essay, as throughout *The Liberal Imagination,* was to put forward the value of the moral without falling into moralizing. It was his argument that morality had more "power and charm" than was granted it in the genteel tradition of the later nineteenth century or in what was understood as the American "realist" revolt against that tradition. Trilling condemned Parrington, Dreiser, and Anderson because, he judged, their notion of the real simplified things; what for Trilling was real was always more complicated. Therefore it was important for him that *Huckleberry Finn* avoids "sentimentality" (103) and the "sentimental" (105). The river brings death as well as life; Huck may wish well to the criminals trapped on the sinking steamboat, but he can't help them and doesn't torture himself about it.

In praising a book known for its everyday, "vernacular," language, Trilling had to choose his own words carefully, and he did. He concluded one phase of his argument by asserting that Huck's "profound and bitter knowledge of human depravity" nonetheless "never prevents him from being a friend to man" (106). This last phrase merits remark. "Friend to man" is a literary allusion, from the ending of Keats's "Ode on a Grecian Urn," but it is also a translation, putting into simple everyday words the idea contained in the Greek five-dollar word *philanthropist*. The stuffy abstraction of philanthropy is what Trilling found in the sentimental simplifications that he and others castigated in the "protest novel." Trilling walked a tightrope in this introduction. He wrote of Huck and Jim as forming a "community of saints," called Huck "morally sensitive" (107), and yet he avoided the simplification, abstraction, and sentimentality that he condemned.

The key to Trilling's antimoralist morality comes as the climax of his section setting forth the greatness of *Huckleberry Finn.* Although W. D. Howells was the first to name chapter 31 a "spiritual struggle" and V. L. Parrington was the first to quote extensively the sequence culminating with "All right, then, I'll *go* to hell," Trilling was the first to develop a full argument for this passage as the book's crucial "moral crisis" (108). In chapter 31, he found the "intensity" of Huck's struggle to indicate that Huck is "deeply involved in the society which he rejects" (107). I am not at all sure that Huck does reject that society, but Trilling's emphasis on Huck's involvement in any case makes the essential point. Huck does not stand apart from it but is in its midst. Precisely for that reason,

Trilling argued, "ideas and ideals" (108) can be of no help to him, because they are the products of the society from which he is breaking away.

In the second chapter of this book, I have made a different argument, namely that Twain achieved a tremendously effective comic simplification of Huck's range of reference by scrupulously omitting from his awareness at this point the two major resources for all American antislavery thought and action—the language of Christian love and the democratic political language of the natural equality of all humankind. In understanding Huck as in the midst of his culture, Trilling staged Huck as an example of the "struggle," the "debate," the "dialectic" that make a culture; he argued further that by containing "both the yes and the no of their culture," certain figures are "prophetic of the future" (7). My argument has been that Twain's *book* is comprehensive in this way—he shows in *Huckleberry Finn* the traces of these alternative and liberatory discourses—but that the consciousness of the character Huck is not, and that taking Huck as moral exemplar has led to an abusive structure of debate when the book has become controversial.

In his 1944 *American Dilemma,* Gunnar Myrdal sketched what he believed to be a typical case, which actually shows a more complex dialectical yes and no than what Trilling attributes to Huck:

> *The moral struggle goes on within people and not only between them.* . . .
> Even a poor and uneducated white person in some isolated and backward rural region in the Deep South, who is violently prejudiced against the Negro and intent upon depriving him of civic rights and human independence, has also a whole compartment in his valuation sphere housing the entire American Creed of liberty, equality, justice. . . . He is also a good Christian and honestly devoted to the ideals of human brotherhood. (lxx, emphasis in original)

And yet I must also note what is wrong with Myrdal here. By making the problem primarily one of how whites feel, he set the keynote for the belief that has dominated most hypercanonizing response to the complaints of African American parents and children, namely, that a proper understanding of Huck's feelings is the key to determining that there is no problem with the book and the way it is used. Blacks figure as the objects of complex white feelings, rather than as independent agents. Moreover, the awkward and antiseptic language Myrdal used to talk about feelings ("compartment in his valuation sphere") exemplifies why the discourse of social science seemed so inimical to major critics of the mid-century, not only Trilling (for example in his critique of the Kinsey report), but also Ralph Ellison (for example in his review of *An American Dilemma*) and James Baldwin (in his critique of the "protest novel"). For Trilling, such language formed part of the tradition of Parrington and Dreiser that misconceived "reality in America." His reading of *Huckleberry Finn* was part of his campaign to rectify the American sense of reality, against those who appealed to "our facile sociological minds" (*Liberal* 183) and conceived of the writer as "Commissioner of Moral Sanitation" (*Gathering* 72).

Trilling's wish to oppose the American canons of realism and to ally "moral realism" with the "moral imagination" led to a powerfully outrageous comparison. Huck no more condemns slavery than such adulterous medieval heroes as Tristram and Lancelot condemn marriage; he is "as consciously *wicked* as any lover of romance" (108). In a prefiguration of Leslie Fiedler's argument, Trilling compared Huck's love for Jim to the great forbidden passions of medieval literature. The comparison heroizes Huck and, we now recognize, also feminizes Jim. The phrase "lover of romance" achieves a strong ambiguity. Lancelot and Tristram are the lovers about whom romances have been written, but enthusiastic readers of romance are also aptly called "lovers of romance," and so the reader willing to accept Trilling's argument has earned this highly honorific title. Trilling concluded by spelling out the logic of romance as he read it in chapter 31. *Huckleberry Finn*, he asserted, "is indeed a subversive book" (108), just as all those genteel librarians had charged, although not for the reasons they had given.

"Huckleberry Finn" II

It is easy to see why Trilling's introduction achieved such circulation within Twain criticism, given Trilling's prestige, given the lucid and compact grace with which the essay ranked this favorite American book at the peak of world literature, while placing it within the contexts of Twain's life, national history, and the development of American literature. Moreover, the terms of praise Trilling found were the gravest ever offered. Trilling's only failure is that he nowhere left room for the reader to imagine that this is a funny book, which has made millions of readers laugh.

It is harder to define what the stakes were for Trilling in "*Huckle-berry Finn.*" By no means all of his essays from the 1940s were incor-porated into *The Liberal Imagination*. What were the ways this essay worked within Trilling's own agenda that led him to include it, while he omitted, for example, his very powerful "Sermon on a Text from Whitman" (1945), as well as his penetrating 1948 reflections on the state of American writing for a *Partisan Review* symposium? Given its placement as the introduction to a text that sold some 300,000 copies in little more than a decade (Blair, *Mark Twain* 375) and that continued to sell equally well for some years more, this essay probably reached more readers than anything else Trilling wrote, on the order of five times more than the 100,000 copies sold of *The Liberal Imagination* (Shumway 277). One might imagine that he put into this popularization some of the most important features of his thought at the time of writing.

To locate the force of "*Huckleberry Finn*" within Trilling's own oeuvre, we must determine what "All right, then, I'll *go* to hell" has to do with anti-Stalinism. For Trilling identified his deepest concern in this period as combating "the commitment that a large segment of the intelligentsia of the West gave to the degraded version of Marxism known as Stalinism" (*Last* 140). He explained in retrospect late in his career, "All my essays of the forties were written from my sense of this dull, repressive tendency of opinion, which was com-ing to dominate the old ethos of liberal enlightenment" (*Last* 141). In another autobiographical formulation, he sketched these notes for the context of *The Liberal Imagination:*

> The liberal intellectual middle-class acceptance of Stalinist doctrine in all aspects of life—in art and thought.
> *The Nation / The New Republic / The New York Times.* (*Last* 240)

Trilling's mention of the *Times* needs some explanation. In his 1945 "Sermon on a Text from Whitman," occasioned by a Communist-sponsored selection from Whitman's poetry, Trilling cited a key for-mulation of Whitman's that he saw as defining what this "Stalin-ist" perspective omitted: the "simple separate person." Along with an overwhelming interest in human life exclusively as a matter of groups rather than of individuals, according to Trilling, the Stalinist perspective also refused "to believe that the adventurous expres-sions of art have an intimate relation to the adventures of political freedom" (*Speaking* 215). The sense of adventure was a keynote of

Trilling's critical thought. He understood his antagonists to believe in a routine, mechanized, predictable morality and history. The deadening paradox of what he called Stalinism was that what should have been a thrilling view of human transformation became instead banal. For the thrill could arise only from also facing the obstacles and improbabilities of achieving classless and conflict-free peace and equality; yet to face those doubts was, as Trilling understood the demand for party discipline, forbidden. In failing to acknowledge these real issues, Stalinism became at once false and dull.

For Trilling, art and politics alike should be invigorating, complex and conflictual, daring and possibly flawed. In contrast, he cited the views of J. Donald Adams, who had been from 1925 to 1943 editor of the *New York Times* book review section, and remained for another twenty years a regular columnist in the "Speaking of Books" feature. Adams's belief in "democracy," Trilling charged, led him to assert that "books of the future will take a certain reassuring shape, specification to be provided by what he calls the 'many'" (*Speaking* 215). Again, for Trilling's sense of Whitman, and of literature more largely, the chance to mean something to the many can arise only from the basis of one's own "simple separate person." What might seem in Adams a fairly ordinary American anti-experimental, middle-brow populism, in this political conjuncture felt to Trilling like something far worse.

One may have some trouble with Trilling's peculiar linkage of democratic optimism and Stalinist party discipline and yet recognize the contours of what he was troubled by. As late as 1960, Adams wrote about Twain with the same unadventurousness, even though he was at this point obviously anti-Communist. Criticizing Soviet comments on the recent new edition of Twain's *Autobiography*, Adams contrasted American freedom to Soviet dictatorship: "Soviet literary officialdom assumes that, as in their own land, American writers are not free agents." Therefore the Soviet press argued that "there is a dreadful conspiracy on the part of the American government to hide from the people the true nature of Mark Twain's contribution to the literature of the United States." According to the "literary dictators of the Soviet Union," Twain was "one of our severest social critics," and they charged that the American image of Twain made him "merely a funny man—a humorist." Adams concluded: the Soviet dictators "see him as a thinker, a conception which might have amused Mark." Adams reversed the spin on the political charge. For him in 1960, even after the work of Trilling, Eliot, Leo Marx, Henry Nash Smith, and Walter Blair, it was Stalinist, or at least Red, to find in Twain anything but simply a funny writer. This anti-intellectual insistence on the lowest common denominator links his position in 1960 to the views that Trilling found Stalinist in the forties.

This 1960 text of Adams suggests that he also wrote a much earlier *Times* statement of the same view. Back in 1935 "Topics of the Times" reflected on centennial assessments of Twain. It was good that he "has been rescued from the hands of the Freudian snatchers" such as Van Wyck Brooks, but even DeVoto's celebratory nationalism did not seem sufficient to the *Times*. Twain has not yet "been restored to the arms of the plain American people where he belongs." Even DeVoto "reveals a strong inclination to claim Mark Twain for an American elite." The *Times* found it elitist for DeVoto to assert that "it is really the author of 'Huckleberry Finn' that counts." The *Times* retorted, "counts with whom?" Hypercanonization had not yet taken hold. For their understanding of the plain American people, Twain lives in his wry aphorisms rather than in any of his books; it is not because he "depicted a whole civilization," as DeVoto argued, that we should care for him, but because of his "laughing magic." This long continuity from 1935 to 1960 may give some gauge of how much cultural work, what a metamorphosis of American culture, it has taken to make *Huckleberry Finn* the iconic text that it has been for less than fifty years, though now defended as if it were an immutable marker of value.

Adams's skepticism toward the extreme critical and scholarly claims made on behalf of *Huckleberry Finn* showed again in a piece from 1957. Adams challenged Hemingway's famous claim that all modern American literature comes from *Huckleberry Finn*. Even though "that statement is always cropping up," every time Adams encountered it he had "further reservations concerning its truth." He pointed out that there was vernacular writing before Twain (citing the Davy Crockett texts, which were fresh in the public mind only a few years after the Walt Disney Crockett revival) and argued that in any case the influence of newspapers would have had the effect on American prose that Hemingway attributed to *Huckleberry Finn*. But above all Adams opposed the restriction Hemingway's claim put on the kind of American writing that should be valued.

Adams argued against the Hemingway canon of American prose in a way that in the 1970s feminist critics would do: "it is a technique limited to certain specific purposes." There are things a book can't do if it limits itself to an uneducated, vernacular perspective. Just a few years before John Steinbeck won the Nobel Prize, Adams cited *The Grapes of Wrath* (1939) against Hemingway. Steinbeck's dialogue is vernacular, but the narrative voice offers "commentary, which adds much to the book's power." And that would have been lost if Steinbeck had written to Hemingway's prescription in the mode of *Huckleberry Finn*. Adams still yearned for national narrative like Stowe's and Steinbeck's, rather than literary narrative like Twain's and Hemingway's.

For Trilling, however, *The Grapes of Wrath* was part of the Stalinist unadventurousness. In 1942 Trilling wrote for the *Kenyon Review*, edited by the politically conservative New Critic John Crowe Ransom, a piece entitled "Artists and the 'Societal Function.'" Despite their different political views, Trilling and Ransom agreed that there was a value in great literature which no one could capture who used social-scientese like "the societal function." Trilling used *The Grapes of Wrath* to exemplify the problem. Like Plato, Trilling took art seriously enough to see its dangers, rather than attributing to it slight but anodyne powers. He argued, "If we are to talk about literature in its relation with social good, and the future of democracy, we ought to be aware how harmful literature can be. A book like *The Grapes of Wrath* cockers-up the self-righteousness of the liberal middle class; it is so easy to feel virtuous in our love for such *good* poor people!" (*Speaking* 189). Socrates had argued in the *Republic* that poetry instead of drying up the passions fed and watered them, and Trilling used a barnyard metaphor to suggest the same: the wrong kinds of feelings are coddled, fostered, and indulged by the wrong kind of art. It is typical of Trilling that what worried him was not a base passion, but precisely a moral passion. Sounding himself a bit the Commissioner of Moral Sanitation, he argued that "we" are made to feel righteous in the wrong way, for the wrong reasons: "The social emotions can provide a safe escape from our own lives and from the pressures of self-criticism," so that we can unawares "feed our little aggressions and grandiosities" (189).

Trilling here elaborated a position he had taken in the 1939 *Partisan Review* symposium "The Situation in American Writing." At that time, he had characterized the entire "literature of social protest" as damaging. Although its "intention of arousing pity and anger" may be "legitimate," the fact is that "because of its artistic failures" it does not aid in engagement with reality. Paradoxically, it "constitutes a form of 'escapism,'" because it "offers a subtle flattery by which the progressive middle-class reader is cockered up with a sense of his own virtue." The reader is "made to feel that he lives in a world of perfect certainties in which critical thought and self-critical feeling are the only dangers" (*Speaking* 118).

Trilling sought in art both reality and adventure. This was what the "moral realism" produced by the "moral imagination" offered; it was what made Henry James's definition of romance so powerful a resource for Trilling, who found in romance "a synonym for the will in its creative aspect," especially of "*moral* creativeness" (*Liberal* 260). This moral creativity of will was what Trilling found in Huck's crisis. Although Huck feels the same "warmly gratifying emotions of self-conscious virtue" as a reader of *The Grapes of Wrath* when he listens to his conscience and determines to write to Miss Watson, Huck finally does not send the letter. It is just because he is "as consciously *wicked* as any illicit lover of romance" that Huck for Trilling embodies the virtue of morally creative will. In praising *Huckleberry Finn* for being a "subversive book," Trilling specified that the "dialectic" of the "great moral crisis" is what counts. "Dialectic" was a term highly valued on the left, which Trilling had made the core of his critique of what he considered the simplistic realism of Parrington and Dreiser, and "subversive" was the term hurled against the left more and more frequently by the reactionary anti-Communists who made life so embarrassing for the liberal anti-Communists, who shuddered to be linked with the reactionaries through their shared enemy.

In his choice of opposingly weighted terms, Trilling tried to steer an independent course, such as he attributed to Huck. In his 1948 response to the *Partisan Review* symposium "The State of American Writing," the same year as "*Huckleberry Finn*," Trilling specified some of the context in which his particular terms of praise may be understood. He was distressed by the current tendency to "reject the traditional method of art," by which he meant in particular "the methods of imagination, symbol, and fantasy"—precisely the elements he considered least congenial to Parrington's criticism or Dreiser's practice, precisely the "romance" elements shared by Hawthorne, James, and Twain. Just here Trilling offered his most

explicit public statement on the pervasiveness of "Stalinism." Drawing on the vocabulary of Matthew Arnold, on whom he had written
his first book, Trilling explained that the current resistance to the
imaginative and adventurous character of art could be called "Phi-
listinism," but, he asserted, it could equally be called Stalinism: for
"Stalinism becomes endemic to the American middle class as soon
as that class begins to think" (*Speaking* 244). Trilling distinguished
this "cultural Stalinism" from any specific "political belief." (This
special usage is crucial to his argument and to his influence but is
not registered, from him or any other source, in the *OED* Supplement.) He ventured that the newly founded liberal Americans for
Democratic Action was no different in its "cultural ideas" from the
old-line-left Political Action Committee of the CIO. In *The Liberal
Imagination*, however, he was both more guarded in brandishing the
specific term *Stalinism* and more insistent on the inseparability of
culture and politics than in this perhaps more casual, or more in-
group, symposium statement.

As early as 1938, Trilling had begun to formulate the mode of resistance that he increasingly valued as his weapon against the dull
conformity he saw around him. In contrast to the "cultural tradition
of the intellectual left" that placed the "collective aspects of life"
above the "individual aspects" (*Speaking* 105), Trilling invoked an
old argument of John Dewey's. Dewey had argued that in certain
kinds of moral situation, the choice cannot be made on the basis of
the possible ends, but only on the basis of "our preference for one
kind of character or another." A person asks, "What sort of an
agent, of a person, shall he be." Although the obvious question is
"what he shall *do*," the deeper question "forces the issue back" to
"the kind of selfhood, of agency, involved in the respective ends"
(*Speaking,* 109). In *The Liberal Imagination,* it seemed obvious to
Trilling that such questions of moral style, of moral character, had
political force, even in cases such as Huck's where the plot of the
novel undoes his *doing,* where it is finally only a matter of personal
style whether he chooses to go to hell or to write to the already dead
woman who has already freed Jim.

Trilling emphasized in the introduction to *The Liberal Imagination*
that "the connection between literature and politics" is "very immediate," for in the current world "the wide sense" of the word politics is "forced upon us." What politics means nowadays is "the politics of culture," that is, "the organization of human life toward

some end or other," and in that organization is involved "the modification of sentiments," which he glossed to mean modifying "the quality of human life" (ix). In the introduction to the *Partisan Reader*, the piece immediately preceding "*Huckleberry Finn*," he joined politics and culture even more forcibly. He asserted that "the cultural program of the Communist Party" in the United States had produced a "divorce between politics and the imagination," which the little magazine must work to undo. As modern people, "our fate, for better or worse, is political" and "our only possibility of enduring it," that is, of making political life also a rich and various and complex life, is "to force into our definition of politics every human activity and every subtlety of every human activity" (*Liberal* 96). Far from targeting the Communists for politicizing imagination, Trilling argued that liberals must activate the imagination in politics, because otherwise there will be only politics but no imagination.

For Trilling, the essence of his desired anti-Communist liberal imagination was its capacity to invent adventurously human beings, rather than the stereotypes of protest fiction. It is Henry James's virtue, and his unwelcome message to actually existing liberalism, that in *The Princess Casamassima* he "represents the poor as if they had dignity and intelligence in the same degree as people of the reading class" (*Liberal* 83). Against the current unimaginative Stalinist-liberal, who defines a "serious book" as one "which holds before us some image of society to consider and condemn" (*Liberal* 208), both James and Twain offer relief. The moral heroism of Huck, against a social order no longer at all a live threat, leaves only the residual message of its posture. Huck's rebellion is subversive because, Trilling believed, "no one who reads thoughtfully the dialectic of Huck's great moral crisis will ever again be wholly able to accept without some question and some irony the assumptions of the respectable morality by which he lives" (108).

The canons of liberal protest fiction, of the Stalinist divorce of politics from imagination, were the respectable morality of his own time for which Trilling offered Huck as antidote. That is, in the historical allegory that emerged from this superimposition, Stalinism for Trilling was to the United States of the mid-twentieth century as the slave system was to the mid-nineteenth. Who now in the 1990s can grasp that this was how the world ever looked to any deeply intelligent and serious people? Yet writing in 1993, Diana Trilling looked back to those days and asserted that in those years "Stalin-ism dominated American culture." Specifically, "in art, journalism, editing and publishing, in the theater and entertainment industries, in the legal profession, in the schools and universities, among church and civic leaders, everywhere in our cultural life, the Soviet Union exercised a control which was all but absolute." She ex-plained that this "submission to Stalinism" was "not always politi-cally conscious" but often arose from the "fashionable trend in what was taken to be enlightened thought" (180–81). So, according to the Trillings, many were Stalinists without knowing it; how handy to have had a category that humiliated those with whom you disagreed, by simultaneously degrading their moral character and jeopardizing their employment.

We have seen a similar logic in Arthur M. Schlesinger, another leading figure in forming the liberal anti-Communist intellectual position: Henry Wallace's Soft on Communism position mapped onto antebellum America as soft on slavery. The remarkable histori-cal irony that I find here comes from the reversibility, not merely the analogy, between the positions Schlesinger and Trilling defined. In the antebellum time in which *Huckleberry Finn* is set, two different committed minorities formed highly influential analyses of the po-litical condition and tendency of the United States. To committed slaveholders, it appeared that things were getting harder for them. Since 1830, an abusive abolitionist press had sprung into existence, and the Free Soil movement threatened to bottle slavery into an in-creasingly limited geographical area, which would prevent its main-taining political parity with nonslave states in Congress. On the other hand, to abolitionists, it appeared that the "Slave Power" dominated American politics, whether in the Compromise of 1850, which reinvigorated the constitutional requirement that fugitive slaves be returned; in the 1854 Kansas-Nebraska Act, which opened all territories to slavery; or in the 1857 Dred Scott decision of the Supreme Court, which excluded African Americans from the life of American citizenship. To each of these adversaries, the other held unquestioned hegemony in the sphere of opinion. If we then map the early 1850s onto the early 1950s, two images superpose. As overwhelming as the abolitionist threat to established American norms seemed to Senator John Calhoun, so strong seemed the Com-munist threat to Senator Joseph McCarthy; as overwhelming as the established slave power seemed to the marginal intellectual

William Lloyd Garrison, so strong seemed the Stalinist establishment to the marginal intellectual Lionel Trilling.

Through this chapter I have analyzed in detail the ways in which
Trilling's "*Huckleberry Finn*" both drew energy from and also contributed to the major concerns of his time with which Trilling was
most deeply involved. His position is powerful and honorable, and
it contains many elements that seem to me, five decades later, exemplary for the criticism of literature in relation to culture and politics.
Yet I cannot accept that we read Huck as wicked. The thrill of chapter 31 comes from following Huck's struggle to become as good as
we are, even if he fails to understand exactly what he is doing. For
readers to whom neither slavery nor damnation is a credible choice,
the moral drama of chapter 31 is greatly diminished, although its
comic force remains great. Trilling, I think, was no less wrong in his
assessment of his own times. For example, Trilling, we have seen,
presumed that the ADA cultural position would not differ from that
of the CIO, yet Schlesinger, an influential founder of ADA, held, we
have seen, the same cultural values as Trilling. For most Americans
around 1950, there existed no Stalinist orthodoxy from which they
needed, daringly, to break free. There are artistic crudities that may
be too easily excused in protest literature, and there are cruelties
that may be too readily excused in protest politics, as Trilling obviously feared; but there are also risks involved in a literary politics
oriented to complexity, risks that involve complacency and the refusal to recognize and to struggle against the real-life crudities of
injustice.

6

Nationalism and Hypercanonization

The Nationalization of Literary Narrative

I am not an Americanist by professional formation, and as in the 1980s I came to focus my teaching and reading in American literature, I was struck by what seemed to me, compared with other national literatures I knew or had studied, a state of hypercanonization. By hypercanonization I mean that a very few individual works monopolize curricular and critical attention: in fiction preeminently *The Scarlet Letter*, *Moby-Dick*, and *Huckleberry Finn*. These works organize innumerable courses in high school, college, and graduate school; they form the focus for many dissertations and books. I have found literary history an important means by which to engage critically with these works and with the professional and intellectual structures that produce their hypercanonicity, to address the works while displacing the terms of address. For literary history, as I try to practice it, these works are not the answers but the problems. My previous chapters have related *Huckleberry Finn*, and discussions by scholars and journalists about *Huckleberry Finn*, to a wide range of social and political contexts—from Huck's time in the 1840s, through Twain's time of writing around 1880, and through the twentieth century (especially since 1948). This chapter is more closely literary in focus, although not exclusively so, since its major concern is the connection Americanists have made between literature and national identity.

In a recently published portion of the new *Cambridge History of American Literature* (volume 2, 1995), I was asked to write on "mid-nineteenth-century American prose narrative." I set myself this problem: How do I account for the emergence, around 1850, of works that count as what readers nowadays recognize as "literature"? I mean here *The Scarlet Letter* and *Moby-Dick*. In contrast to them, other valuable written productions of the time, however much they prove of interest in other ways, do not now widely count as literature. This is not simply an abstract issue of terminology. The designation "literature" is heavy with value. It affects what is studied, taught, and read, and it also greatly determines the terms in which new writing is reviewed in the public press. Books published in the 1990s are praised for resembling *Huckleberry Finn* but not, I believe, any other single work of the later nineteenth century. My historical exploration of this issue involved two areas: the changing definition of "literature," and its relation to differing kinds of writing, that is, a problem of genre. My solution involved reconceptualizing the emerging literary narrative type as one among several different competing generic types. The major narrative form that preceded literary narrative in the United States, and also succeeded it, was what I call "national" narrative, in which the origins, attributes, and future of the United States were made overt themes. At about the time of Andrew Jackson's presidency (1829–37), the historical fiction of James Fenimore Cooper and the *History of the United States* by George Bancroft defined national narrative. Cooper died in 1851, but Bancroft's *History* was written, in ten volumes, from 1834 into the 1880s.

In relation to national narrative, two important smaller types emerged, which differed from it but would have been impossible without it. First in the 1830s what I call "local" narrative, the line from Washington Irving that includes the so-called southwestern humorists of Georgia, Alabama, Mississippi, and Tennessee as well as the northeastern moralist Hawthorne in his shorter works; and second, in the 1840s, "personal narrative," which, contrary to Puritan tradition and twentieth-century expectation, proved to be rather extroverted, first-person reports from the margins of the dominant culture. Important examples of personal narrative include Richard Henry Dana's *Two Years before the Mast* (1840), Francis Parkman's *Oregon Trail* (1849), Frederick Douglass's *Narrative* (1845), and Harriet Jacobs's *Incidents in the Life of a Slave Girl* (1861).

In response to the political crisis of 1850, which produced a compromise intended to subdue controversy, Melville and Hawthorne consolidated elements from their own earlier work and that of Poe and set their works apart from the political optimism and straight-forward patriotic address of national narrative. "The Custom-House" introduction to *The Scarlet Letter* illustrates the point. Through literary narrative, they developed a freely imaginative space of psychological interiority, on the model of what trans-atlantic romantic theory and practice had set forth in the previous two generations. Both local and personal narrative elements could be incorporated under this new principle of integration, by which a self gives order and meaning to elements drawn from other narra-tive modes. The contrast of *Moby-Dick* with another great novel of 1851–52 makes this clear. *Uncle Tom's Cabin* is no less comprehen-sive than *Moby-Dick,* but it integrates local and personal narrative materials under the dominance of a narrative concerning the salva-tion of America, and in Augustine St. Clare it incorporates the figure of the sensitive spectator associated with literary narrative. St. Clare is presented sympathetically but very critically and occu-pies only the middle third of the novel. In contrast, the literary figure of Ishmael engrosses attention from the opening and sur-vives Ahab's quest as witness.

I find that Americans in the twentieth century have—paradoxi-cally—adopted as national exemplars precisely those works that were written in the literary mode so as to differ from national nar-rative, while great national writers such as Bancroft, Cooper, and (until recently) Stowe have been comparatively neglected. This crit-ical distaste for the explicitly national in American writing recalls the problem of "protest" fiction, which I have discussed in the previous two chapters. If we fail to question the assumptions em-bedded in the idolatry of the literary, if we ignore the wide spec-trum of writings of which the literary icons form only a restricted part, we damage our understanding of the present. For many of the productions now associated with multiculturalism are precisely personal, local, and revisionist national narratives—no less than was so in the past.

In Europe as well as in the United States, the nineteenth century was marked by two great cultural transformations that still power-fully shape our lives: the emergence of nationality and the emer-gence of literature (in the specialized sense of imaginative belles lettres, rather than the earlier idea of "letters," which included all culturally valued writing). In our contemporary world of nations in

the last years of the twentieth century, the renewed power of na-
tionalisms throughout what was contained as the "second world,"
no less than the intensified American patriotism spurred by Desert
Stormers requires rethinking this relation. As I understand the last
hundred and fifty years of American history, literary culture and
national culture may be seriously at odds, and they harmonize only
when the nation is given a meaning more psychological than religious or political. (A good example of this tendency was Norman
Mailer's *Why Are We in Vietnam?* [1967], the title of which seems to
promise a national narrative, but which in fact is literary narrative
alluding to *Huckleberry Finn.*) This psychological understanding of
the nation, in turn, has granted America the spiritual legitimacy of
literature, while subordinating literature to an America so conceived as to disarm political criticism.

A line of thought reaches from the middle nineteenth century as
interpreted by my chapters from the *Cambridge History* into the later
nineteenth century. After the reawakening of widespread political
controversy over Kansas in 1854, the hope of avoiding secession
and/or war by stepping back from politics, which had permitted literary narrative to emerge, dried up. As we have noted earlier, this
controversy was what brought Lincoln back to politics and provoked his movement toward the positions that made him a great
national leader. The most ambitious writings of the immediate
post–Civil War years were the volumes of Francis Parkman's national narrative of the struggle for the American forest. The most
captivating writings of the same period were the first books of Mark
Twain. Twain came directly from the newspaper milieu of local narrative. In *Innocents Abroad* and *Roughing It* he strung together bits
any one of which might have been a newspaper sketch, integrating
them through the resources of "personal narrative" (as he characterized *Roughing It* [527]). Meanwhile, a steady trickle of post-
humous materials from Hawthorne's estate kept alive the idea of
literary narrative until Henry James's study of Hawthorne (1879)
marked the moment when James chose to re-produce and occupy
that aesthetic, nonpolitical space with *The Portrait of a Lady.*

Van Wyck Brooks in *The Ordeal of Mark Twain* (1920) and *The Pil-
grimage of Henry James* (1925) set James and Twain as polar contrasting cases of the artist's relation to America. For Brooks, Twain compromised his power as a satirist by yielding too much to the culture
of the East, which was both too genteel and too commercial; while

James preserved his art but lost his subject matter by his trans-atlantic expatriation. More striking than the contrast is the way Brooks made of each a mighty example. As lamented extremes, both Twain and James differ from the devalued middle ground occupied by William Dean Howells, who played a key role in the lives of both of them as friend, editor, and supporter. A moment of American literary history that has still not been adequately thought through is the period of early 1885 when the *Century* magazine published excerpts from *Huckleberry Finn,* while also serializing Howells's *Rise of Silas Lapham* and James's *Bostonians.*

Many causes have made it difficult to grasp how limited an event nineteenth-century literary narrative was. These causes include the establishment of college teaching as the main livelihood of literary scholars and the restriction of college instruction, for much of the twentieth century, to a limited canon of texts extravagantly praised as timeless and studied primarily through close reading. But the causes are not only institutional. They are also political, involving how American intellectuals imagine the place in the world occupied by the culture of their country. For Brooks after the First World War, Twain had sold out literature for America and James had given up America for literature; after the Second World War Trilling, as we saw in the previous chapter, made Twain and James the center of his understanding of the great achievement of American literature. These same causes contributed to the peculiar twentieth-century status of *Huckleberry Finn.* In order to achieve hypercanonization, it had first to be understood as literary, and then its literary value had to be nationalized.

Just like Ishmael's narrative in *Moby-Dick, Huckleberry Finn* is filled with the materials of local humor writing, and it draws for its fundamental mode of presentation on the conventions of personal narrative. Like *Moby-Dick,* too, *Huckleberry Finn* offers the freely aesthetically shaped world of literary narrative, through its technique of representing subject matter that plays an important part in American history (the economics of whaling, the morality of slavery) while cutting off the address to any audience of patriotic citizens who might be engaged to enact the author's vision of nationhood. It is possible to link *Huckleberry Finn* to fundamental national historical experiences, but the link can be made only allegorically, that is, only through an aggressively active process of reader's interpretation, about which readers in fact differ very widely. My name for this allegoric interpretive process is the nationalizing of literary narrative, and it seems to me the means by which hypercanonical idolatry takes place. The hypercanonized literary work is thought to offer an imaginative world cut free from the bounds of specific grievances or goals, so that themes at once eternal and ideally national can be projected onto it. I have tried to identify specific historical pressures in relation to which writers produced the works that have been seen as free of historical pressures, times when writers, and to some degree their readers, wished to sidestep threatening controversies—moments such as the Compromise of 1850, the end of Reconstruction, and the aftermath of World War II.

By recovering limiting contexts for the emergence of literary icons, I want to make trouble for the hypercanonical construction of *Huckleberry Finn*. I hope to say things about *Huckleberry Finn* that can be accepted as true and that, if accepted, make it harder for the book to be treated so readily as an idol, rather than as one very good book among other books, in American culture. The nationalizing of literary narrative, and concomitant psychologizing of politics, produce and reinforce the belief that there is a true America made up by those who take their distance from actually existing America. In this respect, one of the most provocative features of *Huckleberry Finn* is only a heightened instance of what is also true of the other hypercanonized works: its very canonical prestige is connected to the sense that it is "counter"-cultural, or, as Trilling put it, subversive.

For example, let me cite what many scholars still consider the definitive chapter-length treatment of *Huckleberry Finn*, from *Mark Twain: The Development of a Writer* by Henry Nash Smith, one of the founders of the academic discipline of American studies and for a long time in charge of the Mark Twain Papers. Like many academic readers, at least since V. L. Parrington, Smith gave special attention to chapter 31. Here Huck contemplates writing to Miss Watson so that she can recover her runaway slave, but even though this seems to him what religion teaches, he can't do it and decides instead, "All right, then, I'll *go* to hell." Although Smith never referred, here or anywhere else that I know of, to Trilling's 1948 essay, he explicitly credited Trilling's 1955 book *The Opposing Self* for his crucial argument at this point, when he first set it out in his 1958 introduction to the Riverside college edition of *Huckleberry Finn*. Smith quoted Trilling on the "new recognition," in the nineteenth century, of "society as coercion," against which Trilling posed, as Smith noted, "the modern imagination of autonomy," which is based on "selves conceived in opposition to the general culture" (xiii).

Taking from Trilling these terms of the autonomous self opposing social coercion, Smith built the framework for his authoritative interpretation. Smith argued on the basis of chapter 31 that the crux of meaning in the book is Huck's choice between "fidelity to the uncoerced self" and the negative results, the "blurring of attitudes," that are "caused by social conformity" (*Development* 122–23). This "fidelity to the uncoerced self" was the psychological hinge by which Smith connected the literary work *Huckleberry Finn* to a national meaning, as token of an America beyond conformity, an America that, as if it were the star of the world's show, would lead the nations of the world, or perhaps bring history to its destined end. This is the position that led *Big River* to include the song "I, Huckleberry, Me," characterized by David Richards in the *Washington Post* as Huck's "sprightly proclamation of independence."

Twain as Huck: The Uncoerced Self in the California Edition

Smith's critical position helps define the intellectual and institutional context for what I consider an extraordinary anomaly in the major new scholarly edition of *Huckleberry Finn*. For decades now the Mark Twain Project has been conducted from the repository of the Mark Twain Papers, the Bancroft Library at the University of California Berkeley campus, and its editions and scholarship have been invaluable. Yet the California editors have decided that Twain's intentions require the text of *Huckleberry Finn* to include a sixteen-page section that never appeared in the book during Twain's lifetime. (The discovery in February 1991 of the missing portion of the manuscript of *Huckleberry Finn* confirmed the facts but did not affect the logic of the editorial argument, which again surfaces in the new 1996 edition incorporating the new manuscript materials.) This so-called "Raftmen Episode" Twain published in *Life on the Mississippi* (chapter 3), describing it as excerpted from a work-in-progress about Huckleberry Finn, but he then omitted it from *Huckleberry Finn* itself.

The documents concerning Twain's intentions are three letters. The first one is from Twain, insisting that no part of this section be used in publicity materials, since it had already been published and might lead readers to fear that the whole new book would be largely familiar (*Huckleberry* [1988] 442). Next is a letter from his publisher wondering if the section might not be omitted entirely: "I think it would improve" the book (446). In the third letter, Twain replied, "Yes, I think the raft chapter can be left wholly out" (446). The California editors argue that Twain omitted the episode only to "accommodate his young publisher on a practical matter," and that in editorial theory such a decision is equivalent to "accepting the publisher's censorship" (Hirst 450). (Hirst is the general editor of the Mark Twain Project, here explaining in the inexpensive paperback edition the logic of Fischer's textual decision, which Fischer himself explains in the massive, costly scholarly edition to which I otherwise refer.) It is a nagging embarrassment to the editors' scholarly scruple that even where he might have tried to bring the passage back, no evidence exists that Twain ever tried to (*Huckleberry* [1988] 476–77).

I have three points to make about this matter. First, I emphasize that this editorial interpretive attempt to define and magnify the individuality of Twain the author, as a self that should be uncoerced, possessor of intentions and victim of censorship, is perfectly coherent with Smith's critical position taken in interpreting *Huckleberry Finn*. In combating what they consider the publisher's censorship, the editors take upon themselves the spiritual authority of Huck's decision to produce an America by rejecting "social conformity": "All right, then, I'll *go* to hell." Yet the editors take a more complex and accommodating stance in the acknowledgments, the first words of the volume after its dedication and table of contents. They begin, "Our first thanks go to the American taxpayer" (*Huckleberry* [1988] xvii). (This kind of rhetoric led Jonathan Raban, reviewing another product of the Mark Twain Project in the *Times Literary Supplement*, to remark on the "alliance, unprecedented so far as I know, between tax dollars and literary history.") Next the California editors thank "the scholars who recommended federal funding," and the climax comes in thanks to the National Endowment for the Humanities, the "independent federal agency" that granted the funds to make the edition possible (xvii). (That phrase "independent federal agency" is almost a perfect verbal formula for what I have described as the psychological hinge used to connect the literary to the national.)

The rhetoric of acknowledgment is highly interesting. Note the mediating role of the scholarly community. It stands in the unemphasized second position between the strong opening invocation of the citizenry and the climactic summoning of the state. Yet only by means of the scholarly community can citizens receive the benefits of their federated agency, and only the initiative of the scholarly editors opened this possibility. The independence of the NEH is clearly meant to set it apart from the dangers of conformity, and the taxpayers whose "support" (xvii) made the work possible are vicariously co-agents in fighting censorship. So the logic of America as the nation defined by its opposition to itself underwrites this sequence. From economic individual to federal agency, all are free and fight for freedom. I do not think Mark Twain believed anything like this.

My second point is that in insisting on the unfettered individuality of Twain, the editors nonetheless effectively split him in two. If the editors draw glory from being like Twain, he must be protected from being like them. For their scholarly narration of *Huckleberry Finn*'s process of publication constructs quite a different image of Twain from the one they invoke to justify their editorial decision, but more like the selves they acknowledge in giving thanks. Recall that the very name by which Samuel Clemens is known to history as an author, Mark Twain, is itself not just a pen name but a registered trade mark. This economic fact has weighty consequences for the logic of editorial argument. The editors base their decision on a split between "Mark Twain's intentions for his text" and "his publisher's needs." They find "no documentary evidence" that these intentions and needs "coincide" (Hirst 450–51). I read their evidence to different effect, however, as showing that Twain's intentions concerning *Huckleberry Finn* were inseparable from its status as an economic object. The California edition shows that Clemens himself was deeply involved in the whole process by which the book moved from his manuscript to its readers.

The publisher who is supposed to have censored Twain was Charles L. Webster. Webster was a young nephew of Samuel Clemens's, and the publishing concern of Charles L. Webster & Co. was set up by Clemens, according to the very evidence gathered by the California editors, so that the author "could have complete charge of issuing and selling the book" (*Huckleberry* [1988] xlvii). As Webster wrote early in the process, "The Co. . . . is S. L. C. [Samuel Langhorne Clemens]" (xlvii). The correspondence between the two shows, according to the California editors, that "Clemens

was indefatigable in directing every step" (xlvii). There is a contradiction, then: on the one side, the scholarly characterization of the
actual working relation between Clemens and Webster, in which
Clemens was not only active, but the senior, dominant figure, for
whom Webster was basically an agent; on the other side, the claim
that there was no authorial intention in the omission of the passage.
The myth of Frankenstein, the theory of alienation were invented to
deal with such situations, but the editors do not invoke them; they
simply make of Webster the representation of coercively conformist
commercial culture, set against the freedom of the author's creative
intentions. As a result of this defense of Twain's autonomy, the standard MLA certified text of *Huckleberry Finn* is now nearly five percent longer than any edition published during Twain's lifetime, by
virtue of including a passage of some five thousand words that is
identically available in another of his major works.

Here I briefly note the third point. The "Raftmen Episode" involves Huck's witnessing a series of boasts and stories that brilliantly encapsulate Twain's mastery of the local narrative materials
from which his art began. The logic of hypercanonization dictates
that Twain's single greatest book must include as much as possible
of his greatest writing. If some of the most wonderful pages from
Life on the Mississippi are now also to be found in *Huckleberry Finn*,
there will be that much less reason for anyone to read *Life on the
Mississippi*, and the dominance of literary narrative over local and
personal narratives will be further confirmed.

In principle, one might expect so substantial a change in the
canonical text of *Huckleberry Finn* to have drastic consequences for
our critical understanding; in fact it seems that critical argument
has at least a five percent margin of error. I know of no major interpretive argument about *Huckleberry Finn* which depends on the
presence, or the absence, of this episode. However excellent in itself,
it seems in no way essential to the whole—as Mark Twain originally judged in agreeing to omit it.

The Sales Pitch: Local Humor
vs. Literary Subversion

Despite *Huckleberry Finn*'s hypercanonicity, there is
continuing variance in the fundamental terms by which its place in
American literary history is to be understood, that is, in the question that I consider the essential inquiry of literary history, what

kind of work it is. It is now usual to read *Huckleberry Finn* in relation to our contemporary concerns with problems of race and the history of slavery in the United States, and it is hard to doubt that these issues are at least intensely relevant to any apt response to the work. Yet among the documents relating to the distribution of *Huckleberry Finn* is one that I find astonishing precisely because it opens a world of historical difference, which thwarts our expectations.

Clemens, you recall, had set up Webster's company to issue and sell *Huckleberry Finn*. The means of sale was subscription. Agents around the country were set up with territorial rights, and they went door-to-door selling subscriptions. Clemens insisted that the book would not come out until forty thousand subscriptions were sold. To assist in sales, agents were equipped with a prospectus for the book, which included an "abstract" of the book's "story," which I quote in full:

> the adventures of Huckleberry Finn, Tom Sawyer and a negro named Jim, who in their travels fall in with two tramps engaged in *taking in* the different country towns through which they pass, by means of the missionary dodge, the temperance crusade, or under any pretext that offers to *easily* raise a dishonest dollar. The writer follows these characters through their various adventures, until finally, we find the tramps properly and warmly clothed,—*with a coat of tar and feathers,*—and the boys and Jim escape their persecutions and return safely to their friends. (*Huckleberry* [1988], 846, emphasis in original)

Huckleberry Finn is described as a (belated) local narrative of southwestern humor. The King and Duke appear as the central selling point of the book; only the middle third of it in which they appear plays any role in the publicity. Although this description focuses on two rogues, it presents a far less countercultural book than the one that has been read for most of the last fifty years. Huck is never alone with Jim, and the inclusion of Tom suggests that they are not fleeing but frolicking. The issue of slavery is so far buried that Jim's unfree status is not even mentioned, let alone that it might provide any motive for the travels.

I'm not accusing Clemens of misleading advertising; rather, I'm suggesting that these documents point to problems in our historical understanding of how *Huckleberry Finn* came into the world. This abstract was still used in the 1889 *Publishers' Trade List Annual* advertisement (*Huckleberry* [1988] 850), long after it could be likely that the question of Jim's enslavement was being masked because of fear that the subject would not be attractive to potential buyers. (It was by no means uncommon for popular writings of the 1880s to address life under slavery. See, for an overview, the chapters "The South Begins to Write" and "The North Feels the Power of the Pen" in Buck, who, however, does not mention *Huckleberry Finn*, tacitly acknowledging its generic difference.) This critical interpretation of the book's shape and substance, this abstract, was put out by the young publisher whose every arrangement enjoyed, according to the California editors, "the accompaniment of an unremitting barrage of advice, assistance, and interference from his employer" (xlviii), the author, Mark Twain. Even where evidence is not available, the editors are certain that all advertising material had "at least the author's tacit approval" (843).

Literary history exposes radically different understandings of what, in the most basic sense, *Huckleberry Finn* is about, and the efforts of literary historians to place the book expose the argumentative structure of literary history. The dialectic terms most basic to literary history are tradition and innovation, and *Huckleberry Finn* has been placed solidly with both. As tradition, it has been understood as part of American romance, notably by Richard Chase (*The American Novel and Its Tradition* [1957]) and Leslie Fiedler (*Love and Death in the American Novel* [1960]), or as American pastoral by Leo Marx (*The Machine in the Garden* [1964]). As innovation, it has been seen as inaugurating the triumph of the vernacular in American prose, notably by Henry Nash Smith, and, again, Leo Marx, who will be discussed in the next chapter. The sense of Twain as innovative was, in the period before hypercanonization, especially fostered by those who wished themselves to be innovative. I think particularly of the early American prose modernists such as Sherwood Anderson (in his correspondence with Van Wyck Brooks [see Edmund Wilson, *The Shock of Recognition*]) and Ernest Hemingway (in *The Green Hills of Africa*: "All modern American literature comes from one book by Mark Twain called *Huckleberry Finn*" [22]). The issue of linguistic innovation helps elucidate Twain's status as iconoclastic idol.

Twain vs. Cooper: Literary vs. National

I shall come finally to Twain's divergences from national narrative as exemplified by Fenimore Cooper's *The Pioneers*, but my starting point will be Mark Twain's major work of literary criticism, one of the most successful, best-known critical essays in English, "Fenimore Cooper's Literary Offenses." As its title suggests, Twain's essay is a bill of indictment, an act of offense in the guise of judgment. The essay's force springs from the double cross of its opening. Twain begins parodically with three epigraphs, in which the revered Cooper is extravagantly praised by Professors Lounsbury and Matthews and by the famous English novelist Wilkie Collins, but Twain's critique of Cooper makes his readers eventually find in the language of these authorities the same complacent woolliness he has found in Cooper. So Twain offers all the pleasure of a violent assault on the establishment.

But in this essay Twain himself appears not as a wild man, a western rule breaker, but precisely in the role of a pseudo-neo-Aristotelian, enunciator of eighteen inflexible rules that Cooper can be shown to have violated. Twain's rational-technical authority stands against the traditional authority of Cooper, and the English, and the professors. Twain does not himself historicize his argument with Cooper, except for one moment when he speculates that perhaps Cooper's procedures would make sense if it were possible to believe that there ever "was a time when time was of no value to a person who thought he had something to say" ("Fenimore" 592). The very terms of Twain's concession point to its incredibility; time has been money in America at least since Ben Franklin, a century before Cooper. A time in which time had no value would be, by the very words, a worthless time. Twain treats Cooper as a contemporary, that is, as a fellow author confronting a timeless realm of practical rules. Twain attempts to persuade us that Cooper's work is no longer writable and is readable only for those in a state of distraction, their levels of attention set at near zero.

Twain represents Cooper's failings as sensory, failures of eye and ear. Cooper's "ear was satisfied with the *approximate* word" ("Fenimore" 593, emphasis in original), not the "right word," but only its "second cousin" (584). Because of his "poor ear for words," Cooper was guilty of "literary flatting and sharping": "you perceive what he is intending to say, but you also perceive that he doesn't *say* it" (593, emphasis in original). Sensorily handicapped as he was, Cooper "failed to notice that the man who talks corrupt English six days in the week must and will talk it on the seventh, and can't help himself" (592). Mark Twain does not believe in linguistic Sunday best, the flexible usage that scholars know as "code-switching." Cooper was not just half deaf; he was half blind too. Twain ignores the fact that the French novelist Balzac adapted the tense alertness of Cooper's woodsmen to highlight the perceptual intensity required for life in Paris; for Twain Cooper was not "an observer" (586). Cooper could not "see the commonest little every-day matters accurately" (587). If he had, "his inventive faculty would have worked better; not more interestingly, but more rationally, more plausibly" (586). In one episode that Twain mockingly analyzes at length, Cooper's imprecision concerning speed and distance means that "the inaccuracy of the details throws a sort of air of fictitiousness and general improbability" over the whole business (589).

Twain's vocabulary of judgment echoes the etymological history of its terms: *plausible* and *probable* both originated as terms of social approbation but have come to be used as if they were absolutes, and so Twain versus Cooper. Nowadays when to read Cooper at all requires, as Yvor Winters already argued over fifty years ago, "an act of sympathetic historical imagination" (182), it is clear that Twain's terms were those that most effectively served to emphasize the differences between the emerging standards of taste of his time, standards that he was actively fostering in this essay, and the standards of Cooper's time, still residual in Twain's. By downplaying his own innovation, by emphasizing not tradition but rather the eye and ear, the plausible and probable, terms that are conventionally understood as unchanging "nature," Twain sets his critique as little as possible in the realm of the overtly ideological. He might, for instance, have attacked Cooper on the grounds that Cooper was the "American Scott," a liability both on nationalist cultural grounds and, more particularly for Twain, because Twain believed that Scott had exercised a disastrous influence on Southern culture (*Mississippi* 500–502).

But Twain does not address the ethical-national issues raised by the comparison of Cooper to Scott; he shifts the ground to linguistic and aesthetic issues. Yet Twain's technically rational standards of observation and consistency, based on the regularities of the natural world and human nature, rule out of court the possibility that people may speak in several distinct registers for different purposes, at different times, with different interlocutors. Twain insists on linguistic consistency as the index of a psychologically and socially unified identity. In *Huckleberry Finn* the only characters who manifest the variable linguistic usages of which he accuses Cooper are the King and the Duke, and they are frauds. Twain would explain that their variation occurs because they are bad people, not because they are badly written. Cooper, however, offers a different view of linguistic instability. In *The Pioneers,* Cooper notes that Judge Temple, raised as a Quaker, tends to fall into Quaker idiom at moments of passion, as does his daughter to a lesser degree. Neither the Judge nor his daughter is a fraud, but neither has the kind of stability Twain requires. In the United States of the later nineteenth century, as is emphatically the case now, questions of educating immigrants and members of culturally distinct but long settled groups necessarily involved thinking through questions of what it might mean to use situationally variable languages, but this is no concern of *Huckleberry Finn.* Jim speaks for the book when he answers Huck's question, "Spose a man was to come to you and say *Polly-voo-franzy*—what would you think?" Jim answers, "I wouldn' think nuff'n; I'd take en bust him over de head" (97). And yet roughly within what would have been Jim's lifetime, Missouri had been part of the Louisiana territory controlled by France.

The whole book of *Huckleberry Finn,* of course, does not confine itself to a single form of English. Twain's initial note on the language of his book proposes an agenda of dialect accuracy that has been studied and warranted by generations of scholars:

> In this book a number of dialects are used, to wit: the Missouri negro dialect; the extremest form of the backwoods South-Western dialect; the ordinary "Pike-County" dialect; and four modified varieties of this last. The shadings have not been done in a hap-hazard fashion, or by guess-work; but pains-takingly, and with the trustworthy guidance and support of personal familiarity with these several forms of speech.
>
> I make this explanation for the reason that without it many readers would suppose that all these characters were trying to talk alike and not succeeding. (lvii)

For Twain, it is important that characters sound not like each other but each like her or himself.

Yet Cooper, too, in *The Pioneers* made a work to serve as the repository for a great range of voices, as a registry for American idiosyncrasies of speech. Despite all that Twain says against his offenses, Cooper represents in *The Pioneers* a wide range of American immigrant, regional, professional, and ethnic linguistic varieties:

representations of English spoken by American blacks and Indians; the socially pretentious Essex County New England talk of Tabitha the housekeeper and the Jacksonian-Democratic New Englandism of Billy Kirby the Vermonter; the jargons of doctors and lawyers; English as spoken by New York Dutch, a French emigré, and a Cornishman, as well as the cultivated transatlantic English of young Effingham, not to mention again the Temples and Natty.

I want to develop further this comparison of *Huckleberry Finn* and *The Pioneers,* because Twain's stylistic innovation in presenting an extended vernacular narrative of comprehensive scope and great emotional power has effectively rendered invisible a series of extraordinary similarities between these two works. Once these similarities are recognized, it is then possible to define more precisely the divergences of Twain's literary narrative from Cooper's national narrative. Cooper's national narrative is grounded from its words on up in claims that were no longer representable aesthetically or politically to Twain and many of his contemporaries. National narratives held a positive understanding of the course of American history, and their writers believed it was a responsibility of culturally ambitious and important narrative not only to show but also to make explicit this understanding. Literary narratives denied any such responsibility, challenged any such understanding, and developed techniques to supersede such explicitness. American studies has most often struggled to reincorporate literary narrative into a renewed national allegory, undertaking to explicate what was programmatically, even polemically, left silent. William Dean Howells, during Twain's lifetime, humorously predicted and warned against a future of "forming Mark Twain societies to read philanthropic meanings into his jokes, or studying the 'Jumping Frog' as the allegory of an imperializing republic" (Cady 351). Howells memorialized Twain as "the Lincoln of our literature" (*My* 741), but he knew the difference between literature and politics.

The ground of resemblance between *Huckleberry Finn* and *The Pioneers* that I find most primary is the setting in place and time. Each book locates its action a full generation back in the setting that was its author's childhood home. Living in New York City around 1820, Cooper wrote back to the frontier days of Cooperstown, set in 1793. Living in Hartford around 1880, Twain set his action in "the Mississippi valley forty to fifty years ago." Both books are sharply divided between satire and idyll. They satirically portray the small-town social interactions that make up much of the work's fictional substance, but they ecstatically evoke the beauties of the natural world that are set in contrast with town life. Both books locate important values in a smaller social group particularly linked to the natural setting. Moreover, in both books this smaller, marginal group is single-sex and biracial. Leslie Fiedler has made the resemblances in the relations between Chingachgook and Natty Bumppo and Huck and Jim unforgettable points of reference for thinking about the history of American culture. In each case a single individual is made to carry the burden of typifying a whole group. This technique has not been confined to novelists: until the last few years historians almost inevitably wrote of "the Negro," "the Indian," as if there were indeed only one such person.

Both *The Pioneers* and *Huckleberry Finn* establish a crucial scene of conflict between the white outsider and the law, setting up an opposition between human nature and the state which reinforces the contrast between landscape and town. Both works rely on a mystery plot to bring about their conclusions, and in both the white outsider resists remaining within the bounds of the civilized scope that the book has delimited. Natty ends as "foremost in that band of Pioneers, who are opening the way for the march of the nation across the continent" (465). Huck aims to "light out for the Territory" (362). The differences that appear on the ground of these resemblances help to define the historical shift from Cooper's time to Twain's, from a time when national narrative was still emergent to a moment when its authority was again, more effectively than in 1850, challenged by literary narrative. Not that literary narrative wholly superseded national narrative in the 1880s: *The Grandissimes* (1880), by George W. Cable, a writer closely associated with Twain during the later phases of the writing of *Huckleberry Finn,* is much more like Cooper than Twain in the respects I discuss.

In the context of my argument, and developing further the analysis of chapter 2, the outstanding difference between Twain and Cooper is that Twain isolates the historical setting of his book. Cooper through his plot and his narrative voice brings the settlement of 1793 into conjunction with at least three historical epochs: with the period of colonial exploration and initial relations between whites and Indians; with the Revolutionary War that brought the United States into existence as the sovereign authority replacing the British and that also significantly altered property relations within the white world and between whites and Indians; and finally, the narrator acknowledges the changes that have further transformed American life since the time of the novel's action.

In contrast, Twain's aesthetic choice requires that Huck have almost no historical perspective on the land he lives in, either in its local or national dimensions, and there is no narrative presence beyond Huck to open up a deeper past or to link his time and concerns to those of the time Twain was writing in. So rigorously dramatic is Twain's technique, by which any voice that appears must belong to a character, that he requires stage directions to place the novel's events. The title page is inscribed "Scene: The Mississippi Valley; Time: Forty to Fifty Years Ago" (liii).

The Revolution is not part of Cooper's novel, but it is part of what makes the world of that novel intelligible, and it is therefore included by reference. The Civil War is not part of Twain's novel, and it is not in any way textually present, although without its having occurred the meaning we read in *Huckleberry Finn* would be, we think, wholly different. When excerpts from *Huckleberry Finn* ran in the *Century* magazine (December 1884–February 1885), they appeared in issues crammed with Civil War memoirs. In November 1884, the *Century* had begun a massive feature on the Civil War that was so popular it ran for three years; Twain's "Private History of a Campaign That Failed" (1885) was contributed to it. Yet there is no published evidence I know of—whether in the papers of the *Century* editor, Richard Watson Gilder, in Twain's correspondence, or in any reviews or notices—that registered the conjunction of these materials with *Huckleberry Finn*. It is certainly appropriate, even imperative, for historical criticism now to take such juxtapositions into account. My claim, however, is that we have as yet failed to take account of the formal absences and historical silences that are primary data to be interpreted before assimilating the work into a larger context. We must explain the blanks before filling them in.

The difference I have been establishing between *Huckleberry Finn* and *The Pioneers* bears also on the way the mystery plot works in the two books. In *Huckleberry Finn* the mystery—or double mystery, the death of Huck's pap and the freeing of Jim—both take place within the time frame of the main narrative, while in *The Pioneers*, the mysteries have to do with events before the action of the book opens. In Cooper, the revelation of these events gives meaning to what was obscure during the book's narration, but in *Huckleberry Finn,* as many readers and critics have observed, the revelation of the hidden events diminishes the meaning of what seemed the book's action: Huck's flight from his pap, Jim's flight from slavery. In keeping with the tendency of literary narrative to focus on the "sensitive spectator," and in the spirit that Trilling ascribed to Dewey, where the "gesture" of moral style becomes more crucial than what is actually done, these motives are erased as fully as they are in the advertising prospectus. By the same token, the reference in Huck's first sentence to the book *Tom Sawyer,* which initially suggests that an older Huck is narrating from the present time of publication, is nullified by Huck's explanation on the last page that he has composed his narrative almost immediately after the conclusion of its events.

The conflicts between laws of the state and values taken as nature's, that is, as grounded in the American land, are also handled very differently by Twain and Cooper. I find that *The Pioneers* succeeds in making readers feel pulled both ways between the claims of the law as represented by Judge Temple and the claims of custom and nature in Natty Bumppo; in contrast, I do not know of any reader who has believed that Huck should have turned in Jim. Moreover, as argued in chapter 2 of this book, the crisis of judgment in chapter 31 of *Huckleberry Finn* is treated purely internally; Huck is by himself. He describes his decision in terms that evoke the sharp senses Twain valued but denied to Cooper. Huck repeats that he could "see" Jim (270), but this is only in memory; Jim is not there. Moreover, it is a crucial feature of Twain's scene that legal penalties never occur to Huck as he thinks over the situation, only religious retribution. All this is very different from *The Pioneers.* A full courtroom scene is mounted, in which the force and value of the law are presented, even as the actual legal agents are mocked and criticized.

A comparable difference may be defined in the treatment of what I have called the registry of American voices. In *Huckleberry Finn* readers have found no other voice with the authority of Huck's. In *The Pioneers,* however, many readers have found Natty's voice to exceed in authority Judge Temple's or even the authorial narrator's. More broadly, in the terms that Bakhtin has made familiar to recent literary study, we may understand the different voices of *The*

Pioneers as indices for the struggles among different social groups, while in *Huckleberry Finn* this is much less frequently and forcibly the case. Indeed, as early as the narratives of the anti-Jacksonian, Whig congressman Davy Crockett in the 1830s, a written folk voice was put to use for elite politics, while in the 1840s the abolitionist escaped slave Frederick Douglass wrote to a highly formal standard rather than using vernacular. The powerful voices of pap in his tirade against the "govment" (33–34) and Colonel Sherburn against the lynch mob are isolated grotesques rather than integral parts of an action, while the kindly Gospel teachings of Widow Douglas are simply forgotten at the moment Huck's mind turns in crisis to religious terror.

Huckleberry Finn emerges from these comparisons as a much more powerfully centered work than *The Pioneers* in the conjunction it effects between its hero and its narrative language. *Huckleberry Finn* is famous in critical tradition for displacing narrative and linguistic authority from the traditional centers to a character marginal in any number of defined ways, yet it is not certain that *The Pioneers* may not be a much more fundamentally multifocal, and in that sense uncentered, work. Cooper's concern is the process of civilization, which requires many human agents in a variety of roles. For instance, Cooper sets the values of property and mobility into historical tension through contrasting Natty and Effingham. Through the course of the book they live and hunt together with Chingachgook, but after the Indian's death Natty goes out west, while Effingham enjoys marriage and his rightful inheritance after the death of his long-missing and hidden father. Huck, in contrast, both plans to light out for the territory and also finds six thousand dollars rightly restored to him after Pap's death. Twain consolidates the values of Natty's mobility and Effingham's wealth into his single idealized figure of Huck.

Again, *Huckleberry Finn* is famous for bringing crucial moral issues to bear on and in the psyche of it protagonist, yet this too is a further centering; the form and fable of *Huckleberry Finn* reject the very possibility of clashing voices in public debate. After the political failures that led to the Civil War, after the political failures that brought Reconstruction to an end, Twain's literary narrative takes the obliquity of radical ellipsis. In Cooper's national narrative, the light of American nature insures that Natty will feel right about what he did; in the national narrative of *Uncle Tom's Cabin* the light of grace insures that readers who respond properly to the horrors of slavery will "feel right." Huck Finn lives so as to feel right with no sanction beyond his own psyche, the imaginative construction of an autonomous self that is the cultural work of literary narrative, and that Lionel Trilling made the keynote of his anti-Stalinism.

7
Vernacular and Nationality
Comparative Contexts for Chapter 19

This chapter is somewhat intricate. I begin by laying out and considering Leo Marx's argument for Twain's hypercanonization as a founder of American "vernacular." Marx argued that the vernacular revolted against the "genteel tradition," in which Americans adapted old British and European models of high culture. In three phases I challenge this position, which has become a mainstay commonplace of American studies. First, a British context: I contrast Marx's premises for cultural study with those of his British contemporary Raymond Williams. Second, an American context: I argue that the genteel tradition was more complex and vigorous than in Marx's model and that Twain was much closer to the genteel tradition than has been generally granted. Third, European contexts: Twain's relations to the genteel tradition allow useful comparison of *Huckleberry Finn* with work by Twain's European contemporaries, some of whose characteristic techniques and problems he shared.

The Vernacularist Argument

In the previous chapter, I discussed *Huckleberry Finn* in relation to American hypercanonization, the nationalization of literary narrative that defines exemplary national values in works that do not propose them, while neglecting works with an explicitly national agenda, such as Cooper's *Pioneers.* This wish to allegorize, to read into works what the authors have excluded from them, is strengthened by an aesthetic of understatement—the less explicit interpretive guidance the narrator provides, the more room for critics to spell out the implications they see. The technique of understatement worked out by Mark Twain in *Huckleberry Finn* was identified by Henry Nash Smith as a potentially "subversive" mode of "vernacular protest" (*Development* vii).

But what is meant by this laudatory term *vernacular*? How did this term *vernacular* come to occupy a key place in discussions of Twain and other major writers? What is the value of maintaining it? The term was not part of nineteenth-century discussions of what Cmiel calls "popular language" in the United States, nor does it figure with any prominence in such key works as H. L. Mencken's *The American Language* (1919), Constance Rourke's *American Humor* (1931), Walter Blair's *Native American Humor* (1937), F. O. Matthiessen's *American Renaissance* (1941), and B. A. Botkin's *Treasury of American Folklore* (1944). The earliest relevant usage is DeVoto's. In *Mark Twain's America* (1932) he dismissed "dialect" as a small matter but brought "vernacular" to the fore: "the important thing to be observed about Huckleberry's speech is its achievement in making the vernacular a perfect instrument for all the necessities of fiction" (317). DeVoto understood Twain's vernacular "innovation" as beginning to come to "fruition" only "in the last few years," that is, in the twenties perhaps with the work of Twain's great admirers Anderson and Hemingway.

The years after the end of the Second World War were imagined by many to inaugurate the "American Century" that would follow from the rise of the United States to the position of morally best and economically and militarily most powerful state in the world, and the establishment and proliferation of scholarly research in American studies renewed nationalist themes familiar from more than a century earlier, when the United States had first tried to define itself as an independent culture. Only in the years after World War II did *vernacular* emerge with the prominence it still maintains. In that postwar period it functioned among the founding premises for the institutionalization of literary American studies. The two crucial figures, Henry Nash Smith and Leo Marx, were both early graduates of the doctoral program in American civilization, which DeVoto had helped to found in the 1930s before leaving Harvard. Their specific premise is that Twain, together with Walt Whitman, inaugurated what Smith in the 1948 *Literary History of the United States* called, in praise, "the intrusion of the vernacular into consciously literary usage" ("Widening" 650). A decade later, Marx developed this claim in "The Vernacular Tradition in American Literature," which as late as 1988 Marx placed first in the warmly reviewed volume of his collected essays.

Since the early 1950s, no critic has been more identified with the praise and analysis of *Huckleberry Finn*'s vernacular than Leo Marx. Marx was an undergraduate student of F. O. Matthiessen and Perry Miller at Harvard in the late 1930s and then their graduate student after the Second World War, and he was a junior colleague of Henry Nash Smith at Minnesota in the early 1950s. Having won the 1995 lifetime accomplishment award of the American Studies Association, Marx is one of the few figures still active who reaches back to the beginnings of organized American studies. Still in print four decades later, his book of 1964, *The Machine in the Garden: Technology and the Pastoral Ideal in America,* remains a landmark for its combination of economic, technological, and literary history with acute close reading of key passages and a strongly felt contemporary political concern. In 1988 a collection of his influential essays, *The Pilot and the Passenger,* received wide appreciation. His work continues to stand as representative and authoritative. Moreover, despite significant problems that I will raise with it, its quality makes it worth further thought.

In the self-defining introduction (1988) to his essays in *The Pilot and the Passenger,* Marx allied his work with the decisive polemic of Lionel Trilling's "Reality in America" in *The Liberal Imagination* (1950)—despite his severe criticism of Trilling in "Mr. Eliot, Mr. Trilling, and *Huckleberry Finn*," which is included in the collection. The essence of American reality, Trilling argued, is "dialectic." This means, as Marx developed the point, that the most significant works of American culture concern, and contain, a "struggle, or at least debate" central to the culture. Therefore these works will be "dissonant, conflictual," and even "self-contradictory," as I find Marx himself at moments (x). The new-critical notion of paradox is here raised to the point of disruption. Marx updated Trilling by joining his dialectic with the "dialogic" principle of Mikhail Bakhtin, whose work I have discussed in chapter 2. This critical theory of language is then folded back into the American literary tradition: the "masterworks" of Melville and Twain, that is, the hypercanonic *Moby-Dick* and *Huckleberry Finn,* "are brilliant studies (and expressions) of [what Bakhtin calls] 'heteroglossia'" (xi). In particular, *Huckleberry Finn* may be understood as the result of Twain's working through a particular American dialectic, "the prevalence of the conflict between the genteel and the vernacular mindsets in the United States" (xv). This attempt to resolve such a conflict made possible "Twain's greatest invention," the "distinctive, supple, evocative prose style of *Huckleberry Finn*" (xiv).

That style is central to the keynote essay of Marx's collection, "The Vernacular Tradition in American Literature" (1958). Marx began with Cooper, in the spirit of Twain's essay on Cooper's literary offenses. Marx claimed that "the language of Cooper is not all that different" from the language of the British historical novelist Walter Scott, and that therefore in Cooper's generation "the boundary between British and American literature remains uncertain" (3). Twain and Walt Whitman are the "two great seminal figures of modern American writing," because in "Song of Myself" and *Huckleberry Finn*, "the line" becomes "much more distinct." In these works "they establish once and for all the literary usefulness of the native idiom." Because they "fashioned a vernacular mode," they made possible a "national style" (4). This national vernacular, Marx explained, contrasts to what George Santayana had called the "genteel tradition," and therefore its challenge extends more broadly, beyond literature to a whole way of life.

For Marx, the vernacular tradition is not merely a matter of language; it also carries with it social values: "the core of the American vernacular . . . is not simply a style, but a style with a politics in view" (8). This style "is a vehicle for the affirmation of an egalitarian faith so radical that we can scarcely credit it today" (8). Its "political ideal is freedom," both positively and negatively: negatively, "freedom *from* the oppression of society"; positively, "freedom *to* establish . . . egalitarian community" (16). This political agenda is carried by the vernacular "style developed in a new society in a prehistoric landscape," and so Marx found that the vernacular "receives its final sanction from nature itself" (17).

Marx elaborated his claim about Twain's vernacular in the 1956 essay from which his collection takes its title, "The Pilot and the Passenger: Landscape Conventions and the Style of *Huckleberry Finn*." Marx examined several passages from Twain's work describing the Mississippi. The first two are from *Life on the Mississippi*; they set up the problem that, Marx argues, Twain overcame in *Huckleberry Finn*. In *Life on the Mississippi*, the riverboat passenger's conventionally established schemata of landscape description are revealed as false and inadequate by the technically knowledgeable perceptions of the riverboat pilot, but there is no dialectic, only destruction. A brute knowledge eliminates all pleasure and offers instead only human manipulation of nature. Marx argued that through Huck, Twain restored a relation between the two modes of perception. Thereby, in a dialectical synthesis, Twain "regained that unity of thought and feeling he felt himself, along with his contemporaries, to be losing" (32). Marx made this claim despite being well aware that T. S. Eliot, the most admired living critic, had proclaimed any unity of thought and feeling already long lost, since the "dissociation of sensibility" in the earlier seventeenth century (*Selected* 247).

Here is the passage Marx invoked as proof text, the opening of chapter 19, a passage that three decades later Janet McKay asserted had received "more critical attention . . . than any other passage" (153):

> Two or three days and nights went by; I reckon I might say they swum by, they slid along so quiet and smooth and lovely. Here is the way we put in the time. It was a monstrous big river down there—sometimes a mile and a half wide; we run nights and laid up and hid day-times; soon as night was most gone, we stopped navigating and tied up—nearly always in the dead water under a towhead; and then cut young cotton-woods and willows and hid the raft with them. Then we set out the lines. Next we slid into the river and had a swim, so as to freshen up and cool off; then we set down on the sandy bottom where the water was about knee deep, and watched the daylight come. Not a sound, anywheres—perfectly still—just like the whole world was asleep, only sometimes the bull-frogs a-cluttering, maybe. The first thing to see, looking away over the water, was a kind of dull line—that was the woods on t'other side—you couldn't make nothing else out; then a pale place in the sky; then more paleness spreading around; then the river softened up, away off, and warn't black any more, but gray; you could see little dark spots drifting along, ever so far away—trading scows, and such things; and long black streaks—rafts; sometimes you could hear a sweep screaking; or jumbled up voices, it was so still, and sounds come so far; and by and by you could see a streak on the water which you know by the look of the streak that there's a snag there in a swift current which breaks on it and makes that streak look that way; and you see the mist curl up off of the water, and the east reddens up, and the river, and you make out

a log cabin in the edge of the woods, away on the bank on t'other side of the river, being a wood-yard, likely, and piled by them cheats so you can throw a dog through it anywheres; then the nice breeze springs up, and comes fanning you from over there, so cool and fresh, and sweet to smell, on account of the woods and the flowers; but sometimes not that way, because they've left dead fish laying around, gars, and such, and they do get pretty rank; and next you've got the full day, and everything smiling in the sun, and the song-birds just going it!

A little smoke couldn't be noticed now, so we could take some fish off of the lines, and cook up a hot breakfast. And afterwards we would watch the lonesomeness of the river, and kind of lazy along, and by and by lazy off to sleep. Wake up, by and by, and look to see what done it, and maybe see a steamboat, coughing along up stream, so far off towards the other side you couldn't tell nothing about her only whether she was stern-wheel or side-wheel; then for about an hour there wouldn't be anything to hear nor nothing to see—just solid lonesomeness. Next you'd see a raft sliding by, away off yonder, and maybe a galoot on it chopping, because they're most always doing it on a raft; you'd see the axe flash, and come down—you don't hear nothing; you see that axe go up again, and by the time it's above the man's head, then you hear the *k'chunk!*—it had took all that time to come over the water. So we would put in the day, lazying around, listening to the stillness. Once there was a thick fog, and the rafts and things that went by was beating tin pans so the steamboats wouldn't run over them. A scow or a raft went by so close we could hear them talking and cussing and laughing—heard them plain; but we couldn't see no sign of them; it made you feel crawly, it was like spirits carrying on that way in the air. Jim said he believed it was spirits; but I says:

"No, spirits wouldn't say, 'dern the dern fog.'"

Marx emphasized that Huck is a "participant" in the scene, although to my reading this participation is in the mode, discussed in the last chapter, of the "sensitive spectator" of literary narrative. For Marx, this "immediacy" of relation means that the passage is full of "concrete details" that are rendered "as subjective sense impressions" ("dull line . . . pale place . . . little dark spots . . . long black streaks"). Because of Huck's immediate relation to his experience, he has no "abstract conception" of the scene or events, whether the passenger's abstraction of landscape convention or the pilot's abstraction of technical knowledge. Consequently, he can "account for *all* the facts" of the scene: not only songbirds, but also wood-yard cheats and rank dead fish. The features of the scene are not represented as "fixed, absolute, or perfect," but rather as "approximations" in motion over time ("sometimes . . . nearly always . . . likely . . . maybe . . . most always"). As opposed to either the pilot or the passenger, Huck is "literally immersed" in the scene, knee-deep in the water. Marx claimed therefore, that Huck "'belongs' to this landscape in that his language is native to it" (28–29).

In thinking over Marx's argument as a basis for an American cultural history keyed to style, the first question I am struck by is the instability of the key term "vernacular." Marx did not remark its etymological history, which I find provocative. It comes from Latin *verna*, a slave born in the master's house, and it thus carries from its beginnings the problematic of domination and domestication. Moreover, the Latin word is apparently of Etruscan derivation, and thus itself a domesticated, subjugated alien. The current senses listed in *The American Heritage Dictionary* for the noun *vernacular* suggest the problems I find. Sense 1 is "the standard native language of a country or locality"; sense 2 is "the nonstandard or substandard everyday speech of a country or locality." In considering these senses, we might think of the model of Latin vis-à-vis the emerging Romance languages (the "vernaculars"), in order to understand the two senses as perspectival, positional variants of a single situation. From the point of view of the Roman Empire, the second sense ("substandard, everyday") predominated, but from the point of view of nations in formation, the first ("standard, native"). Both senses leave equivocal the issue of "country or locality," that is, in the terms I have been using in this book, whether vernacular is national or local. It would seem that Twain in his note on the dialects of *Huckleberry Finn*, which I discussed in the previous chapter, emphasizes the local, but clearly Marx's argument emphasized the national.

The distinction between standard native language and non- or substandard everyday speech throws back into crisis the whole question of American literary nationality: is there a standard American language, or are there only innumerable everyday variations, differing by "locality"? What does it mean to imply that, as masterpieces of "the vernacular," *Leaves of Grass* and *Huckleberry Finn* have the relation to past British and future American languages that the *Divine Comedy* and the *Decameron* do to past Latin and future Italian? At least it makes us ask whether Marx's praise of vernacular does not in fact work to fix a vernacular *standard*, as the great Renaissance writers did for their European cultures through the prestige they were accorded in critical and educational practices. That is, having been used to define one set of bounds (America versus the Old World), vernacular becomes a means for drawing further bounds within the United States, as to what will count as authentically "American." The question of imperial standpoint remains: for whom will it count? How will it be enforced?

The third sense of vernacular in *The American Heritage Dictionary* further emphasizes this problem of representativeness: "the idiom of a particular trade or profession." In other words, here vernacular means much the same as jargon: not what is common but what is peculiar or particular to a closed group. Marx observes of a word from *Huckleberry Finn, fan-tods,* that he would feel the need to gloss it for a foreign audience, but that "a native audience can be relied on to get the point." Yet in fact the *OED* entry for *fantod* refers to it as a variant of *fantad,* which in turn is documented from specialized glossaries of British sailor talk and for the regions of Leicestershire and Dorsetshire.

The *OED* defines the adjective *vernacular,* as applied to "a language or dialect": "naturally spoken by the people of a particular country or district; native; indigenous." The term "naturally" here startles me by its biologizing, antihistorical tendency. The *OED* glosses the definition by adding, "usually applied to the native speech of a populace, in contrast to another or others acquired for commercial, social, or educative purposes; now frequently employed with reference to that of the working classes or peasantry." This emphasizes what I have already suggested, the extent to which "vernacular" as a notion depends on a system of social stratification and hierarchy. Marx understood vernacular as insurgent, representing popular values that oppose those of an elite. But, on the other hand, as I argued in the previous chapter, Twain's own concern with rigorous dialect consistency (as in the prefatory "Note") suggests that this is not his perspective on the matter. As his attack on Cooper emphasizes, he is programmatically not interested in the interactions within a single speaker of the socially distinct language usages that that speaker may live.

Marx's usages around "vernacular" share the complications that the dictionaries have made explicit. He treated the vernacular as an American "native idiom," and thus the basis for a "national style." But what is the relation between native and national here? First off, we may note that the dictionaries mention vernacular as not only native but also indigenous. What is the difference? Precisely the historical depth of settlement. While the U.S.-born children of immigrants might be native, they are not indigenous. Only those whom we now call "Native Americans" would be indigenous. In the earlier-nineteenth-century discussions of the possibilities of an American literary nationality for the United States, this problem was directly addressed, namely, that the Indians, the historically rooted inhabitants of what had become the United States, spoke as their mother tongues languages that were not the English language of the politically dominant culture. Marx's happy emphasis on Twain's "native" language can only seem an attempt to forget this problem.

But, as I argued in the previous chapter, in Twain's time as in the twentieth century, the opposite problem was also crucial, that is, the problem of immigrant speakers. Marx's definition of vernacular seems to allow no room for this feature of American language and life. Whitman, however clumsily, deliberately incorporated foreign words into his poetry, and many twentieth-century students of American English have found much of its distinctive difference from British English to spring precisely from idioms (words, inflections, syntactic patterns) drawn from other languages. The "creolized" character of American English defines its specific character—but, insofar as this term refers to the process of acculturation by which any two cultures in contact and struggle with each other produce something new, then of course modern British English is itself also a creolized product of intercultural encounters. Marx's emphasis on "native," however useful as a polemical term against the transatlantic import from Britain, ignores the specific clashes and synergies of different language groups in the United States, and thereby inadvertently gives comfort to some of the most distressing tendencies of American nativism—despite his own apt caution against chauvinism.

Marx not only joined the native and the national, but also added the natural to these. The "final sanction" to the vernacular comes from "nature itself" in the "prehistoric landscape." Here Marx idealized and abstracted Twain's text, for steamboats and rafts are inescapably part of Huck's landscape, a copresence that existed only for a few specific decades. So too, when he claimed that Huck, immersed up to his knees in the water, "belongs" to the landscape as "native to it," Marx ignored the force of Twain's note on dialect, namely, that Huck speaks differently from the people he encounters as he goes down the river. He carries Pike County language with him, and he is by now well south of his native Missouri.

The problems with Marx's sense of the "natural" may be seen most clearly in his discussion of a passage from *Life on the Mississippi* that he placed in relation to *Huckleberry Finn*. Twain reports a "strange and tragic accident." Captain Poe and his wife lived on their steamboat. "One night the boat struck a snag . . . and sank with astonishing suddenness." Since there was "water already well above the cabin floor" when the captain got back, "He cut into his wife's stateroom from above with an axe; she was asleep in the upper berth, the roof a flimsier one than he supposed; the first blow crashed down through the rotten boards and clove her skull." Marx argued that in contrast to the "beautiful . . . river" of the conventional sunrise passage, here, in the very next paragraph of *Life on the Mississippi*, is "the murderous river" (*Mississippi* 417–18). In *Life on the Mississippi* the two are segregated textually, but in *Huckleberry Finn* the description of the streaks produced by snags shows that "Huck now accepts that fearful principle of nature responsible for the death of Captain Poe's wife" (30).

Marx seems to have ignored what makes Mrs. Poe's death "strange and tragic" enough to narrate, namely, that its agent was not the river but the captain, acting in the best way he knew how. Had he not smashed in with the axe, the principle of nature that rotted the boards might even have allowed his wife to break through them to safety. It is not nature that deals death here, but the man. Although he is thus more "responsible" than nature is for the outcome, he is no more "murderous" than the river: an accident is no murder. The questions of human agency evaded in Marx's language of the natural open political questions no less than do the instabilities in the sense of vernacular. Marx, who aimed to be a politically aware and engaged critic, has nonetheless joined the national hypercanonization.

I consider it especially important to show this troubling tendency in Marx, because Marx is himself the author of one of the strongest statements against the idolatry of *Huckleberry Finn* that, as he recognized, had begun in American criticism in the years immediately after the Second World War. In 1953, very early in the hypercanonizing process, in "Mr. Eliot, Mr. Trilling, and *Huckleberry Finn*," he argued that the then-recent tendency to "unqualified praise" was as useless for the "problem of evaluating the book" as had been the earlier "parochial hostility" that marked some of its first reception (*Pilot* 38). Proposing as the book's formative impulse the "quest for freedom" (39), which as we have seen he identifies with the vernacular, he found that the long last sequence of the book (in which Tom Sawyer develops an "extravagant mock rescue of Nigger Jim" (38), who has in fact already been manumitted) betrays both the form and the meaning with which the book began. Marx judged, then, that Twain, "having revealed the tawdry nature of the culture of the great valley, yielded to its essential complacency," and he further charged that for modern critics "to minimize the seriousness of what must be accounted a major flaw in so great a work is, in a sense, to repeat Clemens's failure of nerve" (53). This strong phrase, "failure of nerve," echoes a 1943 essay by Sidney Hook. Adapting the phrase from Gilbert Murray's characterization of Hellenistic Greek religion, Hook applied it to criticize the turn away from collective effort to personal concerns with sin and salvation. Marx was criticizing both Eliot's avowed Christian orthodoxy and Trilling's concern with Huck's "knowledge of human depravity."

Despite the valuable analysis achieved in this early essay, Marx in his own later work, as we have seen, fostered rather than combatted hypercanonization. In moving away from his vigorous 1953 critique not only of Trilling and Eliot, but also of *Huckleberry Finn*, he changed positions on several important issues, the most obvious being that Trilling became a source for defining his own position, rather than an object of criticism. Marx had criticized Trilling and Eliot for making of the Mississippi a "god" rather than recognizing that it is merely a "neutral agency" (44), but as we have seen in the discussion of Mrs. Poe's death, Marx himself later treated the river not as neutral but as "murderous." In the earlier essay of critique he identified the social values of loving solidarity between Huck and Jim as "a creed which they bring to the river" and which "neither emanates from" nor "is addressed to" any force of "nature." But in Marx's later praise for Huck's vernacular, he emphasized the native and the natural in the "prehistoric landscape" as a source of value. Most important, in 1953, when he cited Santayana's 1911 essay on the "genteel tradition," he also drew on Santayana's critique of those, such as Twain, who somewhat opposed the genteel but who provided "nothing solid to put in its place" (46). In Marx's essays on vernacular, however, the vernacular ethos and its attendant political values seemed to Marx far more solid than they had a few years earlier, or than they had to their contemporary observer Santayana. Yet over the decades since these pathbreaking essays of the 1950s, Marx remained aware that he was in somewhat of a bind.

Nearly thirty years later, Marx attempted to find a way out of the dilemma that compromised his position. He acknowledged that the "pastoral" literature on which he had focused his lifework represents the views of a "dissident intellectual minority," who stand in opposition to the "dominant culture" ("Pastoralism" 37). By the dominant culture Marx meant not a "majority," but the "most powerful and influential social groups" (67 n. 4). For Marx, the "nation's dominant elites" have held to a "progressive ideology" of material improvement, but classic American literature "does not contain a single work that champions, or even lends much credence" to, that ideology (52–53). Yet Marx found that the literary resistance to the dominant ideology was "confined to the relatively privileged group that would defend (or regain) residual values" (66). If the position of these writers was to become politically effective, he thought, it would require "alliances with the hitherto disadvantaged carriers of emergent values." The point of Marx's commitment to the vernacular had been to try to find, or define, a popular base for what his concern with pastoral has always acknowledged to be a minority concern. This tension, I think, helps to account for the waverings between trenchant cultural criticism and fuzzy populism in Marx's critical writings, and it is crucial for thinking about the standing of *Huckleberry Finn*.

A British Context: Leo Marx vs. Raymond Williams

In the recent essay in which he discussed "emergent" and "residual" social and cultural forces, Marx adopted the vocabulary of his British contemporary, Raymond Williams (1921–88). Williams, from *Culture and Society* (1958) to the end of his career, helped inspire and form the British intellectual movement known as "cultural studies." This movement now has widespread prestige in the United States as an alternative to the critical approaches of the Cold War period, but it closely parallels American studies. Both prefer interdisciplinary work that places literature (and other cultural products) in relation to the insights of the historical and social sciences, and both insist on studying far more than just master-pieces. The Birmingham Center for the Study of Contemporary Culture, the institutional home for British cultural studies, made Marx's *The Machine in the Garden* one of the first texts discussed in the exploratory working group in the middle 1960s out of which the characteristic work of the center emerged. Placing Marx and Williams together offers a first comparative context through which to pose alternative understandings of *Huckleberry Finn.*

Williams's *The Country and the City* (1973) almost seems a British version of *The Machine in the Garden.* Each book articulates two key terms that link the imagination to history, one associated with the past (garden, country), one with the future. Each explores the relations of the two terms over a range of centuries, through extended discussions of major works of canonic culture, but also by means of nitty-gritty from social and economic history, as well as less canonical works of fiction and polemic. Each offers a viewpoint substantially to the left of the established norms of official and academic culture. Each book is importantly concerned with modern versions (from the sixteenth into twentieth centuries) of the classical literary form of *pastoral*—most literally, literature concerned with shepherds, but more broadly, writing representing rural life as, in some sense, leisured. In Williams, this concern is quite direct, in Marx somewhat more oblique. Marx locates a recurrent moment in works by classical American writers: they flee industrialization (the machine) to a green world of nature (the garden), but they are honest enough to see that this green pastoral world never actually succeeds as a refuge but is always broken in on by the impact of industry. In *Huckleberry Finn,* life on the raft is the pastoral, interrupted by the machine when the steamboat runs down the raft. The "natural" values of the vernacular argument are, roughly, the pastoral values.

No doubt this similarity in their work explains why Marx was asked to write a major review essay on *The Country and the City,* which permits our further focus on differences between his position and Williams's that bear on the controversies over *Huckleberry Finn.* Marx found much to praise in Williams's great book, but his criticisms demand attention, for what Williams undertook in *The Country and the City* is a far more erudite and elaborate version of what pained parents and children do when they complain about the hypercanonic role of *Huckleberry Finn* in the schools.

In an interview about *The Country and the City*, Williams explained the "two kinds of judgment" that he thought must both operate in responsible critical work. As historians, we can recognize a work as "a major contribution to human culture" under the past circumstances of its production. Yet we must also be able to make a second judgment that bears less on the past than on the present and on the future. Speaking of a seventeenth-century poem by Ben Jonson discussed in his book, Williams explained, "if I cannot be seriously offended that he wrote out the labourers [by figurative language that made it seem that crops spontaneously offered themselves to the landowner] what affiliation can I now make to labourers?" Without the first, historical, understanding, any response will be merely "naïveté," Williams granted, but without the second understanding, he continued, "if you don't feel offence at his profoundly conventional mystification . . . then what is the meaning of solidarity?" (*Politics* 307). The question that defines *The Country and the City* is "where do I stand?" in relation to the "selective tradition" that cultural authorities have chosen to represent the rural past (*Country* 6, 18).

Marx, in "Between Two Landscapes," saw in Williams "a more sound basis for political than aesthetic judgments." Marx warned that this was a problem, because there is "no rule that obliges artists to concern themselves with the essential determinants of our being," rather than simply with "consciousness." Williams's concern with historical reality (were there really laborers, or did grain spring up as nature's homage to the owner?), Marx worried, "can lead to confusion when dealing with a mode like pastoral," which is a mode of fantasy governed by long-established cultural conventions.

Marx wrote as if he were pointing to a problem that resulted from some inadvertence of Williams's, but in fact he was challenging Williams's whole undertaking. Williams recognized that pastoral is a convention (in Jonson's case, a "profoundly conventional mystification"), and that as a convention it expresses a certain consciousness and also acts further to form consciousness. Williams's project in *The Country and the City* is to confront the convention with the social conditions to which it is obliquely related. If so-called country-house poems like Jonson's, according to a critical tradition derived from Eliot's "dissociation of sensibility" as developed by F. R. Leavis, present an idealized version of social relations, to whose advantage is this? And what are the effects on our current lives if we are taught in school to believe that there was once an organic way of life, expressed in these poems, which has been lost for us by urbanization or industrialization? In the United Kingdom, the myth, as criticized by Williams, involves nostalgia—idealizing the past, in order to claim that there has never been exploitation. In the United States, as I understand the debates over *Huckleberry Finn*, the myth idealizes the present by proposing a nontraumatic relation with the past—things were bad then, but that's all gone, and any sign of that bad past ("nigger") no longer has present power.

Marx deplored the consequences of Williams's "resistance to all that follows from the fact that art, in a bourgeois society, usually lends expression to a minority viewpoint." Marx asked of Williams, "Why should he expect anything else? This is particularly true of literature. After all, who produces it—and who consumes it?" His questions to Williams allowed Marx to formulate a new definition of the political significance of art: "the consciousness of the dominant class is a cardinal fact of political life," and since pastoral serves the social function of "justifying and assuaging the guilt and ambivalence of the dominant class," there is indeed a "political use" for pastoral. In contrast to Williams's exposure of how culture has been used as a means for enforcing and enhancing the social power of the ruling class, Marx explained that literature may permit "a better understanding of the divided state of the minority culture." Marx meant here the division between the members of the dominant class who subscribe to the ideology of material progress, and the members of the dominant class who imagine pastoral critiques of that ideology. This view offers no democratic hope for a literature that reaches beyond the dominant class.

If Williams ever expected that art was good for something other than to serve a minority, one reason would have been that in Britain as in the United States the study of literature is generally justified by a rhetoric of universality. Williams's work played out an angry attempt at rectifying what he had been taught wrongly, whereas Marx's view here seems characterized more by resignation. As Williams explained in the interview, "If you look at the implied relationships of nearly all the books I have written, I have been arguing with what I take to be official English culture" (*Politics* 316). Marx, of course, has claimed such oppositional force for the vernacular, and even for the pastoral, but at least in the case of *Huckle-*

berry Finn, he has failed to take account of the hypercanonization that in the five decades since his critique of Trilling and Eliot has made this book the heart of official American culture.

The last paragraph of Marx's review of Williams further demonstrates the misfit between their two positions. Marx concluded that "one of the ironies of *The Country and the City* is that [Williams] finally adopts a position that can only be called, in the most profound sense of the word, pastoral." In other words, despite his criticisms, Marx admired Williams too much not to embrace him as a fellow member of the anguished, divided, minority yet dominant class. Yet this is so far from Williams's chosen position that the embrace implicitly accuses Williams of a self-unawareness verging on bad faith. To me, this seems possible only because Marx eclipsed the tremendous difference between Williams's position of study and his own. Williams wrote, as does Marx, as oppositional, and he also believed like Marx that the rulers he was opposing were a minority, yet for Williams it was never disabling that those for whom and with whom he stood (as quoted above, "labourers") were not themselves the operative national majority. Perhaps because of his years of adult education teaching experience, Williams had a faith in the accessibility and significance of literature that Marx, perhaps part and parcel of choosing to close out his career at MIT, does not hold.

Marx continued, in glossing his analysis of Williams as crypto-pastoral, "Pastoralism has always held forth the hope of mediation between the complex and the simple" (this is the profoundly influential view of Sir William Empson, as Marx indicated in "Pastoralism" [68 n. 17], a view that Williams rejected in *Country* [36]). Here Marx took the socially based terms of country and city and recoded them into terms (complex vs. simple) that wholly eclipse their social gravity; he weakened the historical specificity of his own best work and all of Wiliams's and cast the genre into eternity ("always"). He continued, "Since Virgil, it has advanced a vision of a whole life balanced, as it were, between two landscapes—one identified with sophistication, art, and the aspiring mind, and the other with simplicity, nature, and the strength to live without ambition." Yet as a reading of *The Country and the City,* Marx's explanation is inept. Williams did not treat the country as a scene of patient endurance, and he certainly did not deny the aspiring mind to rural dwellers. If this is what the pastoral tradition has always held, then Williams was certainly right to oppose it with all possible vehemence, and if his book really turns out—ironically—not to, then Marx owed a much fuller explanation of how it failed. For Williams ended his book not by positing a reconciliation between the terms of country and city, but rather by envisioning a freedom from the divisions that define capitalism, thereby "abolishing the contrast between town and country" (304).

The perspectives of *The Country and the City* help to define my whole critical project in this book, but they also open new possibilities in reading the famous sunrise from chapter 19, Marx's touchstone for vernacular. Williams was much concerned with the process of selection by which what is in life "working country" is turned into "landscape" in art. He emphasized the process of "separation and observation" by which such cultural production occurs (120). Huck and Jim are granted a very special status by Twain. As fugitives, they are sensitive spectators. Their stance toward the world is that of leisured observation, while also that of minority outcasts rather than privileged establishment. Their rafting carries with it a practical routine that both gives them something to do and requires their prolonged inactivity, while also motivating their attentive observation, for there remains a chance that something might come up to threaten them, especially at a time of transition like dawn.

I criticized earlier Marx's characterization of the setting of *Huckleberry Finn* as "prehistoric." Williams's principles direct attention precisely to the features of the passage from chapter 19 that mark it as historic, as showing a world at work more fully than, I believe, any other place in the book—certainly far more than on the Phelps farm or in any of the towns that are encountered along the river. "Little dark spots" become "trading scows," and "long black streaks" are "rafts." Work is signaled by the "sweep screaking," the lumberyard "cheats," the stinking debris of fishermen, a steamboat "coughing along," the "galoot . . . chopping," and the "flash" and *"k'chunk!"* of his axe.

Huck may be, as Marx claimed, "immersed" in the river and thus a "participant" in the landscape, but he is nonetheless a distanced and leisured observer of the world's work in this sequence, in which, I think, the human world at large appears more beautiful and less menacing or foolish than anywhere else in the novel. The distance permits the comfort and beauty. Williams's reflections on the London novels of George Gissing (which are focused on working-class characters) offer a perspective very apt for *Huckleberry Finn.* Even though the book's settings are never themselves urban, we may recognize that *Huckleberry Finn* displays a standpoint intimately related to Twain's adult urban experience. Williams found in Gissing a structure in which "the individual was the person who must escape, or try to escape, from this repulsive and degrading mass," with the result that Gissing's books were characterized by "indignant or repelled observation of men in general; exceptional and self-conscious recognition of a few individuals" (222). It makes a difference that in *Huckleberry Finn* readers are left to make these judgments themselves, on what they gather through Huck's account, but no one has ever claimed that any character but Huck or Jim carries the book's positive values, and there has never been consensus about Jim.

Vernacularists deny the thesis of Van Wyck Brooks that Twain was crippled by his relation to the establishment; they assert that, on the contrary, Twain's strength came from his being much more a cultural nonconformist than Brooks allowed. Williams, in contrast, shows ways to understand *Huckleberry Finn* as participating in dominant cultural practices. This allows a different argument: that Twain was strengthened by his relationship with the establishment. Marx's argument for the oppositional force of the vernacular ethos may have rested on a wishful populism that from the beginning ignored important historical dimensions of Twain's work.

An American Context:
The *Century* and the Genteel Tradition

The sunrise passage from chapter 19 has an especially complex history. As excerpted in the *Century* magazine, it was the first passage from *Huckleberry Finn* presented to American readers. While publication of the American edition of the book was delayed—astonishingly, a craftsman in the printing shop had obscenely altered an illustration—Richard Watson Gilder, editor of the *Century,* was soliciting Twain for material and offered to serialize the book. Twain believed that serialization would kill his subscription sales, but he agreed to let Gilder select some material, and he sent Gilder a full set of page proofs. This editorial work by Gilder has, in the critical tradition, been discussed to ascertain the degree to which Gilder as a respectable, traditional belletrist may have censored Twain's creative idiosyncrasy, but my emphasis now is quite different.

Gilder (b. 1844) had served as assistant editor for *Scribner's* magazine from 1870 to 1881, until the journal was taken over by a new publisher and relaunched as the *Century* under his editorship. He remained editor until his death in 1909. For these three decades, the *Century* was the emblem of what, just after Gilder's death, Santayana epitomized and criticized as the genteel tradition. In the 1870s, William Dean Howells, as editor of the *Atlantic*, had worked hard to recruit contributions from the two contemporary writers he most admired, Twain and Henry James. In the next decade, Gilder, as editor of the *Century*, was equally committed to making his magazine absolutely the best possible, and there were three writers he saw as America's best: Twain, James, and Howells himself, who had become available because he had left the *Atlantic* to devote himself to his fiction. Gilder solicited work from all three of them, so that the excerpts from *Huckleberry Finn* ran in the same volume as the full serializations of Howells's *Rise of Silas Lapham* and James's *The Bostonians* (all three coincided in the February 1885 issue). In addition, Gilder commissioned essays by major critics on each of these three novelists, including what is acknowledged to be the first major critical treatment of Twain, by Howells in 1882.

Gilder devoted the *Century* not exclusively to literature but also to important political issues. Like Matthew Arnold, the British critic who inspirited what became in America the genteel tradition, Gilder maintained an acute concern with what was important in politics while avoiding "the slightest partisan leaning" (Rosamond Gilder 128–29). The journal was not radical, but it was serious and it was not cowardly. At the same time as the excerpts from *Huckleberry Finn*, Gilder launched a tremendously successful several-year-long series of autobiographical accounts of the Civil War, from both sides. This has been understood as working for sectional reconciliation, but he also was aware of endangering the journal's standing in the South by running a serial biography of Lincoln in 1887, which, he explained to a correspondent, "goes into politics more deeply and dangerously than any serial ever published in a magazine for general circulation, so far as I am aware" (Rosamond Gilder 170).

The *Century* strongly supported the restoration of cordial, national feeling between North and South, and so it published not only Joel Chandler Harris but also Thomas Nelson Page and Henry

Grady of Atlanta, the leading exponent of "New South" views. Yet Gilder also published George Washington Cable's "The Freedman's Case in Equity" (1884), a polemical critique of the Southern failure to honor the legal rights of African Americans. Gilder strongly supported Cable against the outcry his essay provoked. He refused to print correspondence abusing Cable and the article, replying with a form letter: "If the South wishes to defame and persecute its brightest literary ornament and leading writer, it is welcome to do so, but the persecution cannot be carried on within our columns" (Herbert F. Smith 70). Nonetheless, despite including in the very first issue of the *Century,* in November 1881, the first publication of Frederick Douglass's account of how he had escaped from slavery (omitted from his 1845 and 1855 narratives because the continuing existence of slavery made it wrong to give away such secrets), Gilder did not bring any African American voices into the controversy provoked by Cable. He turned down a submission by Charles W. Chesnutt, "The Negro's Answer to the Negro Question," on the grounds that it was "so timely and so political" that "it should appear at once," but somewhere else (Herbert F. Smith 71).

In selecting what to excerpt from the proofs of *Huckleberry Finn,* Gilder chose to lead with the feud between the Grangerfords and the Shepherdsons, beginning at the end of chapter 16 and running through the end of chapter 18. But in order to use the material, he had to find a way to introduce the reader to Huck and Jim and their way of life. So Gilder decided to remove this opening sequence of chapter 19 from its position *following* the feud and instead make it inaugurate the sequence. In other words, this sunrise passage, long hailed as quintessentially vernacular in its language and ethos, received its first canonization as exemplary of the work as a whole, as its representative keynote, from the editor of the most established high-culture journal in the United States, the very heart of the genteel tradition.

According to a leading scholar of the genteel tradition, Howard Mumford Jones (b. 1892), who was an expert on cultural relations between the United States and France and a leading proponent of the comparative, rather than exceptionalist-nationalist, perspective within American studies, one characteristic of the genteel tradition that distinguished it from antebellum high culture in the United States was to play down "genius" in favor of a new emphasis on "technique" (220). In the larger intellectual sphere, this

tendency was part of the development in this period of a newly pro-
fessionalized and disciplinary scholarship, such as was discussed
in chapter 4. In literature this emphasis on the "power of craftsman-
ship" was understood to be a lesson to be learned from France—as
Matthew Arnold was emphasizing in his writings addressed to the
England of his time. Henry James is now the best-known practi-
tioner of this mode, but it may be argued that Twain in very important, aggressively nonelitist, ways partakes in the same tendency.

Let us once more return to the sunrise passage. It is an article of
vernacularist faith that Huck's "language is lacking in abstractions"
(Marx, *Machine* 334), but this is simply not so. As day breaks,
Huck's description moves from "a pale place in the sky" to the next
phase of "more *paleness* spreading around." Once day has begun,
Huck and Jim can "watch the *lonesomeness* of the river," and then
later, after a nap, we find them "listening to the *stillness*" (my emphases). These highlighted terms are the very models of abstractions, and they are built into the technique of what Marx called, in
vernacularist praise, rendering the scene through "subjective sense
impressions." If Twain had written "more *light* spreading around,"
he would have prematurely named the result of the process that he
was breaking down and protracting by building it up out of details.
But the latter two abstractions (*lonesomeness* and *stillness*) are even
more noteworthy, for they verbally construct witty figures of paradox, in the mode that in English literature is associated with "meta-
physical" poetry: the abstract conceptions are made the direct objects of sense perceptions ("watch," "listening"). More: they are
privative terms, abstractions denoting an absence; yet these words
of nothingness are made objects of physical verbs.

This is thrilling prose, but it does not have much to do with the
vernacular ethos. It has, however, a curious echo in France in the realist manifesto (entitled simply "Le Roman") with which Guy de
Maupassant prefaced his novel *Pierre et Jean* (1888). Maupassant
criticized a tendency in current French fiction, exemplified by the
Goncourts, to use a "bizarre and complicated" vocabulary as part of
a school of "artistic writing." Against this semantic mosaic work, he
preferred less attention to vocabulary and more to rhythms and
syntax. Twain, as we will discuss later in this chapter, certainly
worked with the rhythms of his prose, but in these powerfully de-
ployed abstractions he practices the technique that Maupassant

criticized in "those who nowadays form images without guarding against abstract terms, who make hail or rain fall on the *cleanness* [*propreté*] of the windows" (21, emphasis in original).

The problem I find here with the vernacularist praise for the concreteness, immediacy, and freedom from "abstract conception" of this sunrise passage may be extended more fundamentally. The passage has been understood by Marx and others as a utopia, conveying in its brief sequence that alternative world to the fraud and force that mark the rest of *Huckleberry Finn*. What has not been remarked, I believe, at least in part because it contravenes the praise words of vernacularism, is the way that the manipulation of the grammatical modes of the verbs gives force to the passage's utopian dimension. The passage is very emphatically and clearly a passage of generalization. The verbs are in forms that indicate repeated action, and the whole sequence is prefaced by "Here is the way we put in the time." The effect is of long habitual actions, and what are characterized as the passage's "approximations" often derive from the plurality conveyed. Yet the very beginning of the chapter delimits the actual time that is thus eternized as "two or three days." This is an extremely skillful use of verb aspect to convey a powerful effect.

This technical relationship between narration and fictional experience Gérard Genette defined as "frequency." This feature measures the ratio between events in the narration and in the narrated action. "Singulative" narrative narrates events the same number of times that they occurred; "repeating" narrative narrates more than once events that occur only once (*Rashomon*); while "iterative" narrative recounts once what happened a number of times (Proust's "I used to go to bed early"). Genette offers an illuminating historical commentary on this iterative mode:

> In the classical narrative and even up to Balzac, iterative sections are almost always functionally subordinate to singulative scenes, for which the iterative sections provide a sort of informative frame or background. . . . The classic function of iterative narrative is thus fairly close to that of description, with which, moreover, it maintains very close relations. . . . Like description, in the traditional novel the iterative narrative is *at the service* of the narrative "as such," which is the singulative narrative. The first novelist who undertook to liberate the iterative from this functional dependence is clearly Flaubert. (116–17)

Certain passages in Flaubert, Genette points out, "take on a wholly unusual fullness and autonomy." Even though the sunrise sequence is often spoken of as descriptive, it would be more exact to call it too iterative in this new sense.

European Contexts:
Twain with and against the French

Can we develop the relations between Twain's work and that of Flaubert further than Richard Bridgman (108) and Brendan Gill have done in a few brief aperçus? Twain no less than Flaubert was devoted, as we noted apropos of Cooper, to the labor of the "right word"—as he said once, there is as much difference in writing between *"almost"* right and *"right"* as there is between the lightning bug and the lightning (*Collected* 1:946). By his turn to Huck as narrator, Twain brought into the narrative not only a vocabulary but also rhythms associated with idiomatic speech. Despite the great difference that Flaubert did not work with a first-person narrator, students of French prose have suggested that the effects achieved by Flaubert in his newly extensive use of the *style indirect libre* also allowed a way to introduce colloquial language that would not have been considered appropriate for the narrator on his own, and also to achieve through ellipsis and the displaced mimicry of speech a movement very different from that of traditionally composed narrative.

More technically oriented students of Twain's style than Marx have emphasized the role in rhythmically modeling his sentences of the parts of speech that carry relatively little semantic weight, especially conjunctions, prepositions, and the adverbs in "two-part" verbs (McKay 155). Beyond the use of *and* so frequently that its occasional omission achieves a powerful impact, some of the striking effects in this mode include: "went by . . . swum by"; "laid up . . . tied up"; "freshen up and cool off"; "softened up, away off"; "lazy along . . . lazy off." In Flaubert's case, no less a student of French prose than Proust emphasized the almost wholly rhythmic role that conjunctions and adverbs played in his innovative sentences and paragraphs. Flaubert's writing, Proust emphasized, might even be considered technically ungrammatical; it would have required correction if he were a student, and yet it allowed for effects so new, so unprecedented, that Proust even judged them a "revolution" (226).

Both Twain, according to Richard Bridgman (106), and Flaubert, according to Jonathan Culler (204), give weight to local units rather than to extensively composed wholes. Attention may even fall on a single word, displaced from its usual position in a sentence, set off, strangely, by commas ("the bull-frogs a-cluttering, maybe"; "being a wood-yard, likely"; "dead fish laying around, gars, and such"). This "fragmentation," as each critic calls it, has been found by other critics, as we have already noticed, to increase the authority given to the individual image and correspondingly to lessen the emphasis on abstract conception.

Of Flaubert's work, the best match for *Huckleberry Finn* is *The Sentimental Education* (1869), as Hispanic-comparatist Stephen Gilman noted. It's not just because Flaubert's novel begins with a steamboat trip. Like Twain's, Flaubert's novel reaches back to the 1840s for an autobiographically linked fiction. There are also notable differences: unlike Huck, Frédéric Moreau is already a young adult when the book begins; the novel's action encompasses a bit more than the whole decade of the 1840s; and its major setting is urban. The beauty, boredom, and terror of Paris play the role in Flaubert's descriptive and iterative passages that the river does in Twain's.

In a letter as he began work on the *Sentimental Education,* Flaubert gives some insight into the meaning of the title: "I want to write the moral history of the men of my generation—or, more accurately, the history of their *feelings*" (*Letters* 80). Known to readers through his feelings more than through any action, Frédéric is a sensitive spectator, whose perceptions Flaubert repeatedly follows as he looks over the city as day breaks. When he is a young man newly arrived in Paris with his friend and rival Deslauriers, "In the morning they strolled up and down their balcony in their shirtsleeves. The sun rose, light mists flowed over the river, they could hear shrill voices in the near-by flower market; the smoke from their pipes curled up into the clear air" (64). Near the end of the novel, he is living with his mistress Rosanette: "the best part of the day was the morning on their terrace" (349). At a moment by himself in the early stages, "he spent hours on his balcony looking down at the river flowing between the grey quays, which were blackened here and there with smudges from drains; or at a pontoon for washerwomen moored to the bank, where children sometimes amused themselves by giving a poodle a mud-bath" (74).

I append the French for this sentence in order to make clear that the English has greatly smoothed out the chopped-up, "frag-mented," prose that results from Flaubert's punctuation:

> Il passait des heures à regarder, du haut de son balcon, la rivière qui coulait entre les quais grisâtres, noircis, de place en place, par la bavure des égouts, avec un ponton de blanchisseuses amarré contre le bord, où des gamins quelquefois s'amusaient, dans la vase, à faire baigner un caniche. (96)

Where in five lines Flaubert has nine commas, his translator has only two commas and a semicolon, and one of those commas is in a relative clause ("which were blackened") that by its grammatical form doubly blunts the French: by smoothing the abruptness of the commas surrounding *noircis,* but also by muffling the intensifying juxtaposition of "grisâtres, noircis" (grey, blackened).

Even these brief passages make obvious that Flaubert's narrative does not rely on *and* for its rhythm as Huck's does, but by highlight-ing punctuation, I have one further point to make about *Huckleberry Finn.* It is only the author, Mark Twain, whom we can imagine as crafting the sentences Huck speaks, even if the words and intona-tions we can imagine as Huck's. For much of the craft in the opening of chapter 19, as everywhere else in the book, depends on how the units of meaning are cut and shaped by punctuation. The sunrise passage lives on its semicolons, the most high-culture mark of punctuation, which is an empirical feature of writing not of speech; the Faulkner-length sentence, beginning "The first thing to see" and running to the end of the passage's first paragraph, gains its proces-sive force in part from contrast with the earlier very short sentences ("Here is the way we put in the time. . . . Then we set out our lines"), which establish that it's not accidental but meaningful when a sen-tence is allowed to run on.

In the previous chapter, I argued that the stylistic differences be-tween Twain and Cooper had kept criticism from attending to the resemblances of *Huckleberry Finn* and *The Pioneers*—resemblances that once acknowledged then provided a ground from which to define important political and cultural differences between the works. Now I hope, on the ground of the stylistic resemblances sketched here, to suggest that Flaubert's *Sentimental Education* may also be placed in meaningful relation of contrast with *Huckleberry Finn.* By bringing Frédéric Moreau's life, even though in an extremely foreshortened way, into the present time of the book's writing, Flaubert establishes a defined perspective from which that past experience may be understood (not a solution to the question of how to understand it, but a point of reference). Even more important, in bringing Frédéric from 1840 to 1851, before the leap in time that leads to the last few pages many years later, Flaubert includes the Revolution of 1848 and the coup d'état of 1851, the French equivalent to the American Civil War. The political trauma that nationalizing critics read into *Huckleberry Finn* is directly represented in *The Sentimental Education*.

One of the most famous theses concerning the history of the novel in the nineteenth century is Georg Lukács's claim, in "Narrate or Describe" and elsewhere, that the shift he defined as that from realism to naturalism may be understood as resulting from the incapacity of the bourgeoisie to hold their ideals as universal any longer. This is the very point Lincoln made in his critique of the empty fireworks of the Fourth of July, which no longer stood for any commitment to universal human equality, but celebrated only the continued comfort of those who, having won their own freedom, no longer cared to end slavery for others. In Lukács's argument, after the moment in 1848 when bourgeois privilege could be preserved only by turning against revolutionary workers, it was no longer possible for the bourgeoisie directly to confront historical action. As Flaubert put it in the letter about the *Sentimental Education* from which I quoted earlier, Frédéric's feelings exemplify "passion such as can exist nowadays, that is to say, inactive" (*Letters* 80). The result I now summarize in formulas drawn not from Lukács but from Lukács's older contemporary, Proust, in Proust's essay on Flaubert's style. The new technique gives "life" to "things," while what before would have been "action" now becomes "impression" (49). For Proust this was a literary advance, but for Lukács exemplary deep subjectivity (what Proust called Flaubert's *subjectivisme*) observed what was happening in a world that no longer supported any hope for leading a decent life, except by a miracle like that of Huck's chapter 31. In the works of Twain and Flaubert, great and profoundly influential, exemplary stylists, only the style rescues readerly pleasure from the horrors of the world represented. Moving away from the praise of vernacular now may help us to new understandings of these connections: the triumphs of national cultures have participated in a process that has been painful for most of those involved in it and that if national in effects has been global in scope—as will be further developed in the next chapter.

Even earlier than Lukács or Proust, another great critic attempted to capture the culture of his age in a generalization that can suggestively embrace both Twain and Flaubert. In his reflections on the "Case of Wagner," Nietzsche tried to relate the new literary techniques of his age to the dominant ideology of the age:

> For the present I merely dwell on the question of *style.*—What is the characteristic of every *literary décadence*? That life no longer dwells in the whole. The word becomes sovereign and leaps out of the sentence, the sentence reaches out and obscures the meaning of the page, the page gains life at the expense of the whole—the whole is no longer a whole. But this is the image of every style of *décadence:* every time, the anarchy of atoms, disgregation of the will, "freedom of the individual" to use moral terms—expanded into a political theory, "*equal* rights for all." Life, *equal* vitality, the vibration and exuberance of life pushed back into the smallest structures, the rest, *poor* in life. (917, my translation)

It might seem improbable that a "decadent" style could be relevant to Twain. Twain's sense of history is a topic too large and complex to treat fully here. But I enter into the record a telegraphic notebook passage that understands the history of the United States in the Gilded Age as a decadence, a falling off, when it should have been something far better:

> [The railroad speculator, Jay] Gould followed CIVIL WAR & California sudden-riches disease with a *worse* one . . . by swindling and buying courts. Cal & Gould were the beginners of the moral rot, they were the worst things that ever befel America; they created the hunger for wealth when the Gr. Civ. had just completed its youth, its ennobling WAR—strong, pure, clean, ambitious, impressionable—ready to make a choice of life-course & move with a rush; *they and circumstances* determined the choice. . . . Circumstance after Vand[erbilt]. wrought railways into systems; then Standard Oil; Steel Trust; & Carnegie. CALIF— causes Pac[ific] R.R. UNCLE TOM WAR TELEGRAPH. to restrict slavery— circum. *abolished* it. (Tuveson 208, quoting from Henry Nash Smith's citation of MT MS. DV127; my additions in brackets)

There is yet a further dimension of this interplay between the international and the national in Twain and in his language. The passage I cited from Nietzsche on decadence is appropriated from the work of Paul Bourget (*Essais* 1:20). Bourget (1852–1935) was a conservative French novelist and intellectual who was a friend of Henry James's and an acute critic of nineteenth-century culture, including the work of Flaubert and Baudelaire. In 1894, Bourget traveled to the United States, writing up his impressions for a French periodical and publishing the results in a book, *Outre-Mer* (1895). The pieces and the book alike were immediately translated, but it seems that Twain probably read them in French in Paris where he was then resident, and while they were still in progress he was moved to a polemical critique, "What Paul Bourget Thinks of Us." The fundamental issue in this piece is whether it is possible, or desirable, to generalize about any nation, but particularly the United States. Twain severely questioned the quasi-scientific mode of generalization and abstraction that Bourget—because, Twain argued, he was French—followed, but Twain also questioned the very idea of a foreigner explaining America to Americans. So one thread of the essay is American nativist, almost jingoistic, but there are two other lines through the essay that are more rewarding. For Twain expounded what he considered the most valuable mode of social reportage, and the wish to push back against Bourget's generalities moved Twain to an intriguing set of claims about the multiplicity of life in the United States.

For Twain against Bourget, only "the native novelist" is the "expert" capable of examining the "souls and the life of a people" and producing a "valuable report." The basis of such work is not "conscious 'observation'" but rather many years of "the slow accumulation of unconscious observation," that is, "absorption." But "even the native novelist" is limited to that area "whose life is familiar to him." Anywhere else in the United States, that writer "becomes a foreigner." Therefore, the novelist cannot generalize: "he lays plainly before you the ways and speech and life of a few people grouped in a certain place—his own place—and that is one book." In contrast to such attempts as those of Emile Zola in a series of novels to work up and cover the life of the whole French nation over a period of years, for Twain only the collective work of many American writers will build up "a hundred patches of life and groups of people in a dozen widely separated cities." Twain offered a catalogue that is both comic and offensive, yet which also strangely prophesies the next century of American multicultural literary practice: "And the Indians will be attended to; and the cowboys;

and the gold and silver miners; and the negroes [*sic* for Negroes]; and the Idiots and Congressmen; and the Irish, the Germans, the Italians, the Swedes, the French, the Chinamen, the Greasers," and this is less than half the list. When "a thousand" such novels have been written, "*there* you will have the soul of the people, the life of the people, the speech of the people" (*Collected* 2:167–68). For Twain, it seems, *the* "vernacular" does not exist.

Against Bourget's search for the uniformities that define Americans and differentiate them from the people of other nations— a search repeated in the 1950s by academic American studies— Twain insisted, "There isn't a single human characteristic that can be safely labelled 'American.'" If, he argued, "you have found what seems to be an 'American' peculiarity," it will not hold: "you only have to cross a frontier or two, or go up or down the social scale, and you perceive that it has disappeared." Nothing is uniformly American, then, and nothing is exclusively American either: "you can cross the Atlantic and find it again" (*Collected* 2:168–69).

Let Bourget here represent the long tradition of reading Twain too exclusively as "quintessentially American." Let Twain's position stand for a double vigilance: far more suspicious of the national and far more attentive to both local and international dimensions.

8

Nation, Race, and Beyond

In the four decades since Leo Marx's essays on vernacular, no discussion of Twain's language has had more impact, reaching beyond the academy as far as *People* magazine, than Shelley Fisher Fishkin's *Was Huck Black? Mark Twain and African-American Voices* (1993). I share her goal of respect for African American voices in public discussions of *Huckleberry Finn,* but I fear that her book is not having a good effect. Instead, people are using her work as a license to keep up the idolatry. In the media buzz when her topic became known, even before the book appeared, Justin Kaplan was quoted in the *Times:* "My understanding . . . is that nigger is a taboo word when used by a white person, but it's an OK word used in a black framework. . . . If you can claim that this is a black voice speaking, I believe the objection to the word nigger is somewhat defused" (DePalma).

Kaplan was tentative, but by 1995 the flagship scholarly journal *American Literature* published an essay which claimed, on the authority of Fishkin's work, "If Huck has any African American linguistic authority, his use of the word 'nigger,' a rallying point for movements to ban *Adventures of Huckleberry Finn* from our high schools, partakes of the privilege any people have to refer to themselves as they choose" (Hoffman 45). So Huck's "black" voice becomes more cultural capital for hypercanonization. But Huck, in referring to himself as he chooses, never names himself as African American and above all never applies the word *nigger* to himself. More broadly, as we shall see, Fishkin's argument relies on sources that argue for the African American component in all American speech. Does this mean every white person might have the linguistic authority to call anyone *nigger*? The social analysis of linguistic history is not the same social analysis that governs human relations in the United States. Whites have been taking possession of elements of black culture for centuries, but it has not ended the structures of inequality from which the pain of name-calling arises.

Fishkin's book troubles me on two grounds, both of which I will address in this chapter. First, it is deeply committed to nationalism: Huck as the representative American, and his book as the exemplary great American book. Of course it is a matter of choice and opinion how one judges this position. I try to make strong arguments for another perspective, but I realize that I am making an unpopular case. So I will delay this part of my argument until I have worked through my other objection. Second, then, I am not persuaded by Fishkin's stylistic and linguistic evidence. I shall lay out my objections in detail so that the issues are available for discussion. Her book's impact and influence make it important that any weaknesses be acknowledged, and I have not yet seen any of my points developed in reviews. But before beginning my criticisms, it is first necessary to define her project.

Fishkin proposed to redefine the "American." She used "America" as her Trojan Horse, to bring new values into *Huckleberry Finn* while still valuing it in the name of "America." She argued that *Huckleberry Finn*, long recognized as fundamentally American, is also fundamentally African American. According to Fishkin, the very possibility of the American vernacular of Huck's narration required the encounter of Samuel Clemens with an African American boy named (perhaps) Jimmy around 1872: Jimmy's lively speech reawakened Clemens's memories of his life among enslaved African Americans in Missouri, and it also directly influenced the particular voice devised for Huck in the novel. Her text for this argument is Twain's brief newspaper sketch of 1874, "Sociable Jimmy," published in the *New York Times*. Fishkin's book is rich in biographical particulars of Clemens's relations with African Americans, especially the intriguing issue of African Americans as an eager audience for Twain (89, 188–89). It also exemplifies a specific political strategy: granted the talismanic power of *Huckleberry Finn* in American culture, Fishkin appropriated that prestige to use for interracially progressive purposes, rather than attempting the uphill battle of questioning the identification of a nation with a book, or of the United States as "American" with this particular book.

Fishkin's argument relies crucially on a writer and thinker who also cared deeply about the interrelations of culture, the nation, and the state: Ralph Ellison, with whom she conducted a lengthy interview in 1991. The second half of this chapter will engage with Ellison, whose views underlie Fishkin's larger position, as opposed to the linguistic detail. She drew on Ellison for two views in particular: his understanding of an overarching American identity in which, as he put it in 1977, "in relationship to the cultural whole, we are, all of us—white or black, native-born or immigrant—members of minority groups" (*Collected* 500), and his conviction that, despite some shortcomings, *Huckleberry Finn* marks a high point of American fiction, both as art and as socially engaged morality. Both of these views are important.

Ellison's understanding of *"Americanness"* (*Collected* 492) is capacious. It stands equally against whites who ignore African American contributions to American culture and against blacks who would define and promote a separatist cultural nationalism. Ellison thus prefigures much emerging work on the culture of the United States as "hybrid." His praise of *Huckleberry Finn* is especially useful for Fishkin in dealing with the challenges that the book has faced in the last forty years because of the historical paradox by now familiar to my readers: In the years after the Second World War *Huckleberry Finn* became for the first time an almost universal classroom text, and yet it uses hundreds of times, in an age of African American struggles for equality and public respect, the highly offensive term "nigger." Ellison, however, cared so little for this verbal issue that he repeatedly in his published criticism referred to Jim as "Nigger Jim" (*Collected* 104, 112, 731), even though Twain's book never itself uses this locution (for lucid reflection on this issue, see David L. Smith 124–25). Ellison's apparent indifference to this concern makes it easier for Fishkin to forge ahead with her positive view on Twain's hybridized antiracism, unencumbered by any defensiveness. Now that the Modern Library has made over eight hundred pages of Ellison's critical prose widely available in a handsome and inexpensive volume, it is clear, a few years after his death, that he was not only the author of a great novel but also one of the major American critics of the period from 1940 to 1980. Fishkin's emphasis on Ellison is one of her book's major contributions.

In thinking about Fishkin's work, it is particularly important to recognize Ellison's views on "the American language," which he summarized in a feature essay for *Time* in 1970. He understood the "American nation" as in important ways "the product" of that language. Even before the Revolution, he argued, this language began as "a vernacular revolt" against the culture of the "mother country." "Much of the sound" of American English, he argued, derives "from the timbre of the African voice and the listening habits of the African ear." Even while "the majority of blacks were still enslaved," Ellison found that "the creators of our [that is, American] great nineteenth-century literature" had "absorbed" into their works the "rhythms, freewheeling diction and metaphors" of African American speech. Ellison's discussion rises to its climax with the claim for *Huckleberry Finn*:

> Mark Twain celebrated [what Ellison calls "the spoken idiom of Negro Americans"] in the prose of *Huckleberry Finn;* without the presence of blacks, the book could not have been written. No Huck and Jim, no American novel as we know it. For not only is the black man a co-creator of the language that Mark Twain raised to the level of literary eloquence, but Jim's condition as American and Huck's commitment to freedom are at the moral center of the novel. (*Collected* 581)

Ellison, however, unlike Fishkin, did not make any specific claim that Huck's voice is distinctively, even uniquely, black. I shall return in this chapter to consider more fully the complexities of Ellison's views about the "American" and its place in a larger, international and global, mode of understanding, but first I need to work through the specifics of Fishkin's case for Huck's black voice.

The Trouble with Fishkin's Linguistics

Fishkin's argument has two main stages. First she laid out the case for the similarity between Huck's language as written in *Huckleberry Finn* and the language of Jimmy in Twain's newspaper sketch. Having established to her satisfaction that Jimmy and Huck share a language, she inquired whether that language is "black." This issue she treated in two dimensions. First, she looked to an article on "Negro English" published in 1884, and she argued that insofar as Huck uses words that this article identifies as "specimen negroisms," his language counts as black. Second, she looked to modern scholars who have established "Black English" as an acknowledged object of linguistic study. Insofar as features of

Huck's grammar match what scholars have defined as Black English, then, his voice is "black." My objections come at every stage of her argument.

My largest problem is that Fishkin's procedure involves almost exclusively the matching of items. There are no hypotheses to be tested; there are no modes of disconfirmation proposed; there is no definition of what overall context is relevant for assessing the issue she was concerned to resolve.

For example, in the initial claim that Jimmy's speech resembles Huck's, Fishkin cited critics' generalizations about Huck's usages and then showed that they also apply to Jimmy. So she cited Richard Bridgman on the feature of "repetition" (16). But Bridgman's treatment of repetition in Twain's writing is unsuitable for her use in two ways. First, Bridgman's book is on what he called "the colloquial style" in American prose. This style was achieved by authors' use in their narrative voices of features that at first, historically, occurred only in directly quoted characters' voices. Since Jimmy's language is presented by Twain only in direct report of his conversation, it is not in the category of Bridgman's primary concern, for Jimmy is a character in a sketch that is narrated by Twain. But second, Bridgman's discussion of "repetition" in Twain is part of a chapter entitled "Henry James and Mark Twain," which argues that James and Twain share distinctive features, including repetition. Thus Bridgman proposed a surprising argument: the master of the genteel, European-influenced high style (James) shares important techniques and emphases with the master of vernacular, native, plain style (Twain). So to show that Jimmy uses repetition makes him as much like Henry James as like Huck.

Fishkin cited Janet Holmgren McKay on characteristic "errors" and "mistakes" in Huck's language and then showed the same usages in Jimmy's language (19). For Fishkin's overall thesis—that Huck's language corresponds to what modern scholars define as "Black English"—this is a wrong move, for the overriding point of modern linguists is to deny that the usages of Black English are "mistakes." Black English, linguists explain, differs from Standard English, and from many other versions of colloquial or dialect English, but it forms a coherent grammatical system.

The instances Fishkin drew from McKay do not seem compelling. Fishkin cited McKay on "Huck's preference for using adjectives in place of adverbs" (19), especially the terms *powerful* and *considerable*. But in several of Fishkin's examples, the terms are not used in place of adverbs:

1. "[They] had such a powerful lot to say": here *powerful* is an adjective, modifying the noun *lot*.

2. "I read considerable to Jim"; "We've heard considerable": in these cases, *considerable* serves as the object of the verb.

Similar instances can be found in all the major reference works as typical and widespread American usages. Mathews's *Dictionary of Americanisms* has almost half a column on *considerable* as used in (2) above, with citations running from 1685. As to *powerful*, the *Random House Dictionary* cites "powerful lot," characterizing it as "chiefly South Midland and Southern US," and the *OED* gives this usage as "dialect and vulgar" both in the United States and Britain, with citations from *Uncle Tom's Cabin* ("dat ar Tom's gwine to make a powerful deal o' trouble") but also from Dickens's *Our Mutual Friend* (1865) ("[he] took a powerful sight of notice"). The *Dictionary of American Regional English* simply defines *considerable*, in some uses, as an adverb, offering citations both from the New England vernacular humor *Letters of Jack Downing* (1834) and from Edward Eggleston's *Hoosier Schoolmaster* (1871), an early example of local color dialect writing from exactly the speech zone Jimmy comes from. So even if Jimmy and Huck share these usages, it says very little about any specially intimate relation between their languages.

In two of her footnotes, Fishkin addressed the kind of issues I have just raised, but the notes seem contradictory. In note 34 she cited an author on *powerful* as "characteristic of Southern speech in general" (156), but she emphasized that only Huck and Jim use the term in *Huckleberry Finn*, making her point that it's a distinctively black usage in the book. But in note 35, she cited another author on the pervasiveness of "uninflected intensifiers" (such as *powerful* and *considerable*) in all the speakers of *Huckleberry Finn*. Here she appealed to quite a different logic: "This fact does not lessen the significance of those terms as characteristic of Huck's speech, however, since *all* speech in the book is ostensibly filtered through Huck and passed on to us in *his* version of it" (156, emphases in original). Not only does note 35 contradict the argument of note 34, but more important, note 35 nullifies Twain's own prefatory note on dialect, where he emphasized his scruple to register precisely seven distinct

types. Twain's note would make no sense whatever if Huck con-
taminates with his own dialect the speech of other characters within
quotation marks, and I am not aware that any other published reading makes such a claim.

Another problem in Fishkin's argument arises from her weak
grasp of the relevant American geography. Fishkin observed that
Jimmy has passed his whole young life around "the same small
midwestern town in which he was born," and that therefore "his
speech is quite different from that of other black speakers whose
voices Twain recreated in his fiction, most of whom hailed from
Missouri or points further South" (36). She here fell into the common identification of Missouri, as a slaveholding state, with the
"South." In fact, Paris, Illinois, where her research led her to believe Jimmy was located, is a bit to the *south* of Hannibal, Missouri
(Paris, 39 degrees, 36 minutes north; Hannibal, 39 degrees, 41 minutes). Moreover, the current scholarly understanding of Black English is based on the fact that across a remarkably wide geographic
range African American speakers share more significant usages
with each other, even at a distance, than with the surrounding
white community.

This problem with geography compromises the next phase of
Fishkin's argument, in which she turned from the similarities between Jimmy and Huck to the question of whether these similarities make their speech identifiably "black." As she explained,
her first test involved whether this speech "manifests . . . lexical
dimensions identified by dialect scholars such as James A. Harrison
in the 1880s as characteristic of 'Negro English'" (168 n. 1). Harrison
published in 1884 an article entitled "Negro English" from which
Fishkin highlighted a list of words he considered typical of American blacks, what he called "specimen negroisms" (Fishkin 43).
Harrison limited himself to a specific geographical area, which did
not include Missouri, since the Mississippi marked his western
boundary. His northern boundary was 39 degrees north latitude,
which Fishkin glossed as "the Mason-Dixon line" (43). And she
noted that the resemblance between Jimmy's speech and Harrison's
list is especially telling because "Harrison's 'sample' is taken from
south of the Mason-Dixon line and Jimmy came from the Midwest" (42). But this is wrong. The Mason-Dixon line is 39 degrees,
43 minutes—in other words rather closer to 40 degrees than to

39. Although Paris, Illinois, and Hannibal, Missouri, are both slightly north of Harrison's area, they are both south of the Mason-Dixon line.

Of Harrison's list, I will not discuss cases where there is evidence for much wider American usage. In Ellison's spirit, I grant the possibility that any American word may have been influenced by black speech. So I comment only on terms that he listed as special "negroisms" but that prove to be widely documented in Britain. In making this critique, I am not suggesting that there has been no African American contribution to the vocabulary or idiom of American English, only that these are not good examples of such contributions. I discuss the majority of those Fishkin cited:

1. Lonesome = depressed: *OED* cites this from Dickens.

2. Tell on = disclose something against: *OED* examples include the 1539 Great Bible and Walter Scott's *Rob Roy*.

3. Let on = pretend: The first *OED* citation is from the Scottish novelist John Galt (1822).

4. Reckon = suppose, think, or fancy: *OED* cites Elizabeth Gaskell (1860) and related usage from Samuel Richardson, *Clarissa* (1748).

5. Monstrous = very: *OED* citations from Shakespeare and Swift.

6. Lay = wager: *OED* cites this as far back as Middle English.

7. Study = meditate: *OED* includes citations from Middle English through Shakespeare.

8. Tolerable = very, pretty: *OED* citation from early-eighteenth-century *Spectator* papers.

9. Disremember = forget: *OED* cites from *Mary Barton* (1848); the first citation is Irish, and it is listed in dialect dictionaries for the Northern Irish county of Antrim as well as for several English counties; the *Dictionary of American Regional English,* citing a *Dictionary of the Scottish Tongue* example from 1584, derives it from Scots.

To be sure, Fishkin defined as her concern only the fact that Huck's usage "manifests a number of expressions and qualities that dialect scholars from the 1870s and 1880s would have identified as African-American" (44). So my *OED* materials may show only why I do not think very much authority should be vested in Harrison. But on Fishkin's own historicist terms, she offered no reasons why Harrison should count as an authority beyond the mere fact of his publication. And there is no evidence to indicate that anyone in Twain's time actually perceived Huck's language as black.

The final stage of Fishkin's argument draws from the recent studies of syntax by which scholars have defined "Black English." Three main topics are addressed. The first comes from J. L. Dillard, whose *Black English* (1972) remains the defining study of the field, although it is not universally accepted. For Dillard, a fundamental difference between Black English and Standard English involves the category of verb tense. He argues that tense is "an obligatory category for Standard English" but that it "can be omitted in Black English sentences."

Dillard's key point is that the fact of something's being an "occurrence in the past" in Black English is "*non-redundantly* marked." He explains this technical term as follows: "whereas in Standard English every verb in a sequence . . . must be marked as either present or past, in Black English only one of the verbs need be so marked." This explains further what he meant by saying that tense in Black English is not an obligatory category: one might have a sequence of sentences, and it is necessary only that one verb in this sequence be marked as to tense. In the Black English statement "he go yesterday," the pastness of the action is marked by *yesterday*, not by the verb *go*, which is in its "base form," not marked as to tense. This is "non-redundant" marking because the information of pastness is given only once, whereas in Standard English ("he went yesterday") it is redundantly marked, both by "yesterday" and by the past-tense form of the verb. Dillard specifically argues against "any facile assumption" about shifts into the "historical present." (All that I have quoted from Dillard is quoted by Fishkin [44–45], although not in the same order or with the same explanation.)

Fishkin's comments show that she did not grasp Dillard's point, which is truly a difficult one for Standard English speakers, because his point is that a language very much like Standard English nonetheless differs from it in very deep ways, so that the most basic categories of Standard English, such as verb tense, are not to be found in Black English. In commenting on her examples, Fishkin wrote that "Huck characteristically shifts tense in a single paragraph or sentence, as do Jimmy and Jim" (45). But Dillard had just been quoted as saying that shifting of tense is not the issue. In a note she explained that "non-redundantly marked verbs in the cases cited here are present-tense verbs in sentences describing actions that clearly took place in the past (and that are described in past-tense verbs earlier in the sentence)" (171 n. 28). But Dillard has just been quoted to the effect that it is pastness as such ("occurrence in the past") that is nonredundantly marked, not the verb. That is, for Dillard, pastness is "non-redundantly" marked by means of the verb's being *un*marked, the marking being done only (in the example above) by the time word *yesterday*, the verb being in the non-tense-marked "base form." Fishkin continued, "Both Jimmy and Jim mark verb tenses with similar non-redundancy." But Dillard has been quoted as saying not that *tense* is marked nonredundantly, but that "tense . . . can be omitted." These are technical matters, but Fishkin invoked technical linguistics to strengthen her case, and if she did not get the technicalities right, then her case is weakened instead.

The suspicion that Fishkin did not understand her linguistic authorities becomes even deeper in the next topics she addressed. The second topic is "deletion of the copula" (46), for which she relied especially on the work of the sociolinguist William Labov, who was like Dillard a decisive figure in establishing the category of Black English. Fishkin did not grasp what Labov (and linguistics more generally) meant by the term *copula*.

In his classic treatment of this topic, Labov defines his inquiry as bearing on the "absence of the copula in the present before predicate nouns and adjectives, locative and comitative phrases, and the parallel absence of the forms of *to be* in the auxiliary *be . . . ing*" (48). He wants to find out what the rules are that account for these features, which differ from Standard English, including such sentences as the following, in all of which Standard English would employ the contraction *He's:* "He a friend [predicate noun]. He tired [predicate adjective]. He over there [locative]. He with us [comitative]. He working with us [auxiliary]" (48). Many pages later, and after much technical grammatical annotation and argumentation, Labov reaches the general rule: "wherever S[tandard] E[nglish] can contract, B[lack] E[nglish] V[ernacular] can delete *is* and *are* and vice versa; wherever SE cannot contract, BEV cannot delete *is* and *are* and vice versa" (73). So what Labov means by *copula* are certain uses of the verb *to be*, forms such as *is* and *are* in specified usages and contexts.

But all the examples of deletion that Fishkin cited for this crucial feature of Black English involve the verb *to have* in its auxiliary usage, not the copula at all. And all her examples involve the past, whereas Labov (as we have noted) defined his concern as "absence of the copula in the present." Her defining example when introducing the concept to her readers is this: "Jimmy's comment 'I ben mos' halfway to Dockery,' would be 'I*'ve* been' in Standard English. Similarly the Standard English version of Jim's comment, 'I ben rich wunst,' would be 'I*'ve* been'" (46, emphases in original). These two examples omit the auxiliary (the contracted form of *have*), but as usages that Labov has called "locative" ("mos' halfway to Dockery") and "predicate adjective" ("rich"), they *include* rather than delete the copula ("ben"). Fishkin continued, "while Huck usually does not delete copulas, it is striking that one of Huck's best known lines . . . '*I been there before*'—uses the zero copula construction" (46). This is incorrect.

There is a third feature of Black English that she also discussed, in connection with the famous closing line just cited: the "remote time construction"using the term *been* in a special way (46). But again, the *Dictionary of American Regional English* shows a wide range of white informants using *been* as Huck does here for *has/have been*. And John Baugh, author of *Black Street Speech*, whose work Fishkin cited several times, in his article on "Black English Vernacular" in *The Oxford Companion to the English Language* discusses this usage in a way damaging to Fishkin's example. He describes the way in BEV "stressed *been* conveys long-standing events with remote pasts," indicating that *before* would not be needed in such a construction; it is redundant (134).

Labov offers the fullest treatment of this special *been*. This usage "appears in contexts that make it seem as if *have* might have been deleted: *He been gone*." But, he notes, it "also appears in contexts where *have* could not have been underlying and the verb could not be a past participle: *I been know your name*." In these contexts, the *been* means "have for a long time," and it implies "and do so now." Labov calls it a "remote present perfect," combining *used to* and *have . . . ed*. Labov's final comment rings true to the inadequacy of Fishkin's attempt to rope Huck's quite different usage into this category: "It is normally not understood at all by speakers of other dialects" (53–54).

Linguistically, then, I do not think Fishkin made a persuasive case that Huck is "black." Nonetheless, her book is important for what it tries to do in larger ways, and in these respects it draws, I

have indicated, on the work of Ralph Ellison, so to Ellison I now
turn. Through Ellison, I want to reflect further on the costs and limits of American cultural nationalism.

Ellison's Cultural Perspective

For *Huckleberry Finn*, Ellison's most important text is
not the much reprinted and cited "Change the Joke and Slip the
Yoke" (1958), which poses the problem of Jim as a minstrel representation, but the earlier essay "Twentieth-Century Fiction and the
Black Mask of Humanity." This essay proposes that the moral history of the United States may be imagined as "a drama acted out
upon the body of a Negro giant" (*Collected* 85), and it argues that after the failure of Reconstruction almost all American writers failed
to do what earlier American writers, from Emerson to Twain, had
done: to conceive of "the Negro as a symbol of Man" (88). Ellison
dwelt on Hemingway's influential formulation that all modern
American writing comes from *Huckleberry Finn*, with Hemingway's
further proviso that the book's ending is just "cheating." Ellison
claimed, in contrast, that only the determination to steal Jim free
once he has been "stolen" from Huck gives the book its great moral
value. Hemingway, thus, lost the "fraternal" meaning of Twain's
book and kept only its "technical discoveries" (91). But Ellison did
not make this an individual shortcoming of Hemingway's, for he
read Hemingway as typical of a phase of national history in which
"by excluding our largest minority from the democratic process,
the United States weakened all national symbols and rendered
sweeping public rituals which would dramatize the American
dream impossible" (92). Readers of *Invisible Man* will recall the crucial scenes of powerful public ritual that articulate that "portrait of
the artist as a rabble-rouser" (*Collected* 220). Ellison's emphasis on
the moral power of public ritual supports, I think, my concern in
chapter 2 with Twain's omission of the Fourth of July from *Huckleberry Finn*.

Huckleberry Finn thus for Ellison represented national value, and
it also took on specific personal value. He wrote that as a youth he
could imagine himself as Huck Finn "(I so nicknamed my brother)"
(112) but not "as Nigger Jim." In his Easy Rawlins series, the
African American writer Walter Mosley revised Ellison's view. In
Black Betty (1994), set in 1961, Easy reflects, somewhat anachronisti-

cally, on the issues that have provoked me to write this book: "I'd picked up *Huckleberry Finn* at a used-book store in Santa Monica. A few liberal libraries and the school system had wanted to ban the book because of the racist content. Liberal-minded whites and blacks wanted to erase racism from the world. I applauded the idea, but my memory of Huckleberry wasn't one of racism. I remembered Jim and Huck as friends out on the river. I could have been either one of them" (13). Ellison, however, could not have been Jim. He further identified his youthful African American milieu as one in which he and his friends were, like Huck Finn, " 'boys'," a "wild, free, outlaw tribe which transcended the category of race" (*Collected* 52). In defining the boys he grew up with in Oklahoma as "Americans" who, because they were also " 'frontiersmen,'" were given equally to "voracious reading" and "quixotic gestures," he may blend Huck with Tom Sawyer (52–53). Ellison's understanding of the particular character of American nationality appears to me highly quixotic, or Tom Sawyerish, insofar as it emphasizes the foundation of the United States and of its American identity, along with the personal identity of its citizens, on a body of resonant texts.

In an important position-taking essay of 1957, "Society, Morality, and the Novel," a title that consciously plays against Lionel Trilling's "Manners, Morals, and the Novel," Ellison defined the crucial feature of American culture: "The moral imperatives of American life that are implicit in the Declaration of Independence, the Constitution and the Bill of Rights were a part of both the individual consciousness and the conscience of those writers who created what we consider our classic novels." Ellison asserted that "these documents . . . inform our language and our conduct with public meaning, and they provide the broadest frame of reference for our most private dramas" (*Collected* 702).

This claim provokes a question that Ellison did not address: Is a critic always right to invoke these national-foundational documents even when the work in question either fails to refer to them or seems to do so only to diminish them? My own arguments on historical distinctions between "national" and "literary" narratives, and my concern with the "nationalization of literary narrative," grow in part from this question. If this national-textual "frame of reference" is simply always there, it would seem hard for Ellison to maintain his distinction between Twain and Hemingway. After all, no more than do Hemingway's narrators does Huck explicitly invoke the founding national documents; their relevance depends on a reader's choosing to place the book in their "frame." Yet as Ellison emphasized in his address upon receiving the 1953 National Book Award, "understatement depends . . . upon commonly held assumptions," but these assumptions are not necessarily available to a writer of "minority status" (*Collected* 152).

In "Society, Morality, and the Novel" Ellison spelled out more fully what in the award speech had necessarily been condensed. For Ellison, the novel as a literary form "is basically a form of communication" (*Collected* 696). But the novel can succeed in communicating "only by appealing to that which we know, through actual experience or through literature, to be the way things occur" (696–97). Therefore, as part of the communicative exchange, there must exist between novelist and reader "a body of shared assumptions," which are possible only because of "the particular circumstances of their mutual society." And at the level of technique, this collaboration "depends upon the reader's acceptance of a set of artistic conventions" (697). Only on the basis of what is "mutual," "shared," and conventional between writer and reader can the discovery of the new occur. But in every society, and certainly in the United States, a "minority" writer may not share the experience, the sense of life, the assumptions, and the specific signals of communication that are those of the majority. This is the problem with understatement—both for minority writers addressing the majority, and no less important, for minority readers encountering the coded understatement of a social group that excludes them.

In Ellison's understanding of American cultural history, the moral energy of nineteenth-century fiction had been muffled by modernists, in whose writings the "energy was turned in upon itself in the form of technical experimentation" (708). In the case of Hemingway in particular, this produced a "confusion." This confusion, Ellison argued, damaged "both Hemingway's imitators and his readers," and its source "lay in the understatement" (708–9). Despite what Ellison considered Hemingway's own high moral seriousness, "the children of the good Americans of the 1880s [precisely the readers who had *Huckleberry Finn* as part of their reading from earliest childhood] had forgotten the historical problems which made Hemingway's understatement fully meaningful" (709).

In his protracted meditation on Hemingway and understatement, Ellison framed in relation to race an issue that had long, and has since, been much discussed in relation to gender. Typically critics have contrasted the hyperbolic overstatement of sentimental writers following Stowe against the elliptical understatement of ironical writers following Hawthorne. Toni Morrison (*Playing*) and Kenneth Warren have recently done important work in bringing out the barely spoken racialist frame of reference that shapes prestigious work in the more elliptical line.

In "Society, Morality, and the Novel," Ellison placed the literature of the United States in a larger context, about which the same interpretive problem may be posed—that is, what frame may be assumed? Consider this statement: "In the nineteenth century, during the moment of greatest middle-class stability . . . the novel reached its first high point of formal self-consciousness" (*Collected* 700). This is already a notable formulation. For the modernism that made "formal self-consciousness" a feature to be noted and valued generally failed to find this virtue in the literature of the nineteenth century. Ellison, like Trilling, used modernist aesthetic categories to appreciate freshly the classics of the nineteenth century, while—again like Trilling—carrying forward the nineteenth-century critical commitment to the link between literature and society.

There is a further remarkable element in this sentence of Ellison's, for I have omitted a long interpolation. The sentence actually reads as follows:

> In the nineteenth century, during the moment of greatest middle-class stability—a stability found actually only at the center, and there only relatively, in England and not in the colonies, in Paris rather than in Africa, for there the baser instincts, the violence and greed could destroy and exploit non-European societies in the name of humanism and culture, beauty and liberty, fraternity and equality while protecting the humanity of those at home—the novel reached its first high point of formal self-consciousness. (700)

More anticipating Edward Said than echoing Lionel Trilling here, Ellison framed the culture of the novel around the turbulence of imperialism, and he recognized that even as the novel may be a form of truth telling, novels could also "reconstruct an image of experience which would make it unnecessary for one to be aware of the true reality upon which society rested" (701).

In this essay, as we have already noted in the discussion of Hemingway and understatement, Ellison was emphatic concerning both the moral importance of the novel as a form and also the possibility that writers or readers or both may fail fully to grasp and promote that moral significance. Like Trilling on "moral realism," Ellison saw a novel as admirable to the extent that it "intensifies our sense of the real" (697), but he also recognized that a novel may win popularity "to the extent that [it] justifies our desire to evade certain aspects of reality which we find unpleasant beyond the point of confrontation" (697, italicized in original).

Ellison, like Trilling, admired *Huckleberry Finn* for its power of confronting fundamental moral issues. My concern is less to argue against this view than to emphasize that the tradition of idolatry has made this kind of claim by the authorities a matter more of ritual invocation than of actually renewed moral exploration. It is striking that Ellison's most unequivocal statement about the moral importance of *Huckleberry Finn* came in his earliest discussion, and over the many years following, while he never came out "against" *Huckleberry Finn*, he continued to emphasize the shortcoming he found in the figure of Jim and the limitations that this shortcoming marked even in Twain's very great accomplishment. That is, he did not take part in the hypercanonization.

In Ellison's concern with the novel's task to make readers aware "of the true reality upon which society rested," we recognize again the problems of convention and understatement: What can be assumed as a shared basis and what must be said *explicitly* in order to invoke a frame of reference?

Ellison's complex sense of global geopolitics as the enabling condition for formal accomplishment in the nineteenth-century novel matched his understanding of his own time. Since the failure of Reconstruction, the accomplishment of *Huckleberry Finn* remained an isolated landmark, and therefore, Ellison wrote, "now in the 1950s, at a time when our world leadership has become an indisputable and perplexing fact, we have been forced to return to problems, in the form of the current desegregation issue, which should have been faced up to years ago" (*Collected* 705). The national first-person plural is deeply rooted in Ellison's discourse here. As he tentatively ("perplexing") tries on the burden of "world leadership," I am unhappily reminded that his powerful praise of Twain and critique of Hemingway first appeared in a magazine edited by Henry Kissinger.

In Ellison's *Paris Review* interview (1955), he observed in a similar vein, "Our so-called race problem has now lined up with the world problem of colonialism and the struggle of the West to gain the allegiance of the remaining non-white people who have thus far remained outside the Communist sphere" (*Conversations* 18–19). Such statements mark Ellison's continuity with the moment of 1948, analyzed in relation to Lionel Trilling in chapter 5. They demonstrate what we might call the liberal Compromise of 1948: the link binding the politics of social—including racial—justice in the United States to a policy and rhetoric of domestic anti-Communism and Cold War abroad.

Ellison's Cold War liberalism takes on a fuller intricacy in his 1958 interview with the French journal *Preuves*. He emphasized that African Americans were "the only black peoples" in the world who were "not fighting for separation from the 'whites,'" and this goal of integration was sought "precisely in terms of American constitutionalism" (*Collected* 299). In 1964, Ellison observed that "Negroes' struggle . . . for freedom [has] *always* been moral; what is new is that their efforts now have sanction in national law." The "protection" afforded by "the ultimate force of federal troops" had become available to African Americans for the first time "since the end of Reconstruction" (*Collected* 570).

The most authoritative current historian of Reconstruction, Eric Foner, has sketched a history of the relations of African Americans to the power of the national government in the United States that underlines the significance of Ellison's point, even as it shows the relation of Ellison's thinking to issues still very much alive in the U.S. politics of the 1990s as I write.

> The redefinition of federalism and establishment of a national principle of equality before the law worked a profound transformation in blacks' political outlook. Before 1860, most blacks had feared federal power, since the government at Washington seemed to be controlled by the Slave Power. Indeed, some Northern states in effect nullified the national fugitive-slave law before the Civil War. But with emancipation and equal rights coming through unprecedented exercises of central authority, blacks fully embraced the nationalism of the Civil War era. Until Americans abandoned the idea of "the right of each state to control its own affairs," wrote Frederick Douglass, "no general assertion of human rights can be of any practical value." The states' inability to suppress political violence during Reconstruction reinforced this tendency to look to Washington for salvation. This identification with the national government, reinforced during the modern civil-rights

movement, remains to this day a major difference between black and white political traditions. Their distinct historical experience leads most blacks to fear unrestrained localism far more than an activist government at Washington, even while, as President Reagan demonstrated, talk of curbing national authority can still, two centuries after the American Revolution, galvanize white votes. ("Blacks" 71)

Foner's incisive overview provides important context for the emotion one feels in Ellison's comments: it is a great historical privilege to feel oneself and one's people so directly the beneficiary of the power of the state, and to participate in the wise exercise of such power.

The thrilling success of the ideals of the civil rights movement may explain the triumphalism when in 1977 Ellison wrote of "the irrepressible movement of American culture toward the integration of its diverse elements" (*Collected* 505). As the key term of the civil rights movement in the decade after 1954, "integration" gives one meaning to Ellison's sentence. Yet "integration" also has a less attractive meaning, as a process of breaking down resistances and assimilating local diversities into a homogeneous totality. Ellison participated in this more fearsome sense of integration as well, in his studied distance from protests against the war in Vietnam, in his decision in 1969 to speak at West Point, and with his 1968 contribution to the volume honoring Lyndon Johnson. In that tribute to Johnson, he explained further his priorities concerning the uses of state power: "As a charter member of the National Council of the Arts, I felt that governmental aid to the American arts and artists was of a more abiding importance than my hopes that the Vietnam War would be brought to a swift conclusion" (*Collected* 554).

In earlier writings, Ellison had shown what seems to me a more nuanced sense of how the ambivalent process of integration works, for example in the observation, apropos of Richard Wright's *Black Boy*, that "the welfare of the most humble black Mississippi sharecropper is affected less by the flow of the seasons and the rhythm of natural events than by the fluctuations of the stock market" (*Collected* 139). Here the integration is not political but economic, integration not into a nation but into global capital flows.

In his assessment of Lyndon Johnson, however, Ellison did not reckon that the economic cost of the Vietnam War might nullify his conviction that Johnson was "the greatest American President for the poor and for Negroes" (*Collected* 562). Ellison's Tuskegee contemporary and later friend and intellectual associate Albert Murray, a retired air force officer and important author, took common ground with Ellison on this point in a way that resonates with Foner's historical perspective and that further indicates what many African Americans may have felt was at stake:

> Negro voters and political bird watchers had some hopes for FDR and JFK, felt stuck with Ike, are still philosophical about Truman; *but they put their money on LBJ*—and were somewhat saddened to find how many of their Northern liberal friends insisted that LBJ's civil rights record counts for nothing and that Negroes should *hate* him because of his blunders in Vietnam. Many suspected that much of the opposition to Johnson's foreign policy was really another sneaky backlash trick to weaken his *domestic* policy! (119)

This provokes many sad reflections: above all, that it was precisely Johnson's success in pursuing (although not accomplishing) his chosen foreign policy that did most to weaken, to diminish the long-term benefits of, his domestic policy, once the costs of an underfunded war economy began to be felt. This to me is a case of global economics unhinging American nationalism. However, in the realm of culture—which as a member of the National Council on the Arts he recognized to be related in complex ways to politics—Ellison's assessment of his own inheritance as an author is emphatically not nationalist: his roots are not just black and not only American but include Marx and Freud (*Collected* 666), Malraux and Dostoevski (211–12).

A remarkable instance of Ellison's fully internationalist, cosmopolitan cultural commitment came in the question period of an extraordinary roundtable discussion. In 1968, at the annual convention of the Southern Historical Association, C. Vann Woodward convened his friends Ellison, Robert Penn Warren, and William Styron—three prize-winning, Southern-born, Northern-based, liberal novelists—to discuss "The Uses of History in Fiction." The motive for the panel was the controversy over Styron's *The Confessions of Nat Turner* (1967), which had been widely praised and won the Pulitzer Prize, before being blasted in a volume of ten black writers' responses. This is one marker of the transition from the integrationist civil rights movement to the complexities of Black Power, which seemed—to many blacks and whites who had been active in civil rights—to split the community of goodwill far more than it achieved further progress. And yet, in ways still at issue in current debates over *Huckleberry Finn,* many well-meaning whites wholly failed to recognize the authoritarian paternalism in their wish to define for African Americans how they should feel, and be grateful for, the best efforts of whites on their behalf. Ellison himself was a friend of Styron but pointedly stated that he had not yet read *The Confessions of Nat Turner.*

Ellison spoke with great grace and tact about the general difficulty of using named historical figures in a novel. He also restated, yet more emphatically, the problem of assumptions and conventions, joining it to his dissatisfaction with Twain's Jim:

> When a novelist moves into the arena of history and takes on the obligation of the historian he has to be aware that he faces a tough rhetorical problem. He has to sell *me,* convince me, that despite the racial divisions and antagonisms in the U.S., his received version of history is not drastically opposed to mine. . . . I can . . . accept Sam Feathers or Lucas Beauchamp in Faulkner in ways that I couldn't accept Jim in *Huckleberry Finn.* (*Conversations* 154)

A questioner asked whether Ellison thought that Twain's "creative imagination was limited . . . by the historical moment, and that this is what has changed" (172). Ellison's answer boldly cuts against the grain of hypercanonization and nationalism. He declared that Twain was also "limited . . . by his being not quite as literary a man as he was required to be" (172). Ellison had explained that even historical fiction "isn't written out of history" alone; as a form of art, it is also "written out of other art forms" (171). Therefore, Ellison found, the shortcoming that limits even Twain's great accomplishment is not simply a matter of his historical period. There were artistic resources available to Twain that he did not make use of. Ellison mentioned some of the literary resources Twain could have used as "touchstones" to assist him in "filling out the complex humanity of that man who appeared in his book out of his own imagination, and who was known as Jim" (172). In using the term "touchstones," Ellison alluded to Matthew Arnold's high-cultural perspective, and the specific predecessor Ellison named is equally out of the usual orbit of American discussion of *Huckleberry Finn.* Twain "could have gone to Walter Scott." I wish Ellison had said more here. His statement is like Huck's conscience saying he could have gone to Sunday school, for Twain loathed Scott, as we have seen, and it is commonplace to connect his blast against Scott in *Life on the Mississippi* with the mockery, in *Huckleberry Finn*, of Tom Sawyer's love for transatlantic historical romance. But Ellison called his own shots, regardless of this nativist tendency in Twain's cultural ideology, which has been magnified by hypercanonization.

Edward Said in Counterpoint

To recognize the strengths of Ellison's concerns for the international, and the problems it poses for his commitment to the national, opens a critical perspective on Fishkin's nationalist use of Twain. Her book ends: "Will Huck become an emblem of a society that is now, and has always been, as multiracial and multicultural as the sources of the novel that we have embraced as most expressive of who we really are?" (144).

To push beyond this populist finale in Fishkin and to further reflect on Ellison, I draw on Edward W. Said's *Culture and Imperialism* (1993). In reflecting on American nationalism, it is salutary to bring in a writer who is an American citizen not born in the United States. His own particular experience of "the politics of dispossession" (as he titled a 1994 book) gives Said a perspective that complements Ellison's. Said's *Orientalism* (1978) inaugurated in the United States, and in many other nations, the kind of work that has become known as "postcolonial studies," and for decades he has also been the most prominent and humane voice within the United States for the cause of the Palestinian people, a serious critic of Arafat as well as of Israeli and American policies. Contrast Said's final sentences with the one I just quoted from Fishkin: "It is more rewarding—and more difficult—to think concretely and sympathetically, contrapuntally, about others than only about 'us.' But this also means . . . above all, not constantly reiterating how 'our' culture or country is number one (or not number one, for that matter). For the intellectual, there is quite enough of value to do without *that*" (336). Since my reflections on Said and Fishkin aim to challenge the nationalism of established American literary historiography, it is exactly to my purpose that *Culture and Imperialism* deals rather little with the United States. For that very reason those who care about American culture will benefit by considering the alternatives it makes possible.

The key methodological notion of *Culture and Imperialism* is what

Said calls "contrapuntal criticism." Taken from musical vocabulary, the adjectival form of counterpoint has several important resonances. It emphasizes not resolution, but rather the interplay of parts that would be independent were they not brought together into a larger composition. In this respect, the notion of the contrapuntal is quite distinct, I think, from the unifying rhetorics and models that dominate Americanist discussions of the relations between the story elements of *Huckleberry Finn* and its historical or political "meanings." This emphasis on the contrapuntal as bringing together through an act of will two distinct elements is closely allied with the notion of the "hybrid." Said makes a distinction between "cultural identities," which attribute an organic unity to culture or its products, as if they were natural growths, and cultures or cultural works considered as "contrapuntal ensembles" (52), which are assemblages put together by human beings. "Contrapuntal" suggests that the interrelated parts have active and intricate relations to each other and to the whole that they together are parts of. The term thus allows a large scale of thinking that still does not claim to be all-embracing. In a crucial formulation, Said proposes that "the whole of a culture" is "disjunct," but that "many important sectors of it can be apprehended as working *contrapuntally* together" (194).

In contrapuntally joining imperialism with the institution of the novel in Britain and France in the nineteenth century, Said deploys a notion rather like what Raymond Williams called "structures of feeling," but I think Said manages greater material precision with what he calls "structures of attitude and reference." One structure of attitude and reference, for example, is a tendency that "fixes socially desirable, empowered space in metropolitan England or Europe and connects it by design, motive, and development to distant or peripheral worlds . . . conceived of as desirable but subordinate" (52). As another such structure, he cites the sentiment that "subject races should be ruled, that they *are* subject races, that one race deserves and has consistently earned the right to be considered the race whose main mission it is to expand beyond its own domain" (53). This language of space and expansion registers a fundamental concern in Said's book that brings him closer to some themes of American literary and cultural study than to the traditions of synoptic comparative literature which provide most of his own methodological models, even as he deviates from them.

Said, throughout his career, has been concerned that criticism be what he terms "secular." This term contrasts to *religious,* and more broadly to the connotations of veneration and givenness. It is not the task of critics to praise works as if they were divine, or even as if they had grown through the laws of nature. As a "secular" critic, he acknowledges works of culture as great but not as transcendent (or, in the usual critical phrasing, "timeless")—neither out of human control and judgment, nor on the other hand wholly subject to the human will, for humans are not omnipotent. By thus recognizing the necessary limits and imperfections of all human activities, Said takes a strong position against what he calls the "rhetoric of blame." This is a critical position that has hurt feelings and provoked debate among some readers who have previously used Said's work and felt themselves allied with him. Here is the strongest moment on this topic:

> It would be silly to expect Jane Austen to treat slavery with anything like the passion of an abolitionist or a newly liberated slave. Yet what I have called the rhetoric of blame so often now employed by subaltern, minority, or disadvantaged voices, attacks her and others like her, retrospectively, for being white, privileged, insensitive, complicit. Yes, Austen belonged to a slave-owning society, but do we therefore jettison her novels as so many trivial exercises in aesthetic frumpery? Not at all, I would argue, if we take seriously our intellectual and interpretative vocation to make connections, to deal with as much of the evidence as possible . . . above all to see complementarity and interdependence instead of isolated, venerated, or formalized experience that excludes and forbids the hybridizing intrusions of human history. (96)

This perspective on Austen, along with Said's extended appreciation of the "pleasures of imperialism" in Kipling's *Kim* (132–62), suggests that it might be possible to discuss *Huckleberry Finn* without hyperboles of either outrage or defensiveness. By forgoing the rhetoric of blame, one may acknowledge the great value of *Huckleberry Finn* without feeling obligated to construct for it a historically impossible purity. (As Ellison observed, "Usually when you find some assertion of purity, you are dealing with historical, if not cultural ignorance" [*Collected* 443]). And I would emphasize that in my reading of the controversies over *Huckleberry Finn,* it is not simply the parents and children who object to the book who use a rhetoric of blame. The rhetoric of defensive blame, the accusation of "not

206 Nation, Race, and Beyond

actually reading," is just as bad—and worse, insofar as it comes from the more authoritative side in the nondebate.

Said's reference to "hybridizing intrusions" recalls the pain that is part of historical action and process. Yet there remains a question he has not yet worked out, I think. Grant that *Culture and Imperialism* magnanimously refuses the "rhetoric of blame" that has marked so much recent socially and politically concerned criticism, and grant, too, that this refusal by no means diminishes the book's power to make critical political judgments. Nonetheless, the book's practice of "connection" rejoins the realm of pain (empire, slavery, war, etc.) to the realm of pleasure (the separated aesthetic sphere). Once the connection is reestablished, what can assure that the pain does not overwhelm the pleasure? The continuing present vividness of America's historical racism is what provokes the pain that leads students and their parents to protest the classroom prestige of *Huckleberry Finn*.

What could contrapuntal American literary history be like? Said addresses the contemporary United States, but from the nineteenth century he discusses only Britain and France; yet the nineteenth-century literature of the United States has provided the ground on which later-twentieth-century American nationalism has been most eager to build its sense of a powerful "we." As early as the 1930s, in his nationalist recuperation of Twain from the charges of Brooks, DeVoto claimed that Twain differs from the writers before the Civil War precisely because his is an age of empire, not merely of national consolidation. Adapting historical periodizing terms more familiar from French history, DeVoto asserted, "Emerson is the classic literary man of the First Republic," and "Mark Twain was the classic writer of the Empire that succeeded it" (*Forays* 357). This historical difference, DeVoto argued, had cultural consequences, "Yet criticism curiously went on expecting America to speak with that self-same voice" of the antebellum period. Both genteel critics and the "liberal" critics such as Brooks who succeeded them foolishly "expected the transcontinental America, the melting pot, the industrial revolution, the American empire," to sound like Emerson or Thoreau. In his estimation, criticism was "fifty years" behind Twain (356) (that is, not until DeVoto's own *Mark Twain's America* was the account finally reckoned right). The figure now perceptible to Americans, "the Mark Twain whom it is at last possible to see, when his work has been over for forty years and he has been dead for twenty-five," is "the great writer who was shaped by the experience of a westward-making people during the great years of their rise to empire, and who shaped their experience to the finest, fullest, and greatest art the empire produced" (362).

Since DeVoto, this imperial theme has not been welcome to American cultural critics, but the historical geographer D. W. Meinig argues in his three-volume work in progress, *The Shaping of America: A Geographical Perspective on Five Hundred Years of History*, that the United States is better understood as an empire than as a nation, especially because the model of nation has been a model of homogeneity, while the model of empire has required confronting, as a "geopolitical challenge," the issue of "diversity" (194).

No work has been at once more revered and more loved in America's process of national-imperial self-reinforcement than *Huckleberry Finn*, even when the national self is proclaimed as "hybrid," as by Fishkin. No work is more regularly referred to by the upper-middlebrow establishment of the *New York Times* that also proclaims America's continuing imperial mission. But where in the book is the place to set the imperial counterpoint? In concluding this chapter, I will sketch two areas for exploration. The first involves rethinking the issues of language that have been so much at the fore in these last several chapters. The second involves reconceiving the Mississippi in the imaginative geography of Mark Twain's America. Together they lead to an understanding of Twain's United States as produced from a global history of empire and as itself producing a new empire.

Creole vs. Vernacular

Unlike the nationalist emphasis in Fishkin's work that tends to erase Africa from the African American and to erase England from American English, Dillard's work on Black English supports the comparative study of the culture of the United States. Dillard makes an elaborate and challenging argument that situates Black English in a long global history, in which most Americans will be surprised to discover that the Portuguese language plays a key role. The Portuguese were the first modern Europeans involved in exploration and slave trading in Africa, starting in the fifteenth century, and to make communication possible as the Portuguese encountered various African peoples, a new language grew up, spoken by both parties: "Portuguese Trade Pidgin." According to Dillard's analysis, this language formed the basis for the new language used for similar purposes by English sailors and merchants, "Maritime Pidgin English" (14–15). This was the language Africans encountered, sooner or later, in the anglophone slave trade, and it in turn provided a basis for a new pidgin spoken by recently enslaved Africans among themselves, when (as was common) groups of slaves included Africans with no other language in common. American Black English, then, like the varieties of Black English of the West Indies, arose among the children of slaves who spoke this pidgin. Dillard emphasizes that this version of English came via West Africa, not "directly from Great Britain"; it arrived by slave ships, "not . . . the Mayflower" (6).

In the terminology of linguistics, a language that arises in this way, as the mother tongue of the children of pidgin speakers, is called a "creole" or "creolized" language. This antiseptic usage in the science of language comes from an earlier usage that carries more evidently the smell of struggle, as evidenced in an *OED* citation from the age when colonies were not yet "post": "a language of a civilized people, especially European, mixed with that of one or more savage tribes." The term *creole* has a long history in modern Western languages, dating from the first European settlements in America. It has much the same etymological meaning as *vernacular*: *creole* comes to English from French *créole*, from Spanish *criollo*, from Portuguese *crioulo*, "animal or person born at home, then . . . a black African slave in Brazil who was born in his or her master's house" (McArthur 270). Despite their similar etymologies, the quite different history and connotations of *creole* and *vernacular* make *creole* more salutary and stimulating for current critical use. Anthropologists have adapted the term *creolization* as an alternative to "acculturation" to refer to the conflicts "between ways of life and the compromises or blends that result" (Mullin 4). "Acculturation" carries the suggestion of one way of life being made over into another, on the model of assimilation, but *creolization* connotes "mixture" rather than "purity," the making of something new rather than maintaining a tradition.

Although the term *creole* is known to most who live in the United States as relevant only to Louisiana (and a very valuable book on the topic concerns New Orleans [Hirsch and Logsdon]), the basic sense of *creole* refers to peoples in all the North and South American and Asian areas colonized by Europeans, specifically to individuals born in the colonized area whose parents came from Europe or Africa. The term in itself carries no specification of color or race, except insofar as it distinguishes the creoles both from immigrants or transients from the colonizing area and from the indigenous population of the colonized area. Part of its force as a term, then, is that its model is not binary—as in that of vernacular vs. genteel—but involves three or more terms (keeping both England and Africa in mind when dealing with the relations between American English and African American English). A creole perspective not only registers more clearly the complex mixtures forming American language and culture; it also links America to a globally transformative history.

To think about American literature and culture through the term *creole* rather than through the term *vernacular* would place less weight on the exceptionalist, nationalist project of distinguishing the culture of the United States from the cultures of Britain and Europe and more on relating, both as similar and as different, the cultures of the United States to those of other areas once held as colonies of Britain and European nations. Moreover, in recognizing that questions of empire were not terminated by the Revolutionary War, a creole perspective would foster the understanding of the United States not only as itself a postcolonial nation but also as itself an imperial nation.

In the previous chapter, instead of using "vernacular" as an intellectual and political tool by which to link *Huckleberry Finn* to America, as part of nationalist hypercanonization, I linked Twain, through an international process of modernity, to great French writing quite contemporary with his own activity. The creole perspective does far more than the vernacular perspective to help understand why the link to Flaubert and the link to Black English may both be illuminating and important approaches to Twain. Although the notion of creole has indeed at times been used as part of an ideology of racial purity, its wider connotations, as seen in its usage in linguistics, suggest "mixture" rather than "purity." Thus a creole perspective encourages thinking about Twain and the emergence of American literary nationality not as something in the first place unique and exceptional, but instead as one among many occasions—around the globe and over centuries—where colonialism precipitated resistances that became nationalism. Yet the process of nationalism has not been uniquely (post)colonial; it has also transformed the colonizing powers.

Putting the River on New Maps

Meditating on his own beginnings in Oklahoma and on Bessie Smith's song of "Going to the Terr'tor'," Ralph Ellison noted the key role of "geography" in the "symbolism of our [in this context, African American] folklore" (*Collected* 601), and Roy Harvey Pearce long ago laid out the relations between boomer land-grabbing and Huck's plan to "light out for the Territory." Just as Dillard's global perspective allowed us to open the subject further than Fishkin's nationalism permitted, Said's "contrapuntal" way of reading helps us further to connect *Huckleberry Finn* to the moment of Mark Twain's writing, a few years before the 1890 census reported the "closing of the frontier," the moment of consolidating America's continental empire before the United States began overseas imperialism.

An important connection may be found in the very freedom to move on the Mississippi through the heart of North America. Although Mark Twain published *Huckleberry Finn* in 1884–85, it is set forty to fifty years earlier, 1835 to 1845. Only in 1803 had the Louisiana Purchase brought *into* the United States the river that had previously marked the western *border*, and that purchase came only after a period of crisis in which for six months the Spanish governor of Louisiana had forbidden U.S. use of the port of New Orleans and closed the Mississippi to U.S. traffic. As of 1835, when Samuel Clemens was born, Missouri was the westernmost state of the Union: Iowa to its north and Arkansas to its south were still territories; and by the "Platte Purchase" of 1837 Missouri extended itself yet further west (becoming until the annexation of Texas the largest state), federally expropriating from Indians (several thousand Iowa and Sac and Fox, along with smaller groups) and converting to slaveholding the corner of the state that extends north and west from Kansas City.

Huck and Jim, although under some constraints, have access to the river, but in 1861 Samuel Clemens had to give up his career as a Mississippi pilot, only two years after he had begun it, because the Civil War so disrupted river traffic and because he dreaded being drafted as a gunboat pilot. When *Huckleberry Finn* was excerpted in the *Century* magazine, from December 1884 through February 1885, it was in the same volume that began a three-year series of memoirs of the Civil War which won tremendous circulation for the journal. The first excerpt from *Huckleberry Finn* was the account of the murderous Grangerford-Shepherdson feud; the next month the *Century*, along with a second piece from *Huckleberry Finn*, ran a lengthy account of the "Operations of the Western Flotilla," that is, the series of engagements that allowed the Union to control the Mississippi from Cairo to Memphis. The main map used to illustrate this *Century* article centers on the Madrid Bend (Walke 441), exactly the portion of the river that is illustrated in the map provided in the standard scholarly edition of *Huckleberry Finn* ([1988] 369) to show the location of the Grangerford-Shepherdson feud, where Huck landed after the raft was run through by the steamboat. The Grangerfords lived in Tennessee, a Confederate state; a mile away the Shepherdsons lived in Union Kentucky. So the democratic racial harmony of Huck and Jim's America-on-a-raft is overturned, and they are cast into the midst of bloody and terrible combat, exactly at the point where secession split the Mississippi.

The contrapuntal approach I am trying to develop differs from the line of criticism, from Trilling to Fishkin (69, 144), that has found *Huckleberry Finn* "subversive." I would not want to take the feud as a miniature model of the Civil War, which would allow us to picture Twain as a daring, self-aware social critic, subverting commonplace pieties. Rather, I take the silence about the history of the Mississippi to be one of the most telling things about this sequence, and about the book more largely. This absence permits reflection on what Said calls the "structure of attitude and reference" by which free movement on the Mississippi is understood as so essential a part of American identity that the book invites readers to give no special thought to the recent purchase of the river valley from France, or of the Civil War that actually obstructed traffic for several years and threatened to reimpose on the river all the complexities of international travel that Jefferson's purchase of Louisiana had hoped to end. By putting historical study to new, contrapuntal use, the element of *Huckleberry Finn* most frequently considered antipolitical, anticonventional, oppositional, or primordially natural, Huck's rafting, comes obliquely against, and is modified by, the national-imperial possession of "our" continent.

Coda

The Memories of *Huckleberry Finn*

We remember *Huckleberry Finn*, even as the book itself seems an act of memory. *Huckleberry Finn* is the "most remembered" work of American fiction. Among the few hypercanonized texts, it is at the top; and the book's subject matter arises from Mark Twain's memories of the small-town and river life Samuel Clemens knew in the 1840s and 1850s. These two memories are connected. One reason *Huckleberry Finn* has become canonically remembered is the shape its remembering gives to the largest ongoing felt problem in the modern history of the United States.

From its publication in 1885 into the 1930s, as we have seen, *Huckleberry Finn* was greatly admired by leaders of advanced literary practice and opinion, and it was greatly loved by many young readers, but it became a universal school text only in the years after the Second World War. The first college text edition of *Huckleberry Finn* was introduced by Lionel Trilling, who opened a wholly new interpretive field when he characterized Huck and Jim as forming a "community of saints." This appropriation of *Huckleberry Finn*, I have argued, makes it into a "national narrative," but Twain wrote it as a "literary narrative." As a literary narrative *Huckleberry Finn* did not directly address the concerns of its time with race and nation, as for example George Washington Cable did in his national narrative *The Grandissimes* (1880), and precisely the obliquity of *Huckleberry Finn*'s relation to its own time has made it more readily amenable to our time's reshaping remembering of it. Such reshaping remembering, what I call "the nationalization of literary narrative," is a tremendously useful technique for empowering a national first-person subject—"we Americans." The wish for such a place to speak from, a national-cultural first-person plural subject, can be found across a wide range of commentators on the current life of the United States, ranging from the liberal pragmatist post-philosopher Richard Rorty to Newt Gingrich. In its standing as "our" most beloved and admired book, *Huckleberry Finn* is not only a cultural treasure, but also a resource for power.

The year 1985 helped me to register the hypercanonization of *Huckleberry Finn*, as I encountered the range of scholarly and more widely public attention to the book's centennial. That year another topic for memory and commemoration appeared even more prominently in the press. It was the fortieth anniversary of the ending of the Second World War. President Ronald Reagan of the United States paid respectful tribute to the graves of German SS soldiers at Bitburg. That scandal spurred intense discussion, and in 1986 there erupted in Germany what became known as the "historians' controversy." It seemed to many Germans and observers abroad that some scholars were using the discipline of history for dangerous political purposes. These scholars were making historical arguments that tended either to "relativize" or to "normalize" the Nazi German state's attempt to kill all Jews. By doing so, these historians, it was feared, were weakening the commitment of the German people to humane politics in the future.

For example, the historian Hans-Peter Schwarz, biographer of West Germany's Cold War leader Konrad Adenauer, was reported to have argued: "precisely in the last decade West Germans have been visibly longing to reassure themselves of their roots in an unabridged German history that can be experienced in living terms, but they are constantly reminded only of the twelve years [i.e., 1933–45] on which patriotic feelings of self-esteem cannot be based. When national consciousness is replaced by consciousness of guilt, patriotism is programmed to degenerate into defeatist pacifism" (quoted in Habermas 247). To an American, this statement seems uncanny because 1985 was just a "decade" after the end of the war in Vietnam, which had been a period of "twelve years," from 1963 to 1975, that had damaged American patriotic feelings of self-esteem, and which some feared had already led to defeatist pacifism (the "Vietnam Syndrome").

Our attempt in the United States to find terms for articulating a deep commitment to democratic political values and practices while avoiding the rhetorical and political pitfalls of "we Americans" is longstanding—at least since Randolph Bourne's pained, polemical reflections on World War I ("the patriot loses all sense of the distinction between State, nation, and government" [357]). More recently, the leading senior figure in literary American studies Sacvan Bercovitch has asked, "What would happen . . . if 'America' were severed once and for all from the United States?" (65). Such reflections can gain strength from the contribution to the German historians' controversy by Jürgen Habermas. Habermas asked boldly, "Can one become the legal successor to the German Reich and continue the traditions of German culture without taking on a historical liability for the form of life in which Auschwitz was possible?" (236). Habermas proposed the term "constitutional patriotism" to define a newly arm's-length relation between national politics and national culture, a patriotism that "now relates not to the concrete totality of a nation," that is, to the "blood and soil" so tainted by the Nazis, but rather to "abstract procedures and principles" (261), democratic rather than traditional in basis.

Yet in moving from the German debate back to the United States, I run a risk spelled out by several of the distinguished American scholars of German Jewish origin who joined the controversy. Geoffrey Hartman warned of "a more subtle revisionism . . . all around us that mitigates the horror of the camps, not by denying it but by using equalizing comparisons. So Vietnam . . . is dubbed a 'holocaust'" (6). All comparative study runs this risk. I have no wish to equalize. But the German debate over patriotism and national self-esteem casts light on the attempts in the United States to come to terms with long-protracted policies and practices of the nation-state that block a happily patriotic understanding of "we Americans." As my whole book has suggested, it need not have taken the war in Vietnam to provoke a crisis within patriotism. The Harvard historian Charles Maier incisively characterized the perspective of the German neoconservative historian Ernst Nolte, whose work helped provoke the "historians' controversy." Maier explained that for Nolte, "Auschwitz need preoccupy the Germans no more than Hiroshima or antebellum slavery, say, haunts Americans" (18).

We may remember that a landmark in the historiography of the enslavement of Africans and African Americans in the United States, *Slavery: A Problem in American Institutional and Intellectual Life* by Stanley Elkins, developed an extended comparison between the practices of enslavement and the techniques of Nazi camps. Elkins argued that the results were destructive to African American personality, producing a "Sambo" character type. Since then, decades of research have uncovered the vitality, integrity, and strength of resistance within the slave community. Yet comparative perspective underlines a disquieting ambiguity in such a notion of "resistance." Recent German studies of "everyday life" under the Third Reich have argued that Germans outside the camps, despite not actively rebelling against their dictatorial regime, did not wholly support it either. Precisely the term *Resistenz* has been used to characterize this situation (Maier 93).

Insofar as Maier disagrees with Nolte and believes that Auschwitz must remain a focus of moral concern, he apparently also believes that antebellum slavery should haunt Americans. And readers of the American Nobel Prize-winning authors William Faulkner and Toni Morrison know that it does. Morrison's dedication of *Beloved* to the "sixty million and more" asserts that the scale of inhumanity in the centuries-long, circumatlantic process by which Africans were enslaved and brought to the Americas fully merits comparison with that of the inhumanity practiced by twentieth-century totalitarian regimes. What if Germany's most beloved and widely taught book were an Aryan boy's Bavarian vernacular account of his adventures in 1944 with an escaping Jew? *Huckleberry Finn* has been put to work in the public culture of the United States as the attempt to transform haunt into idyll. Huck's decision in chapter 31, "All right, then, I'll *go* to hell," has been authoritatively read for decades as the cry not of a demon but of Trilling's saint, a holy fool.

That moment of decision, the most hypercanonical moment in *Huckleberry Finn,* is also the most powerful moment of memory in the book, for the decision is motivated by Huck's vivid recall of his times with Jim, set as counterweight to the voice of conscience, which speaks for the practices and values of a culture that regularly and resolutely enslaved African Americans. You may recall that Conscience tells Huck, "There was the Sunday School; you could a gone to it; and if you'd a done it they'd a learnt you, there, that people as acts as I'd been acting about that nigger goes to everlasting fire." Conscience tells Huck what he would have learned if he had gone to school, but apparently he knows it anyway. Twain here offers a model of something that might be called "cultural memory." Such memory need not arise directly from the individual experience of the persons whose memory it nonetheless forms part of; it is an intimate part of the person, so much so that it may manifest itself unbidden, and yet it is a part that one may debate with or even override, for as chapter 31 makes clear, cultural memory is not automatically a good thing.

The noun *memory* comports as well with the verb *to commemorate* as with the verb *to remember*, and *to remember* may mean to "bear in mind." Thus the "memory" of any group is commonly understood as what from the group's past members of that group can bring to mind. In a context that seems to me quite distinct from any idea of racial identity but that does acknowledge political continuity, the president of the then–Federal Republic of Germany, Richard von Weiszäcker, spoke in the Bundestag as part of the 1985 commemoration of the fortieth anniversary of the end of the war in Europe: "May 8 is a day of remembrance. Remembering means recalling an occurrence honestly and undistortedly so that it becomes a part of our very beings" (Hartman 263). That is, memory takes the form of an imperative as well as an indicative: part of memory in culture is, at times, heeding the injunction, "remember this."

It is extremely important that there exist, as von Weiszäcker's phrasing suggests, a form of cultural, historical memory that is not based on "blood," the filiative structure of ancestry and descent that forms the armature around which so much racist argument wraps itself. In his 1858 Senate campaign Abraham Lincoln developed an idea like von Weiszäcker's, in order to explain how the Declaration of Independence worked to make fellow Americans of those who had come to the United States since independence (and by implication, those who—as was the case with enslaved African Americans—had been in the colonies that became the United States but had not directly participated in the Revolution).

Speaking in Chicago on 10 July, Lincoln looked back to the holiday just past. He began rather tentatively. Perhaps he imagined an audience that felt about Independence Day as he had himself just a few years earlier, in the 1855 passage I quoted in chapter 2, in which Lincoln had mocked the holiday as good only for firecrackers:

> Now it happens that we meet together once every year, sometime about the 4th of July, for some reason or other. These 4th of July gatherings I suppose have their uses. If you will indulge me, I will state what I suppose to be some of them.

Evidently Lincoln's struggle against Douglas had reinstilled meaning into the holiday:

> We hold this annual celebration to remind ourselves of all the good
> done in the process of time[,] of how it was done and who did it, and
> how we are historically connected with it.

Here Lincoln made the crucial distinction that separates his interpretation of the Declaration from that of Douglas and of the Dred
Scott decision:

> We have, besides these men—descended by blood from our ances-
> tors—among us perhaps half our people who are not descendants at
> all of these men. . . . If they look back through this history to trace their
> connection with those days by blood, they find they have none, they
> cannot carry themselves back into that glorious epoch and make them-
> selves feel that they are part of us.

Not "blood" but only the founding, abstract principles of the
United States bring *all* American citizens together:

> When they look through that old Declaration of Independence . . . then
> they feel that that moral sentiment taught in that day evidences their
> relation to those men, that it is the father of all moral principle in them,
> and that they have a right to claim it as though they were blood of the
> blood and flesh of the flesh of the men who wrote that Declaration.

Lincoln employed the language of biological connection, but only
as an evident figure of speech: "as though" the same flesh and
blood were shared. His final metaphor conveys the thrilling stimu-
lus of this "historical connection," but the language is closer to
that of a scientist's laboratory than to the ordinary language of
family. The "moral sentiment" that new citizens now feel and share
with the Founders serves as "the electric cord" in the declaration "that links the hearts of patriotic and liberty-loving men together" (1:455–56). Yet I cannot end simply by praising Lincoln.
For Lincoln is the president whose patriotic leadership in the Civil
War did most to create that confusion among "State, nation, and
government" that Bourne condemned.

Against that terrible power—in the Civil War, the Spanish-
American War, World War I, World War II, the Cold War, the Vietnam War, or the "New World Order"—Twain's literary strategy of
the private heart offers welcome relief, which innumerable readers have taken with gratitude. But, I have argued, Twain's literary

strategy has over the last fifty years been nationalized by cultural authorities—critics, teachers, and journalists—and there is a double cost. There is a literary cost: If we force *Huckleberry Finn* to carry national-political burdens it wasn't made for, we cannot rightly appreciate its sublime moments of moral comedy and stylistic mastery, as I have argued in chapters 2 and 7. And there is a political cost: Lionel Trilling dwelt on the need to bring imagination into politics, but cultural authorities now seem to believe that in teaching *Huckleberry Finn* as a "weapon against racism" imagination is already politics enough. Huck, as "quintessentially American," is made to represent the innocent heart that validates the moral goodness of the (we wish) no longer so terrible national power. This covert politics of complacency allows a little bit of fictional feeling to purify what is still unjust in the social and economic life of the United States. To remedy such a state of affairs, the "Lincoln of our literature" must yield to the Lincoln of our politics. Principles and actions, and public debates over principles and actions, are more important to remember than *Huckleberry Finn* if we wish to end racism and to be citizens who can take pride in our country in a world that is not wholly "ours."

Acknowledgments
Works Cited
Index

Acknowledgments

As a work of scholarship that has much to say about classroom issues, this book owes much to the stimulation and challenge I enjoyed in several introductory courses at the University of Illinois at Chicago, especially from 1979 to 1981. Actual work on this project began only in the late 1980s, and I thank the graduate students at Columbia University and the University of Pittsburgh who greatly contributed to my learning in our seminars together. Among those students, several have shared with me materials that actually or almost got into the book: Lynn Casmier-Paz, John W. Giles, Steve Parks, Christine Ross, and Julia Sawyer.

Without a Fellowship from the National Endowment for the Humanities, which took me from the classroom, I could not have ended my work. Institutional support for research expenses from Columbia University and the University of Pittsburgh has been indispensable. I am especially grateful to my research assistants: Eleni Coundouriotis, Peaches Henry, Rebecca Dean, Cela Mascarenhas, Gwen Gorzelsky, Lisa Roulette, Sara London, Kelly Amienne, Roger LePage, and Lynn Harper.

Lectures and colloquia with colleagues provided very helpful occasions to try out portions of my argument. First thanks must go to Janice Carlisle and the Society for the Study of Narrative Literature and to Michael Riffaterre and the School of Criticism and Theory, whose invitations provoked my earliest chapter drafts in 1990. Along the way, thanks to many others who invited or welcomed me, some more than once, to their campuses: Paul Armstrong (University of Oregon); Susan Balée (Beaver College); Lauren Berlant, Bill Brown, Christopher Looby, and Laurence Rothfield (University of Chicago); David Bromwich and Carl Hovde (Columbia University Trilling Seminars in Criticism); Christopher Castiglia (Bryn Mawr College); Pat Crain and Eric Haralson (Columbia University Columbus Circle); Wai-Chee Dimock and Masao Miyoshi (University of California-San Diego); John Eperjesi (Carnegie-Mellon University); Betsy Erkkila and Jay Grossman (University of Pennsylvania); Michael T. Gilmore (Brandeis University); Gunter Lenz (Humboldt University); Kathryne Lindberg (Wayne State University); Daniel O'Hara (Temple University); Donald Pease (Dartmouth College); Q. S. Tong (Hong Kong University); Herbert F. Tucker (University of Virginia). Also welcome were invitations to speak at meetings, from Shelley Fisher Fishkin, Cyrus Patell, Bruce Robbins, and Wang Ning.

This book would not have been possible without the advance commitment and enthusiasm for the project, and the long-term patience, shown by Frank Lentricchia, editor of the American Writers Project, and Allen Fitchen, Director of the University of Wisconsin Press. My thanks also to the editors and publishers in whose pages preliminary versions of a few portions have appeared: Paul Bové, editor of *boundary 2*, Donald Pease, editor of the special issue, and Duke University Press for "Nationalism, Hypercanonization, and *Huckleberry Finn*" (a first version of chapter 6), from *boundary 2* 19.1 (1992): 14–33; Betsy Erkkila and Jay Grossman, volume editors, and Oxford University Press for "Whitman and Problems of the Vernacular" (from which I draw a few pages on vernacular in chapter 7 and on creole in chapter 8) in *Breaking Bounds: Whitman and American Cultural Studies* (1995): 44–61; Marshall Brown, volume editor, and Duke University Press for "What Is the History of Literature?" (from which I draw a few pages in the Coda), in *The Uses of Literary History* (1995): 23–33; Gordon Hutner, editor, and Oxford University Press for "Putting the River on New Maps: Nation, Race, and Beyond in Reading *Huckleberry Finn*" (used in part in part of chapter 8), *American Literary History* 8.1 (1996): 110–29.

This book is not an attack on the community of scholars who work on Mark Twain. Although I may seem ungrateful, I must emphasize that the members of this community with whom I have had contact have been uniformly gracious and collegial. Since my concern has mainly been to argue with prestigious writings that, however valuable in themselves, have contributed to a state of public discussion that I lament and oppose, it would have overburdened my pages also to detail all those whose published work on *Huckleberry Finn* I admire. But I must mention Wayne Booth, Forrest Robinson, and Steven Mailloux for work in which I recognize kindred concerns, whether they agree with me or not. As I began to write on Ralph Ellison, Robert J. Corber and Alan Nadel offered supportive criticism.

I have been very lucky in my friends. Over the years I pursued this work, several of my fellow editors at *boundary 2* were engaged in closely related projects: Paul Bové on Henry Adams, Ronald Judy on slave narrative, Kathryne Lindberg on African American revolutionary writing, Daniel O'Hara on Henry James, and Donald Pease on the reconstruction of American culture from Stowe to Twain. And my Pittsburgh colleague Nancy Glazener was working on American realism. All this made possible unusually searching and knowledgeable criticism of work in progress, which they have repeatedly offered, and for which I can never give enough thanks. Other friends and colleagues also lent crucial support, including Sacvan Bercovitch, James Cox, Susan Gillman, Fredric Jameson, and Karl Kroeber. For my ambitions in this book, one example has been most important. For decades, Edward W. Said's work as a writer has combined a scholar's learning, a critic's discernment, and an intellectual's passion for justice. In thanks for all this and more, I dedicate this book to him.

I cannot end without again thanking Carol Kay, whose searching thoughts on liberal politics have persuaded me to greater nuance in my assessment of the decades after World War II, and whose willingness to read this work has made it seem worth writing.

Works Cited

Adams, J. Donald. "Speaking of Books." *New York Times Book Review*, 10 March 1957, 2.

Adams, J. Donald. "Speaking of Books." *New York Times Book Review*, 29 May 1960, 2.

[Adams, J. Donald?]. "Topics of the Times." *New York Times*, 3 Nov. 1935.

Applebee, Arthur. "Stability and Change in the High School Canon." *English Journal* 81.5 (Sept. 1992): 27–32.

Arac, Jonathan. "Narrative Forms." In *Cambridge History of American Literature*, ed. Sacvan Bercovitch. Cambridge: Cambridge UP, 1995. 2: 607–777.

Arnold Matthew. *The Portable Matthew Arnold*. Ed. Lionel Trilling. New York: Viking, 1949.

Arvin, Newton. "Mark Twain: 1835–1935." *New Republic* 83 (1935): 125–27.

Ayers, Edward L. *The Promise of the New South: Life after Reconstruction*. New York: Oxford UP, 1992.

Bakhtin, Mikhail. *The Dialogic Imagination*. Trans. Caryl Emerson and Michael Holquist. Austin: U of Texas P, 1981.

Baldwin, James. "Everybody's Protest Novel." 1949. In Phillips and Rahv 326–32.

Ballard, Allan B. Letter. *New York Times*, 9 May 1982.

Baugh, John. "Black English Vernacular." In McArthur 133–35.

Beaver, Harold. "Run, Nigger, Run: *Adventures of Huckleberry Finn* as a Fugitive Slave Narrative." *American Studies* 8 (1974): 339–61.

Bellinger, Frances Trotter. Letter. *Washington Post*, 20 March 1995.

Bercovitch, Sacvan. *The Rites of Assent: Transformations in the Symbolic Construction of America*. New York: Routledge, 1993.

Berland, Evan. "Mark Twain Museum Mounts 'Huckleberry Finn' Defense." *Pittsburgh Post-Gazette*, 20 July 1995, A5.

Berman, Paul. Review of *Big River*. *Nation*, 1 June 1985, 682–84.

Berthoff, Warner. "The People's Author: Attempting to Find Mr. Mark

Twain." *American Trajectories: Authors and Readings, 1790–1970.* University Park: Pennsylvania State UP, 1994. 21–38.

Blair, Walter. *Mark Twain and Huck Finn.* Berkeley and Los Angeles: U of California P, 1960.

Blair, Walter, ed. *Mark Twain's Hannibal, Huck, and Tom.* Berkeley and Los Angeles: U of California P, 1969.

Boorstin, Daniel J. *The Americans: The National Experience.* 1965. Harmondsworth: Penguin, 1969.

Booth, Wayne. *The Company We Keep: An Ethics of Fiction.* Berkeley and Los Angeles: U of California P, 1988.

Bourget, Paul. *Essais de psychologie contemporaine.* 2 vols. 1883. Paris: Plon, 1919.

Bourget, Paul. *Outre-Mer: Impressions of America.* 1894. Translator not named. New York: Scribner, 1895.

Bourne, Randolph. *The Radical Will: Selected Writings, 1911–1918.* Ed. Olaf Hansen. New York: Urizen Books, 1977.

Bradbury, Malcolm. "Huckleberry Finn: An Epic of Self-Discovery." *UNESCO Courier,* June 1982, 15–17.

Bradley, David. [Untitled]. *New Yorker,* 26 June 1995, 133.

Bradley, Sculley, et al., eds. *Adventures of Huckleberry Finn.* Norton Critical Edition. 2d ed. New York: Norton, 1977.

Branch, Taylor. *Parting the Waters: America in the King Years: 1954–1963.* New York: Simon and Schuster, 1988.

Bridgman, Richard. *The Colloquial Style in America.* New York: Oxford UP, 1966.

Brooks, Van Wyck. *The Ordeal of Mark Twain.* 1920; rev. 1933. New York: Meridian, 1955.

Brooks, Van Wyck. *The Times of Melville and Whitman.* New York: Dutton, 1947.

Brown, Robert B. "One Hundred Years of Huck Finn." *American Heritage,* June–July 1985, 81–85.

Buck, Paul H. *The Road to Reunion, 1865–1900.* Boston: Little, Brown, 1937.

Budd, Louis J. *Mark Twain: Social Philosopher.* Bloomington: Indiana UP, 1962.

Budd, Louis J. *Our Mark Twain: The Making of His Public Personality.* Philadelphia: U of Pennsylvania P, 1983.

Budd, Louis J., ed. Introduction. *New Essays on "Huckleberry Finn."* Cambridge: Cambridge UP, 1985. 1–33.

Buder, Leonard. "'Huck Finn' Barred as Textbook by City." *New York Times,* 12 Sept. 1957, 1, 29.

Cable, George W. *The Grandissimes: A Story of Creole Life.* 1880. New York: Hill and Wang, 1957.

Cady, Edwin H., ed. *W. D. Howells as Critic*. London: Routledge and Kegan Paul, 1973.

[Canby, Henry Seidel?]. "Mark Twain, Radical." *Saturday Review of Literature* 1 (1 Nov. 1924): 241.

Cardwell, Guy A. *Twins of Genius*. East Lansing: Michigan State College P, 1953.

Carey-Webb, Allen. "Racism and *Huckleberry Finn:* Censorship, Dialogue, and Change." *English Journal* 82.7 (Nov. 1993): 22–34.

Carkeet, David. "The Dialects in *Huckleberry Finn*." *American Literature* 51 (1979): 315–32.

Carnes, Jim. "Arrest That Book!" In *Teaching Tolerance* 5.1 (Spring 1996): 19.

Chace, William M. *Lionel Trilling: Criticism and Politics*. Stanford: Stanford UP, 1980.

Champion, Laurie, ed. *The Critical Response to Mark Twain's "Huckleberry Finn"*. Westport, CT: Greenwood, 1991.

Chesnut, Mary. *Mary Chesnut's Civil War*. Ed. C. Vann Woodward. New Haven: Yale UP, 1981.

Cmiel, Kenneth. *Democratic Eloquence: The Fight over Popular Speech in Nineteenth-Century America*. Berkeley and Los Angeles: U of California P, 1991.

Cooper, Anna Julia. *A Voice from the South*. 1892. New York: Oxford UP, 1988.

Cooper, James Fenimore. *The Pioneers*. 1823. *The Leatherstocking Tales*, vol. 1. New York: Literary Classics of the United States, 1985.

Cox, James M. *Mark Twain: The Fate of Humor*. Princeton: Princeton UP, 1966.

Craft, William. *Running a Thousand Miles for Freedom*. In *The Great Slave Narratives*, ed. Arna Bontemps. Boston: Beacon, 1969. 269–331.

Culler, Jonathan. *Flaubert: The Uses of Uncertainty*. Ithaca: Cornell UP, 1974.

Current, Richard, ed. *Reconstruction in Retrospect: Views from the Turn of the Century*. Baton Rouge: Louisiana State UP, 1969.

Davis, David Brion. *Slavery and Human Progress*. New York: Oxford UP, 1984.

Degler, Carl N. *The Other South: Southern Dissenters in the Nineteenth Century*. 1974. Boston: Northeastern UP, 1982.

DeMott, Benjamin. *The Trouble with Friendship: Why Americans Can't Think Straight about Race*. New York: Atlantic Monthly P, 1995.

Denning, Michael. *Mechanic Accents: Dime Novels and Working-Class Culture in America*. London: Verso, 1987.

DePalma, Anthony. "A Scholar Finds Huck Finn's Voice in Twain's Writing about a Black Youth." *New York Times*, 7 July 1992, A16.

DeVoto, Bernard. *Forays and Rebuttals*. Boston: Little, Brown, 1936.

DeVoto, Bernard. *Mark Twain's America*. Boston: Little, Brown, 1932.

Dillard, J. L. *Black English: Its History and Usage in the United States*. 1972. New York: Vintage, 1973.

Dixon, Thomas, Jr. *The Leopard's Spots: A Romance of the White Man's Burden, 1865–1900*, New York: Doubleday, 1902.

Doctorow, E. L. [Untitled]. *New Yorker*, 26 June 1995, 132.

Douglass, Frederick. *Autobiographies*. Ed. Henry Louis Gates, Jr. New York: Library of America, 1994.

Doyno, Victor A. Afterword to Mark Twain, *Adventures of Huckleberry Finn*. The Oxford Mark Twain. New York: Oxford UP, 1996. 1–25.

Doyno, Victor A. Textual Addendum to Twain, *Huckleberry Finn* (1996). 365–418.

Eaton, Clement. *The Freedom-of-Thought Struggle in the Old South*. 1940. Rev. and enlarged ed., New York: Harper and Row, 1964.

Edwards, June. "Morality and Huckleberry Finn." *Humanist*, March-April 1984, 35–36.

Egerton, John. *Speak Now against the Day: The Generation before the Civil Rights Movement in the South*. New York: Knopf, 1994.

Eliot, T. S. Introduction to *Huckleberry Finn*. 1950. In Bradley et al. 328–35.

Eliot, T. S. *Selected Essays*. New York: Harcourt Brace and World, 1964.

Elkins, Stanley. *Slavery: A Problem in American Institutional and Intellectual Life*. Chicago: U of Chicago P, 1959.

Ellison, Ralph. *Collected Essays*. Ed. John F. Callahan. New York: Modern Library, 1995.

Ellison, Ralph. *Conversations with Ralph Ellison*. Ed. Maryemma Graham and Amritjit Singh. Jackson: UP of Mississippi, 1995.

Emerson, Ralph Waldo. *Emerson in His Journals*. Selected and edited by Joel Porte. Cambridge: Harvard UP, 1982.

Fairchild, Hoxie N. Letter. *New York Times*, 14 Sept. 1957.

Fender, Stephen. "African Accents, Tall Tales." *TLS*, 16 July 1993, 27.

Fiedler, Leslie A. "Come Back to the Raft Ag'in, Huck Honey!" 1948. In Graff and Phelan 528–34.

Fiedler, Leslie A. *Love and Death in the American Novel*. 1960. Cleveland: Meridian, 1962.

Fiedler, Leslie A. *What Was Literature? Class Culture and Mass Society*. New York: Simon and Schuster, 1982.

Fields, Barbara Jeanne. "Slavery, Race, and Ideology in the United States of America." *New Left Review*, no. 181 (May–June 1990): 95–118.

Fischer, Victor. "Huckleberry Finn Reviewed: The Reception of *Huckleberry Finn* in the United States, 1885–1897." *American Literary Realism* 16 (1983): 1–57.

Fishkin, Shelley Fisher. *Lighting Out for the Territory: Reflections on Mark Twain and American Culture*. New York: Oxford UP, 1996.

Fishkin, Shelley Fisher. "Twain in '85." Op-Ed, *New York Times,* 18 Feb. 1985.

Fishkin, Shelley Fisher. *Was Huck Black? Mark Twain and African-American Voices.* NY: Oxford UP, 1993.

Flaubert, Gustave. *L'Education sentimentale.* 1869. In *Oeuvres,* vol. 2, ed. A. Thibaudet and R. Dumesnil. Paris: Gallimard, 1952.

Flaubert, Gustave. *Letters, 1857–1880.* Selected, edited, and translated by Francis Steegmuller. Cambridge: Harvard UP, 1982.

Flaubert, Gustave. *Sentimental Education.* 1869. Trans. Robert Baldick. Harmondsworth: Penguin, 1964.

Fluck, Winfried. *Aesthetische Theorie und literaturwissenschaftliche Methode: Eine Untersuchung ihres Zusammenhangs am Beispiel der amerikanischen Huck Finn-Kritik.* Amerikastudien/American Studies no. 43. Stuttgart: Metzler, 1975.

Foner, Eric. "Blacks and the U.S. Constitution, 1789–1989." *New Left Review,* no. 183 (Sept.–Oct. 1990): 63–74.

Foner, Eric. *Reconstruction: America's Unfinished Revolution, 1864–1877.* New York: Harper and Row, 1988.

Franklin, John Hope. *The Militant South, 1800–1861.* Cambridge: Harvard UP, 1956.

Franklin, John Hope. *Race and History: Selected Essays, 1938–1988.* Baton Rouge: Louisiana State UP, 1989.

Frederickson, George M. *The Black Image in the White Mind: The Debate on Afro-American Character and Destiny, 1817–1914.* 1971. New York: Harper and Row, 1972.

Frederickson, George M. *The Inner Civil War: Northern Intellectuals and the Crisis of the Union.* 1965. New York: Harper and Row, 1968.

Freehling, William W. *The Reintegration of American History: Slavery and the Civil War.* New York: Oxford UP, 1994.

Freehling, William W. *The Road to Disunion: The Secessionists at Bay, 1776–1854.* New York: Oxford UP, 1990.

Genette, Gérard. *Narrative Discourse: An Essay in Method.* 1972. Trans. Jane E. Lewin. Ithaca: Cornell UP, 1980.

Geng, Veronica. "Idylls of Minnesota." *New York Times Book Review,* 25 Aug. 1985, 1, 15.

Genovese, Eugene D. *From Rebellion to Revolution: Afro-American Slave Revolts in the Making of the New World.* 1979. New York: Vintage, 1981.

Genovese, Eugene D. *Roll, Jordan, Roll: The World the Slaves Made.* New York: Random House, 1974.

Gibson, Donald B. "Mark Twain's Jim in the Classroom." *English Journal* 57 (Feb. 1968): 196–99, 202.

Gilder, Rosamond, ed. *Letters of Richard Watson Gilder.* Boston and New York: Houghton Mifflin, 1916.

Gill, Brendan. Review of *Big River*. *New Yorker*, 13 May 1985, 128.

Gilman, Stephen. *"Adventures of Huckleberry Finn*: Experience of Samuel Clemens." In Sattelmeyer and Crowley 15–25.

Goldberg, Carey. "Welcome to New York, Curse Capital." *New York Times*, 19 June 1995, B12.

Gottesman, Ronald, et al., eds. *The Norton Anthology of American Literature*. 2 vols. New York: W. W. Norton, 1979.

Graff, Gerald, and James Phelan, eds. *Mark Twain, Adventures of Huckleberry Finn: A Case Study in Critical Controversy*. Boston: Bedford Books, 1995.

Habermas, Jürgen. *The New Conservatism: Cultural Criticism and the Historians' Debate*. Ed. and trans. Shierry Weber Nicholsen. Cambridge: MIT P, 1989.

Handlin, Oscar. *Race and Nationality in American Life*. Garden City, NY: Doubleday, 1957.

Hardwick, Elizabeth. "Faulkner and the South Today." 1948. In *Faulkner: A Collection of Critical Essays*, ed. Robert Penn Warren. Englewood Cliffs, NJ: Prentice-Hall, 1966. 226–30.

Harris, Joel Chandler. *On the Plantation: A Story of a Georgia Boy's Adventures during the War*. 1892. Athens: U of Georgia P, 1980.

Hartman, Geoffrey, ed. *Bitburg in Moral and Political Perspective*. Bloomington: Indiana UP, 1986.

Hearn, Michael Patrick. "Expelling Huckleberry Finn." *Nation*, 7–14 Aug. 1982, 117.

Hechinger, Fred. "Irrationality, Futility and Huck's Censors." *New York Times*, 4 June 1985, 20.

Hemingway, Ernest. *The Green Hills of Africa*. New York: Scribner, 1935.

Henry, Peaches. "The Struggle for Tolerance: Race and Censorship in *Huckleberry Finn*." In Leonard et al. 25–47.

Hentoff, Nat. "The Trials of 'Huckleberry Finn.'" *Washington Post*, 18 March 1995, A17.

Herbert, Hilary A. "The Conditions of the Reconstruction Problem." In Current 29–51.

Hill, Hamlin, ed. *Adventures of Huckleberry Finn*. Centennial Facsimile ed. New York: Harper and Row, 1987.

Hill, Hamlin, and Walter Blair. Introduction. *The Art of Huckleberry Finn: Text of the First Edition; Sources; Criticisms*. San Francisco: Chandler, 1962. 1–19.

Hirsch, Arnold R., and Joseph Logsdon, eds. *Creole New Orleans: Race and Americanization*. Baton Rouge: Louisiana State UP, 1992.

Hirst, Robert H. "A Note on the Text." In Mark Twain, *Adventures of Huckleberry Finn*. Mark Twain Library edition. Berkeley and Los Angeles: U of California P, 1985. 447–51.

Hitchens, Christopher. "American Notes." *TLS*, 9 March 1985, 258.

Hoffman, Andrew J. "Mark Twain and Homosexuality." *American Literature* 67.1 (1995): 23–50.

Hook, Sidney. "The New Failure of Nerve." 1943. In *The 1940's: Profile of a Nation in Crisis,* ed. Chester E. Eisinger. Garden City, NY: Doubleday, 1969. 352–62.

Howe, Lawrence. Letter. *New York Times,* 25 July 1992, A20.

Howells, William Dean. *My Mark Twain.* 1910. In Edmund Wilson, *Shock* 674–741.

Hutchinson, Stuart, ed. *Mark Twain: Critical Assessments.* 4 vols. Mountfield, East Sussex: Helm Information, 1993.

Irving, Washington. *History, Tales and Sketches.* Ed. James W. Tuttleton. New York: Library of America, 1983.

Jacobs, Harriet. *Incidents in the Life of a Slave Girl: Written by Herself.* 1861. Ed. Jean Fagan Yellin. Cambridge: Harvard UP, 1987.

Jehlen, Myra. "Banned in Concord: *Adventures of Huckleberry Finn* and Classic American Literature." In Robinson, *Cambridge* 93–115.

Jones, Howard Mumford. *The Age of Energy: Varieties of American Experience, 1865–1915.* New York: Viking, 1971.

Jordan, Winthrop D. *Tumult and Silence at Second Creek: An Inquiry into a Civil War Slave Conspiracy.* Baton Rouge: Louisiana State UP, 1993.

Kamiya, Gary. "The 'Lincoln of Our Literature': Mark Twain Exhibition at Blackhawk Is Awe-Inspiring." *San Francisco Examiner,* 22 September 1994.

Kammen, Michael. *A Season of Youth: The American Revolution and the Historical Imagination.* 1978. New York: Oxford UP, 1980.

Kaplan, Justin. *Born to Trouble: One Hundred Years of Huckleberry Finn.* Center for the Book Viewpoint Series, no. 13. Washington: Library of Congress, 1985.

Kaplan, Justin. Introduction to Twain, *Huckleberry Finn* (1996). vii–xi.

Krutch, Joseph Wood. "Speaking of Books." *New York Times Book Review,* 23 May 1954, 2.

Labov, William. *Language in the Inner City: Studies in the Black English Vernacular.* Philadelphia: U of Pennsylvania P, 1972.

Lemann, Nicholas. *The Promised Land: The Great Black Migration and How It Changed America.* New York: Knopf, 1991.

Leonard, James S., Thomas A. Tenney, and Thadious M. Davis, eds. *Satire or Evasion? Black Perspectives on Huckleberry Finn.* Durham, NC: Duke UP, 1992.

Lincoln, Abraham. *Speeches and Writings.* 2 vols. New York: Library of America, 1989.

Longinus. *On the Sublime.* Ed. D. A. Russell. Oxford: Clarendon P, 1964.

Lorch, Fred W. *The Trouble Begins at Eight: Mark Twain's Lecture Tours.* Ames: Iowa State UP, 1968.

232   *Works Cited*

Lukács, Georg. "Narrate or Describe." 1936. *Writer and Critic*. Trans. Arthur D. Kahn. New York: Grosset and Dunlap, 1971.

Lynn, Kenneth S. "Huckleberry Feminist." *TLS*, 17 May 1996, 3–4.

Lynn, Kenneth S. "Welcome Back from the Raft, Huck Honey!" 1977. *The Air-Line to Seattle: Studies in Literary and Historical Writing about America*. Chicago: U of Chicago P, 1983. 40–49.

Lynn, Kenneth S. "You Can't Go Home Again." 1959. In Bradley et al. 398–413.

Lynn, Kenneth S., ed. *Huckleberry Finn: Text, Sources, and Criticism*. New York: Harcourt, Brace and World, 1961.

Maier, Charles S. *The Unmasterable Past: History, Holocaust, and German National Identity*. Cambridge: Harvard UP, 1988.

Mailer, Norman. "Huckleberry Finn, Alive at 100." *New York Times Book Review*, 9 Dec. 1984, 1, 36–7.

Mailloux, Steven. *Rhetorical Power*. Ithaca, NY: Cornell UP, 1988.

Marx, Leo. "Between Two Landscapes" [review-essay on Williams, *Country*]. *Journal of the Royal Institute of British Architecture* (1973): 422–24.

Marx, Leo. "Huck at 100." *Nation*, 31 Aug. 1985, 150–52.

Marx, Leo. *The Machine in the Garden: Technology and the Pastoral Ideal in America*. New York: Oxford UP, 1964.

Marx, Leo. "Pastoralism in America." In *Ideology and Classic American Literature*, ed. Sacvan Bercovitch and Myra Jehlen. Cambridge: Cambridge UP, 1986. 36–69.

Marx, Leo. *The Pilot and the Passenger: Essays on Literature, Culture, and Technology in the United States*. New York: Oxford UP, 1988.

Marx, Leo, ed. *Mark Twain: Adventures of Huckleberry Finn*. Indianapolis: Bobbs-Merrill, 1967.

Mason, Bobbie Ann. [Untitled]. *New Yorker*, 26 June 1995, 130.

Matthews, Brander. Review of *Huckleberry Finn*. 1885. In Bradley et al. 291–95.

Maupassant, Guy de. *Pierre et Jean*. 1888. Ed. Pierre Cogny. Paris: Garnier, 1959.

McArthur, Tom, ed. *The Oxford Companion to the English Language*. New York: Oxford UP, 1992.

McCandless, Perry. *A History of Missouri, 1820 to 1860*. Volume 2 in *Sesquicentennial History of Missouri*, ed. William E. Parrish. Columbia: U of Missouri P, 1972.

McCullough, David. *Truman*. New York: Simon and Schuster, 1992.

McDowell, Edwin. "From Twain, a Letter on Debt to Blacks." *New York Times*, 14 March 1985, 1, 16.

McKay, Janet Holmgren. *Narration and Discourse in American Realistic Fiction*. Philadelphia: U of Pennsylvania P, 1982.

McLaurin, Melton A. *Celia: A Slave*. Athens: U of Georgia P, 1991.

McPherson, James M. *Battle Cry of Freedom: The Civil War Era. Oxford History of the United States*, vol. 6. New York: Oxford UP, 1988.

Meier, August, and Elliott Rudwick. *Black History and the Historical Profession, 1915–1980*. Urbana and Chicago: U of Illinois P, 1986.

Meinig, D. W. *The Shaping of America: A Geographical Perspective on Five Hundred Years of History*, vol. 2: *Continental America 1800–1867*. New Haven: Yale UP, 1993.

Messent, Peter. *New Readings of the American Novel: Narrative Theory and Its Application*. London: Macmillan, 1990.

Miller, Perry. *Nature's Nation*. Cambridge: Harvard UP, 1967.

Moore, Molly. "Behind the Attack on 'Huck Finn': One Angry Educator." *Washington Post*, Metro section, 21 April 1982, 1, 6–7.

Morrison, Toni. *Beloved*. 1987. New York: New American Library, 1988.

Morrison, Toni. Introduction to Mark Twain, *Adventures of Huckleberry Finn*. The Oxford Mark Twain. New York: Oxford UP, 1996. xxxi–xli.

Morrison, Toni. *Playing in the Dark: Whiteness and the Literary Imagination*. Cambridge: Harvard UP, 1992.

Mosley, Walter. *Black Betty*. 1994. New York: Pocket Books, 1995.

Mullin, Michael. *Africa in America: Slave Acculturation and Resistance in the American South and the British Caribbean, 1736–1831*. Urbana: U of Illinois P, 1992.

Murray, Albert. *The Omni-Americans: Black Experience and American Culture*. 1970. New York: Vintage, 1983.

Myrdal, Gunnar, with the assistance of Richard Sterner and Arnold Rose. *An American Dilemma: The Negro Problem and Modern Democracy*. 1944. New York: Pantheon, 1972.

Nadeau, Robert. "*Huckleberry Finn* Is a Moral Story." *Washington Post*, 11 April 1982. In Champion 141–42.

Nast, Thomas. "A Dead Issue" [cartoon]. *Harper's Weekly* 29. 1497 (29 August 1885): 576.

New York Times. "G.O.P.'s Rising Star in the House Pledges to Right the Wrongs of the Left." 10 November 1994, B3.

New York Times. "Huck Finn's Friend Jim." 13 September 1957, editorial page.

New York Times. "A Little Kind of Low Chuckle." 16 April 1982, editorial page.

New York Times. "Nominees Sought to Top School Job." 13 Sept. 1957.

New York Times. "Think Back, Too." 1 Jan. 1984, editorial page.

New York Times. "Truman Predicts Income Tax Rise." 15 Nov. 1957.

New York Times. "Wagner Supports Board of Education on Dropping 'Huckleberry Finn' as Textbook." 14 Sept. 1957.

Nietzsche, Friedrich. *Der Fall Wagner. Werke in Drei Bänden,* ed. Karl Schlecta. Munich: Carl Hanser, 1966. 2:901–38.

Nightline. 4 February 1985. In Champion 147–55.

Noble, Kenneth B. "Issue of Racism Erupts in Simpson Trial: Prosecutor and Defense Lawyer Clash in Arguments over Epithet." *New York Times,* 14 Jan. 1995, 7.

Noble, Kenneth B. "A Man Dead, a Man Jailed, a City Divided." *New York Times,* 11 Dec. 1995, A8.

Noble, Kenneth B. "Simpson Judge Permits Evidence on Racial Bias of Detective." *New York Times,* 21 Jan. 1995, A10.

Novick, Peter. *That Noble Dream: The "Objectivity Question" and the American Historical Profession.* Cambridge: Cambridge UP, 1988.

O'Hara, Daniel T. *Lionel Trilling: The Work of Liberation.* Madison: U of Wisconsin P, 1988.

Orwell, George. *Collected Essays, Journalism, and Letters.* 1968. 4 vols. Rpt. Harmondsworth: Penguin, 1970.

Page, Thomas Nelson. *The Old South: Essays Social and Political.* 1892. New York: Scribner, 1918.

Paine, Albert Bigelow. *Mark Twain.* 1912. 3 vols. Rpt. New York: Chelsea House, 1980.

Patterson, James T. *Grand Expectations: The United States, 1945–1974. Oxford History of the United States,* vol. 10. New York: Oxford UP, 1996.

Pearce, Roy Harvey. " 'The End. Yours Truly, Huck Finn': Postscript." 1963. In Bradley et al. 358–62.

Perry, Thomas Sergeant. Review of *Huckleberry Finn.* 1885. In Bradley et al. 289–90.

Phillips, William, and Philip Rahv, eds. *The New Partisan Reader, 1945–1953.* New York: Harcourt, Brace and Company, 1953.

Podhoretz, Norman. *Doings and Undoings: The Fifties and After in American Writing.* New York: Noonday, 1964.

Podhoretz, Norman. "The Literary Adventures of Huckleberry Finn." *New York Times Book Review,* 6 Dec. 1959, 5, 34.

Poirier, Richard. *A World Elsewhere: The Place of Style in American Literature.* New York: Oxford UP, 1966.

Potter, David M. *The Impending Crisis, 1848–1861.* New York: Harper and Row, 1976.

Potter, David M. *The South and the Sectional Conflict.* Baton Rouge: Louisiana State UP, 1968.

Proust, Marcel. "A propos du style de Flaubert." 1920. In *Flaubert,* ed. Raymonde Debray-Genette. Paris: Marcel Dider, 1970. 46–55.

Quirk, Tom. *Coming to Grips with "Huckleberry Finn": Essays on a Book, a Boy, and a Man.* Columbia: U of Missouri P, 1993.

Raban, Jonathan. "Speaking for America." *TLS*, 21–27 Sept. 1990, 991–93.

Rabinovitz, Jonathan. "Huck Finn 101, or How to Teach Twain without Fear." *New York Times*, 25 July 1995, B1, B4.

Rainwater, Lee, and William L. Yancey. *The Moynihan Report and the Politics of Controversy.* Cambridge: MIT P, 1967.

Rhodes, James Ford. *History of the United States from the Compromise of 1850,* vol. 1: *1850–1854.* 1892. New York: Harper and Brothers, 1896.

Rich, Frank. "Dropping the N-Bomb." *New York Times*, 16 March 1995, A15.

Rich, Frank. "Hoping Again for Generosity of Spirit in a Brutal Land." *New York Times*, 23 March 1990, B1–B2.

Richards, David. Review of *Big River. Washington Post,* 12 May 1985. G1, G4.

Richards, Leonard. *"Gentlemen of Property and Standing": Anti-Abolition Mobs in Jacksonian America.* New York: Oxford UP, 1970.

Robinson, Forrest G. *In Bad Faith: The Dynamics of Deception in Mark Twain's America.* Cambridge: Harvard UP, 1986.

Robinson, Forrest G., ed. *The Cambridge Companion to Mark Twain.* Cambridge: Cambridge UP, 1995.

Rogers, Joseph H. Letter. *New York Times*, 24 Sept. 1957.

Rorty, Richard. "The Unpatriotic Academy." Op-Ed, *New York Times*, 13 Feb. 1994, 15.

Ryan, William. "Savage Discovery: The Moynihan Report." 1965. In Rainwater and Yancey 457–66.

Said, Edward W. *Culture and Imperialism.* New York: Knopf, 1993.

Sattelmeyer, Robert, and J. Donald Crowley, eds. *One Hundred Years of "Huckleberry Finn": The Boy, His Book, and American Culture.* Columbia: U of Missouri P, 1985.

Saxton, Alexander. *The Rise and Fall of the White Republic: Class Politics and Mass Culture in Nineteenth-Century America.* London: Verso, 1990.

Schlesinger, Arthur M., Jr. "The Causes of the Civil War: A Note on Historical Sentimentalism." 1949. In Phillips and Rahv 314–25.

Schlesinger, Arthur M., Jr. "The Failure of Statesmanship." *Saturday Review of Literature* 30 (18 Oct. 1947): 9–10.

Schlesinger, Arthur M., Jr. "The Opening of the American Mind." *New York Times Book Review,* 23 July 1989, 1, 26–27.

Sewell, David R. *Mark Twain's Languages: Discourse, Dialogue, and Linguistic Variety.* Berkeley and Los Angeles: U of California P, 1987.

Shumway, David. *Creating American Civilization: A Genealogy of American Literature as an Academic Discipline.* Minneapolis: U of Minnesota P, 1994.

Silber, Nina. *The Romance of Reunion: Northerners and the South, 1865–1900.* Chapel Hill: U of North Carolina P, 1993.

Skvorecky, Josef. "Huckleberry Finn: Or, Something Exotic in Czechoslovakia." *New York Times Book Review.* 8 Nov. 1987, 47–48.

Smagorinsky, Peter. *Standards in Practice Grades 9–12.* Urbana, IL: National Council of Teachers of English, 1996.

Smiley, Jane. "Say It Ain't So, Huck: Second Thoughts on Mark Twain's 'Masterpiece.'" *Harper's* 292. 1748 (Jan. 1996): 61–66.

Smith, David L. "Black Critics and Mark Twain." In Robinson, *Cambridge* 116–28.

Smith, Henry Nash. Introduction. *Adventures of Huckleberry Finn.* Boston: Houghton Mifflin, 1958. v–xxix.

Smith, Henry Nash. *Mark Twain: The Development of a Writer.* 1962. New York: Atheneum, 1972.

Smith, Henry Nash. "The Widening of Horizons." In *Literary History of the United States,* ed. Robert E. Spiller et al. 1948. 3d ed. New York: Macmillan, 1963. 639–51.

Smith, Henry Nash, and William M. Gibson, eds. *Mark Twain–Howells Letters: The Correspondence of Samuel L. Clemens and William D. Howells, 1869–1910.* 2 vols. Cambridge: Harvard UP, 1960.

Smith, Herbert F. *Richard Watson Gilder.* New York: Twayne, 1970.

Stampp, Kenneth M. "The Fate of the Southern Antislavery Movement." *Journal of Negro History* 28 (1943): 10–22.

Stampp, Kenneth M. *The Peculiar Institution: Slavery in the Ante-Bellum South.* New York: Alfred A. Knopf, 1956.

Steinberg, Stephen. *Turning Back: The Retreat from Racial Justice in American Thought and Policy.* Boston: Beacon, 1995.

Stewart, Sally Ann. "Court Airs Fuhrman Racial Slurs." *USA Today,* 30 August 1995, A1.

Stowe, Harriet Beecher. *Uncle Tom's Cabin.* 1852. Ed. Ann Douglas. Harmondsworth: Penguin, 1981.

Strauss, Valerie. "Twain Classic Bounced from Class Again: Prestigious Girls School Joins Debate over 'Huckleberry Finn.'" *Washington Post,* 4 March 1995, A1, 12.

Styron, William. [Untitled]. *New Yorker,* 26 June 1995, 132–33.

Sundquist, Eric. Introduction. *Mark Twain: A Collection of Critical Essays.* New Century Views. Englewood Cliffs, NJ: Prentice-Hall, 1994. 1–14.

Sutton, Roger. "'Sivilizing' *Huckleberry Finn.*" *School Library Journal,* 1984. In Champion 145–46.

Teres, Harvey. *Renewing the Left: Politics, Imagination, and the New York Intellectuals.* New York: Oxford UP, 1996.

Thompson, George. *Prison Life and Reflections; Or, a Narrative of the Arrest, Trial, Conviction, Imprisonment, Treatment, Observations, Reflections, and Deliverance of Work, Burr, and Thompson, Who Suffered an Unjust and Cruel Imprisonment in Missouri Penitentiary, for Attempting to Aid Some Slaves to Liberty.* 1847. 3d ed. Hartford: A. Work, 1849.

Trilling, Diana. *The Beginning of the Journey: The Marriage of Diana and Lionel Trilling.* New York: Harcourt Brace and Company, 1993.

Trilling, Lionel. *Beyond Culture: Essays on Literature and Learning.* New York: Viking, 1965.

Trilling, Lionel. *A Gathering of Fugitives.* Boston: Beacon, 1956.

Trilling, Lionel. *The Last Decade: Essays and Reviews, 1965–1975.* Ed. Diana Trilling. New York: Harcourt Brace Jovanovich, 1979.

Trilling, Lionel. *The Liberal Imagination: Essays on Literature and Society.* 1950. Garden City, NY: Doubleday, 1953.

Trilling, Lionel. *The Opposing Self: Nine Essays in Criticism.* New York: Viking, 1955.

Trilling, Lionel. *Speaking of Literature and Society.* Ed. Diana Trilling. Oxford: Oxford UP, 1982.

Turner, Arlin. *George W. Cable: A Biography.* Durham: Duke UP, 1956.

Turner, Frederick Jackson. *Frontier and Section.* Ed. Ray Allen Billington. Englewood Cliffs, NJ: Prentice-Hall, 1961.

Turner, Frederick Jackson. *The United States, 1830–1850: The Nation and Its Sections.* 1935. Gloucester, MA: Peter Smith, 1958.

Tuveson, Ernest Lee. *Redeemer Nation: The Idea of America's Millennial Role.* Chicago: U of Chicago P, 1968.

Twain, Mark. *Adventures of Huckleberry Finn.* Introduction by Justin Kaplan. Foreword and Addendum by Victor Doyno. New York: Random House, 1996.

Twain, Mark. *Adventures of Huckleberry Finn.* Ed. Walter Blair and Victor Fischer. *The Works of Mark Twain,* vol. 8. Berkeley and Los Angeles: U of California P, 1988.

Twain, Mark. *Collected Tales, Sketches, Speeches, and Essays.* Ed. Louis J. Budd. 2 vols. New York: Library of America, 1992.

Twain, Mark. "Fenimore Cooper's Literary Offenses." In Edmund Wilson, *Shock* 582–94.

Twain, Mark. *Following the Equator: A Journey around the World.* Hartford: American Publishing, 1897.

Twain, Mark. *The Innocents Abroad and Roughing It.* New York: Library of America, 1984.

Twain, Mark. *Mark Twain's Autobiography.* Ed. Albert Bigelow Paine. New York: Harper and Brothers, 1924.

Twain, Mark. *Mississippi Writings.* New York: Library of America, 1982.

Twain, Mark. "A Scrap of Curious History." *Complete Essays,* ed. Charles Neider. Garden City, NY: Doubleday, 1963. 517–23.

Tyler, Anne. "An American Boy In Gangland." *New York Times Book Review,* 26 Feb. 1989, 1, 46.

Veysey, Laurence. "The Plural Organized Worlds of the Humanities." *The*

Organization of Knowledge in Modern America, 1860–1920, ed. Alexandra Oleson and John Voss. Baltimore: Johns Hopkins UP, 1979. 51–106.

Walke, Henry. "Operations of the Western Flotilla." *Century Magazine* 7 (1885): 423–46.

Walker, David. *Walker's Appeal, in Four Articles, together with a Preamble, to the Colored Citizens of the World, but in Particular, and Very Expressly to Those of the United States of America.* 1829. 2d ed., 1830. In *Walker's "Appeal" and Garnet's "Address" to the Slaves of the United States of America.* 1969. Salem, NH: Ayer, 1994.

Wallace, John. "*Huckleberry Finn* Is Offensive." *Washington Post,* 11 April 1982. In Champion 143–44.

Warren, Kenneth W. *Black and White Strangers: Race and American Literary Realism.* Chicago: U of Chicago P, 1993.

Warren, Robert Penn. *Who Speaks for the Negro?* New York: Random House, 1965.

Washington, Booker T. "Tribute to Mark Twain." *North American Review,* 1910. In Hutchinson 2:462–63.

Washington Post. "Selling Huck Down the River." 9 April 1982, A18.

Washington Post. "Mark Twain School Trying to Censor Huck." 8 April 1982, A1, A10.

Wecter, Dixon. *Sam Clemens of Hannibal.* Boston: Houghton Mifflin, 1952.

Wendell, Barrett. *A Literary History of America.* 1900. New York: Greenwood, 1968.

Will, George. "Huck at a Hundred." *Newsweek,* 18 Feb. 1985, 92.

Williams, Raymond. *The Country and the City.* New York: Oxford UP, 1973.

Williams, Raymond. *Politics and Letters: Interviews with "New Left Review."* London: Verso, 1979.

Wills, Garry. *Lincoln at Gettysburg: The Words That Remade America.* New York: Simon and Schuster, 1992.

Wilson, Edmund. *Classics and Commercials: A Literary Chronicle of the Forties.* New York: Farrar, Straus and Company, 1950.

Wilson, Edmund. *The Shores of Light: A Literary Chronicle of the Twenties and Thirties.* New York: Farrar, Straus and Young, 1952.

Wilson, Edmund, ed. *The Shock of Recognition: The Development of Literature in the United States Recorded by the Men Who Made It.* Garden City, NY: Doubleday, 1943.

Wilson, Woodrow. *Division and Reunion: 1829–1889.* 1892; 11th ed., 1898. New York: Collier Books, 1961.

Wilson, Woodrow. "The Reconstruction of the Southern States." In Current 3–28.

Winters, Yvor. "Fenimore Cooper, or The Ruins of Time." *In Defense of Reason.* 3d ed., 1947. Denver: Swallow, n.d. 176–99.

Woodward, C. Vann. *The Burden of Southern History.* Rev. ed. Baton Rouge: Louisiana State UP, 1968.

Woodward, C. Vann. "The Elusive Mind of the South." *American Counterpoint: Slavery and Racism in the North/South Dialogue.* 1971. New York: Oxford UP, 1983. 261–83.

Woodward, C. Vann. "Southerners against the Southern Establishment." 1987. *The Future of the Past.* New York: Oxford UP, 1989. 280–94.

Wyatt-Brown, Bertram. *Southern Honor: Ethics and Behavior in the Old South.* New York: Oxford UP, 1982.

Yardley, Jonathan. "Huckleberry Finn and the Ebb and Flow of Controversy." *Washington Post,* 13 March 1995, D2.

Yardley, Jonathan. "Huckleberry Finn Doesn't Wear a White Sheet." "Prejudices" column, *Washington Post,* 12 April 1982. C1, C4.

Index

Abolition Movement: analogy to Cold War, 114–15, 131–32; Elijah Lovejoy murdered, 42; emergence of Garrisonian, 42; Howells on, 95, 97; in Clemens family, 49–50; in Hannibal, MO, 47–49; in Missouri, 46–47; revisionist history and, 114–15; Wendell on, 94. *See also* Slavery in United States

Accuracy: as basis for critical argument, 26–27, 77. *See also* Realism

Action: contrasting models in *HF* and *Uncle Tom's Cabin*, 102–5; Eliot on, 103; Fiedler on, 35; in Flaubert, 177, 179; in *HF* and Jacobs, 46; in *HF* undermined by ending, 35, 129, 151; Marx on, 163; problem of African American agency, 103–5; Said and, 206; Trilling cities Dewey on, 129, 151

Adams, Charles Francis: on Stowe, 94

Adams, J. Donald (*New York Times*), 125–27

Adventures of Huckleberry Finn. See "All right, then, I'll *go* to hell"; Chapter 19; Chatper 31; Editions; Ending; Hypercanonization; Language; Jim; Pedagogic Issues; Racial Issues; Self; Raftmen Episode; and names of individual critics, novelists, and scholars

African Americans: agency of, 11–12, 103–5; American language and, 185–86; Black English, 186–93; challenge HF, 19–21, 205–6; in Civil War, 103–5; July Fourth and, 55–58; migration to North, 109–10; opposed to "whole community," 39; relation to US government, 199–200; stereotypes of, 24, 194; struggle for civil rights of, 21, 61–62, 110–11, 199–201. *See also* Civil Rights Movement; Slavery in United States

Aldrich, Thomas Bailey, *The Story of a Bad Boy*, 57

All in the Family, 33

"All right, then, I'll *go* to hell" (*HF* ch. 31): quoted, 6, 17, 18, 33, 52–53, 72, 74, 86, 121, 138, 140, 215; anti-Stalinism and, 124; as emblematic of America, 18; greatest moment in American literature, 17; irony of, 33, 35; pedagogy for, 86; as rejection of conformity, 140. *See also* Chapter 31 Moral Crisis (*HF*)

Allegorization, 137–38, 148, 154, 179

America: Ellison on, 185, 194–201; Fishkin redefines, 184; identified with Huck and *HF*, vii, 3, 14, 36, 77, 81, 87–88, 112, 139, 184, 212, 217; logic of, 141; Mississippi River and, 210–11; MT as Uncle Sam, 5; MT on, 181–82; patriotism, 214; vernacular authenticates, 160–62. *See also* National Narrative; Nationalism; "Quintessentially American," *HF* as

The Wisconsin Project on American Writers

Frank Lentricchia, General Editor